RIOTS, DEATH AND BASEBALL

To Les,

Robert H. Griffiths,
22/2/2019.

By the same author:

The Story of Kinmel Park Military Training Camp
1914–1918

Welsh Soldiers, Civilians and Eisteddfodau in WWI

'The Enemy Within'
German POW's and Civilians in North Wales
during WWI

Riots, Death and Baseball –

The Canadians at Kinmel Park Camp 1918 to 1919

Robert H. Griffiths

First published in 2019

ISBN: 978-1-84524-297-8

Cover design: Eleri Owen

Published by Gwasg Carreg Gwalch,
12 Iard yr Orsaf, Llanrwst, Wales LL26 0EH
tel: 01492 642031
email: books@carreg-gwalch.cymru
website: www.carreg-gwalch.cymru

DEDICATION

To Ruth, my very special cariad, and wife now of forty years. AND to our wonderful grandson, Jackson Antony, with whom we both spend many hours of absolute joy. He is always such a delight to be with.

This book is also dedicated to the memory of two children of my dearest friends, Colin and Judith. Namely, Delyth Ann, who died in 1988, aged eight, and, Gareth Wyn, who died in 2018, aged thirty-three.

ABOUT THE AUTHOR

Robert H. Griffiths is a former police officer who now spends his time as a military historian, author and genealogist. He lives with his wife, Ruth, in Denbigh, North Wales.

Robert H. Griffiths

A little bit of Heaven

I've been at Grove Park Barracks,
I've been at Bromley too;
I've soldiered down at Pennington
Which was none too grand its true.
But the place I shall remember
And remember with a frown,
Is that Mud-bound God forsaken
Kinmel Park, near Abergele Town.

T'was Kil-E.M, Camp they called it
That described it to a 'T',
Had it been a few yards further
T'would have been right in the Sea.
And the man who first discovered
This interesting spot,
Should rank as an explorer
With Shackleton and Scott.

We never see a 'Civvy',
We never see a Pub,
We never see a paper
And we do not see much grub.
But now we're Isolated,
That we all agree is true
We might have been encamping
In the Wilds of Timbuctoo.

The wind is simply icy
As through the 'Jerks' we bend,
The only chance of getting warm
Is when we go to bed.
The cold is so intense here
An unusual sight we saw,
A Seagull from exposure
Had 'Snuffed it' near our door.

A little bit of 'Heaven',
North Wales has now been named,
The Author's p'raps not seen 'World's End',
If so, he can't be blamed;
But I'll make a sweeping statement
And all the world I'll tell,
If Kinmel is a bit of Heaven
Then give me a bit of H . . . !

(Attributed to G.W.D. – M.T., A.S.C.)

Though written almost certainly prior to the arrival of the Canadians at Kinmel Park Camp in the late Summer of 1918, it would be a slapstick 'poetic account' of the camp with which the Canadians would not have disagreed with in the slightest!

Contents

Introduction

When I wrote my first Kinmel Park Camp related book, published in 2014, I purposely entitled it, *The Story of Kinmel Park Military Training Camp 1914 to 1918*, and only touched upon the Canadian presence at the camp, with only 1914 to 1918 in the title. The Canadian's time at the camp having been from September 1918 until late June 1919, with the 'infamous' riots/disturbances occurring there on 4 and 5 March 1919, which resulted in the violent deaths of five soldiers, many others injured and over fifty later to face court martials on serious charges.

I had intended this second book on the camp now looking back one hundred years, to focus purely on these riots/disturbances, and upon the many Canadian soldiers who died mainly from illness, whilst at Kinmel Park Camp, and who are buried nearby in the churchyard of 'The Marble Church', Bodelwyddan.

However, after extensive research I found that the 'Canadians at the Camp' was not just a story of the riots/disturbances, and of deaths through illness, almost all the result of the Spanish Flu pandemic, but of much more – of highly decorated Canadian soldiers passing through the camp, including the Victoria Cross recipients, Tommy Holmes and Alexander Picton Brereton. Nor is it just about white Canadian soldiers, a number of whom were British born and had emigrated to Canada, but a great deal more ethnically diverse than that. For the Canadians at Kinmel Park Camp is also the story of First Nations Canadian soldiers, fearless in battle, but unorthodox as soldiers; of Black Canadian soldiers, a number born in the United States and also the West Indies, including hundreds from the now iconic No.2 Construction Battalion – 'the Black Battalion';

of women, Canadian Nursing Sisters, nicknamed 'Bluebirds', and of Canadian War Brides, British women who in their thousands married Canadian soldiers of the Canadian Expeditionary Force (the C.E.F), and returned with them to Canada, to begin new and very different lives. A few of these women were local Welsh ones, who married Canadian soldiers who were at Kinmel Park Camp.

There are thousands of individual stories to be told of the men and women of the C.E.F who passed through Kinmel Park Camp prior to their return to Canada. Some stayed at the camp for just a few weeks, whilst others had to endure months at the camp awaiting their turn to be repatriated.

I have endeavoured in this book to reveal a collection of diverse stories, concentrating on the people themselves, every one of whom have now of course passed from this earth. I firmly believe they deserve to be remembered today and for years to come, not just as mere names on weather beaten gravestones or upon war memorials, which most people only glance at, and then only on or around Remembrance Sunday, but as important entities in history.

Robert H. Griffiths,
November 2018

Chapter One

Canada's sacrifice in the First World War

Canada at the time of the outbreak of the First World War was a somewhat divided country, riven with factionalism. French speaker against English speaker; Protestant against Catholic; Rural farming type people against Urbanites; Soldiers against Civilians. Canada during the First World War was still a Dominion, a semi-independent country under the British Crown and part of the British Empire.

It was with this backdrop that Canada and many thousands of Canadian citizens male and female, 'answered the clarion call of the British Empire' to fight against Germany and the Central Powers in August 1914. Particularly eager to volunteer and enlist in the C.E.F (the Canadian Expeditionary Force) were Canadians of English, Irish, Scottish or Welsh birth, or those of British ancestry.

The figures generally accepted as being the most accurate are that a total of 619,636 Canadians served in the Canadian military during the First World War, from a population of approximately 7,879,000, with 424,589 of them serving overseas. Of this huge number of men and women in the C.E.F, 59,544 died during the war, 51,748 of them as a result of 'enemy action'. A further 172,000 Canadians were wounded with the medical authority figures of approximately 138,000 as being battle casualties. The remainder being injuries sustained away from any war zone.

The figures for those who lost limbs are 3,461 men and women. One soldier, Ethelbert (Curley) Christian, a black soldier, a wonderfully stoic man was the only Canadian soldier, though actually United States born, to lose all four limbs and miraculously survive being a quadriplegic. There are in addition, also those who suffered psychological problems from their war service. The medical authorities identified at least 9,000 who suffered from what is called 'shell shock', though those who actually suffered such trauma was almost certainly many thousands more, but they went undiagnosed. Many Canadians returning home were said to be 'broken in mind and body'.

The small Royal Canadian Navy reported a total of 150 war deaths and some 1,388 Canadians died whilst serving with the British flying services. There are no figures for Canadians who volunteered to serve, not with any of the Canadian military forces, but in the British army or Royal navy – which many did.

During the First World War, the Canadian military authorised the formation of 260 different infantry battalions over the vast expanse that is Canada, to serve with the

Recruitment Poster (Enlist Now)

Canadian Expeditionary Force (the C.E.F). Very many of them were locally formed and named accordingly. But only a few of these 260 battalions ever reached France & Flanders as an entity to serve at the Front. For they arrived in England and were quickly broken up, and absorbed into an existing reserve battalion. Though some, such as the Canadian Mounted Rifles were not broken up, but instead converted into infantry battalions to serve in the Canadian Corps. Other Canadian combat units in the C.E.F included some cavalry and mounted infantry regiments, artillery brigades and machine gun battalions.

Of the first contingents of Canadian soldiers who very promptly volunteered for the C.E.F and fought on the Western Front in 1914, about 70% of them were British born men residing in Canada who 'heeded the clarion call of the mother country'. This though was a reflection of just how many British born people pre-1914 had emigrated to Canada to begin a new life for themselves or gained employment there. At the end of the First World War, even including those conscripted into the C.E.F, only 51% were Canadian born. The ties to Britain however were not universal throughout Canada. The Province of Ontario had particularly close ties, whilst the opposite was true of the Province of Quebec. Here many were French-Canadians, who spoke French very much as their first language, and those monoglot French speakers who did enlist found their lack of English an impediment when they joined the English language dominated C.E.F. In the Province of Quebec amongst those in power, politically and culturally, there was little or no appetite for being directly involved in a 'European War' between Britain and Germany, to them both far off countries with empires. The city of Montreal being an exception, for here recruiting for the C.E.F was reasonably successful.

The Canadian has always, and Canadian soldiers are no exception to this, greatly disliked being mistaken by their accents for Americans. The First World War Canadian soldier wished to be set apart from others and fully excepted if not enjoyed it, when they were referred to as 'Canadas', 'Tommy Canucks, or 'Canucks'. Canucks being a slang term for Canadians, originally spelt 'Kanucks', an Americanism to describe French or Dutch Canadians dating back to the 1830's.

Canadian Conscription

When the British Empire went to war on the last occasion before the First World war, it was for The South African War of 1899–1902, also known as The Second Boer War. For this war, Britain, nor any of its then Dominions needed to bring in any form of military conscription, and several thousand Canadian men volunteered to fight for the British Empire.

The same was true of the first eighteen or so months of the First World War, but the losses of men over this period and the on-going stalemate and madness of trench warfare meant that in January of 1916, in Britain, conscription was introduced by The Military Service Act. Then, by late 1916, the Canadian military were now running short of ample numbers of soldiers to replace their dead and wounded, and voluntary enlistments were slowing. It was now that the Prime Minister, Sir Robert Borden who was born in Nova Scotia, Canada, decided that a form of conscription was required, for what was then the Dominion of Canada. The debate over conscription in Canada was a fierce and divisive one, both politically and with the Canadian public Those in favour of conscription accused their opponents of being cowardly and lacking loyalty, whilst those opposed to conscription accused their opponents of being imperialists or warmongers. But it was not always as clear-cut as that, for there were many Canadians who opposed conscription, but supported the war effort against the belligerent enemy, Germany and the Central Powers. It was the compelling of Canadian men to go to fight which they opposed. The bitter debate over the introduction of conscription raged on even after Prime Minister Borden and his political supporters pushed through the 12th Canadian Parliament, The Military Service Act, and it came into force in late 1917. Though it was not until 1 January 1918, that the recently formed Unionist Government under Prime Minister Borden began to enforce the act.

Basically, this act stated that all male citizens of Canada who were aged between twenty and forty-five were now subject to military service for Canada for the duration of the war, if they were required. We now know of course that the war ended in November of 1918, but they were not to know that then, for it looked like dragging on for many more months if not years to come. Some groups such as farmers sought exemption from compulsory military service for their sons, and there were serious protests by French-Canadians who used the introduction of conscription as another reason why Quebec should become a sovereign country within Canada. Tens of thousands of young French-speaking Canadians refused to register for possible conscription. When efforts were made to arrest what were called then 'draft dodgers' across Quebec, some rioting and street battles took place in Quebec City, resulting in the loss of lives.

In truth, conscription did not have much of an effect upon Canada's overall war effort. Records show that by the Armistice, only some 48,000 conscripted men had been sent overseas as part of the C.E.F. It is estimated that only half of these ever got to be at the Front. Whilst more than 50,000 other conscripts never actually left Canada. But I am sure if the war had dragged on into 1919, these conscripts would in due time have been sent overseas to replace the dead and wounded, which would have resulted from the war's continuation.

A number of the Canadian soldiers who found themselves at Kinmel Park Camp in late 1918 and into 1919, were draftees into the C.E.F under The Military Service Act 1917, and some of them died as a result of illness at the camp. Drafted (conscripted) into the C.E.F, and only weeks, or at most a few months later, they were 'dead and buried' in a churchyard, in a quiet corner of North Wales.

Chapter Two

The Canadians at Kinmel Park Camp

Kinmel Park Camp during the First World War was the largest military training camp in Wales and one of the largest in Britain. It was and still is, though now not much of it remains, situated in northern Wales, lying between St Asaph, some three miles away, and Abergele, some three and a half miles away. The seaside resort of Rhyl is some five and a half miles away in a north easterly direction.

Kinmel Park Camp was built from scratch in late 1914, into 1915, on former lush parkland, much of the land from the Kinmel Park estate, with some from the Bodelwyddan Park estate. The camp even had its own railway, the KCR, the Kinmel Camp Railway, which ran right into the centre of the camp itself, between the hutments. At first a line was laid to the camp across the Rhuddlan Marsh from a junction with the main Chester to Holyhead line, at Foryd Station, near Kinmel Bay. Later a deviation of the northern section of the railway was laid, meaning the KCR now went to the town of Rhyl by connecting with the Vale of Clwyd line at Foryd Junction.

The KCR was a great boon in bringing in the vast amount of supplies needed to keep the camp running. It also was very much used for the transportation of the many thousands of Canadian soldiers who arrived and departed when it was being used as a staging/transit camp. The KCR was very popular with the Canadian soldiers at Kinmel Park Camp who would travel on it to get to the 'local hotspot' of Rhyl, especially at weekends. There are eye-witness accounts from locals of the last KCR train back to the camp from Rhyl on Saturday nights being regularly so full, that many of the Canadian soldiers had to be transported on the roofs of the carriages, or they would have had to walk back to camp.

The 'elephant in the room' so to speak when considering the Canadians at Kinmel Park Camp, 1918–1919, is the aberration that was the rioting, also called 'the disturbances' that occurred on the evening of Tuesday 4th March, and the following day, Wednesday, 5th March 1919.

But I believe that the deplorable events at Kinmel Park Camp on 4 and 5 March 1919, should not be allowed to cast a shadow over the fine achievements of those Canadian men and women who gave such great service during the First World War. A main body of rioters, who had in fairness to them good reason to be angry at their treatment, joined by many 'hangers on', must not be permitted to tarnish the reputation of the vast majority of Canadian military personnel. For, as my research has found, a number of these 'rioters' had actually been brave soldiers, some even having fought in battles regarded today as being 'iconic ones' for the Canadian infantry in France & Flanders.

There was also so much more to the Canadians at Kinmel Park Camp during 1918 and 1919 than the two days of sporadic rioting and looting which so tragically resulted in five deaths and at least twenty-three others suffering wounds, some serious.

Kinmel Park Camp from August 1918, until Armistice Day 11 November 1918, was used as a 'segregation' camp for Canadian soldiers arriving on the British mainland from Canada. Here incoming 'drafts of soldiers' who had mostly arrived at the Port of Liverpool, underwent a form of quarantining for any infectious diseases; were provided with some further military training, and completed their kitting out, before they were to be moved on to one of the Canadian camps in the south of England. Well, that is until the war went very much the Allies way, and defeat for the enemy, and the Armistice beckoned.

Post-Armistice for the Canadians, Kinmel Park Camp was no longer on a war-based footing, but a 'staging' camp', also referred to as a 'transit camp', or 'concentration camp' (as in, where there was a large concentration of soldiers). This was a supposedly very temporary camp for those who were passing through it. There was a procedure at this camp and other similar Canadian camps in Britain as the soldiers awaited ship transport back to Canada from ports around Britain such as Liverpool, Southampton and Glasgow.

Kinmel Park Camp was now divided into 'wings', corresponding to the dispersal areas of what was then the Dominion of Canada.

From its outset Kinmel Park Camp had its own military hospital, located at camp No.10, close to Engine Hill, Bodelwyddan. The Shorncliffe Military Hospital, Kent, England, was taken over by The Canadian Army Medical Corps and was renamed, No. 9 Canadian General Hospital, Shorncliffe. It operated as such from 10 September 1917, until 17 December 1918, when it was wholly transferred to Kinmel Park Camp because of the huge Canadian presence now here post-Armistice. It now operated from 17 December 1918, until its closure on 26 June 1919, as No. 9 Canadian General Hospital, Kinmel Park Camp.

Demobilization

One might think that Canadian soldiers, female nurses or other military personnel, post-Armistice awaiting their return to Canada from the Western Front, or from a camp in Britain, merely had to find their way to a 'staging/transit camp' and they would soon be on their way. No, there was a set process to be gone through, especially with so many thousands of such Canadians needing to be transported back to their homeland.

The Canadian soldier was required to fill out a rather lengthy twenty question application form for him to receive any war service gratuities due to him, and to register himself for the purpose of having his documentation completed. This was a process which involved the compiling of his military history since he had joined the C.E.F whether as a volunteer or as a conscript. He was also required to parade before the medical officer of his unit or draft, for a preliminary medical examination.

He then went before a medical board for a full assessment of his medical condition and this was fully documented. This medical board, before which each and every Canadian soldier appeared, officer or other rank, sat and decided upon establishing the physical condition of the man at that time, prior to his return to Canada. This was for the soldier a vital decision, for on it depended any claim he wished to make for a war pension or for assistance he sought from the Department of Soldiers' Civil Re-establishment. He also underwent a full dental check-up and went before a dental board. Great significance was made of this and his dental records were fully recorded. Clothing and equipment he was considered to require for his stay at Kinmel Park Camp, or other staging camp was issued to him. Kinmel Park Camp for most of the year was a cold, windswept place, but in Winter quite unbearable. The Canadian soldier then received his issue of pay and now he was now to go on furlough (leave) for two weeks – one could fairly call it 'demobilization leave'.

On his return from the two weeks of leave, he reported back to Kinmel Park Camp or other staging camp and was provided with the details of a specific shipping company to await a specified sailing back to Canada. He was subsequently given an embarkation card which entitled him to a berth on a particular ship back to Canada.

But in reality, many thousands of Canadian soldiers at Kinmel Park Camp, especially from February 1919, waited weeks if not months before receiving this embarkation card – often sailings would be cancelled due to a docks' strike or the unavailability of certain troop transport ships, some being found to not be in a fit state to be used. Then the issued embarkation card would be 'worthless', causing great frustration to men eager not surprisingly to return to their far away homeland, and to their families, friends and 'hopefully normality again!'.

It was just over a week after the Armistice, that a special service was held at St Asaph Cathedral, held primarily for the Canadians stationed at the nearby Kinmel Park Camp, which the *Denbighshire Free Press* of 23 November 1918 reported upon:

> St Asaph News
> MILITARY THANKSGIVING SERVICE
> There was a memorable service at the Cathedral last Friday, on the occasion of a thanksgiving service for the cessation of hostilities, specially arranged for the Canadian troops stationed at Kinmel Camp. The troops under the command of Colonel Colquhoun, had a fine reception in the be-flagged city, and the venerable edifice was filled to overflowing. Even the organ loft being occupied by worshippers. Brigadier-General E. B. Cuthbertson, C.M.G., M.V.O. was present in his capacity as commander of the camp.
>
> The service was conducted by the Dean of St Asaph, with the assistance of Reverend W. E. Kidd, M.C., senior

> chaplain of the Canadians at Kinmel Camp. The Bishop of St Asaph in the course of an address based on the text, 'Thy sons shall come from afar' (Isaiah 60), paid a glowing tribute to the services and sacrifices of Canadians on behalf of the Motherland in its time of greatest need. He said, 'One of the most wonderful chapters ever written in connection with the history of the war would be that dealing with the way in which the sons of the Motherland had come from afar to save and serve her. Germany thought that one of our greatest difficulties in the war would be that colony after colony would break away and leave the Mother Country to fight alone. In that, however, as in many other respects, Germans were simply judging us as they judged themselves, taking our standard to be a purely selfish standard'.

The Edmonton Bulletin, Edmonton, Alberta, Canada, edition of 25 February 1919, some one week before the riots/disturbances at Kinmel Park Camp, had an extensive article with the heading 'How the Boys are being Demobilized', written by a recently returned Canadian soldier who signed the article 'THE VETERAN'. Here is an extract from this which involves Kinmel Park Camp:

> … From Bramshott we knew we would first go to Rhyl, North Wales, where I might call the 'Canadian Demobilization Collecting Centre' had been established. A nine-hour train ride from Liphook landed us at Abergele, which is the station for our Rhyl camp, and when we detrained there, we found we had three and a half, or four miles to march, and when that distance had been covered – it took two hours – we were a very tired, dusty, hungry and footsore bunch of boys,

as we had to carry all our equipment, and rifle, plus a kit bag, and the whole, I judge, weighed about 85 pounds. Upon ultimately reaching the camp we were assigned huts and were soon sleeping the sleep of soldiers, 'all in'. Next day when looking over the camp, we found we were in Camp No. 13, which is 'the receiving camp', and during the day had a muster parade, to see all had survived the heavy march of the previous night. There were no absentees. On Thursday at noon we were told to parade immediately with full kit., and upon doing so we were lined up in 'military districts', and were escorted to Camp No. 9, which looks after all those for Saskatchewan, Alberta and British Columbia. Shortly after arriving at Camp No. 9, we were warned for a medical inspection, and the entire afternoon was spent on this examination, which was very thorough, and in the nature of a final medical examination. The next day, Friday, was a 'quiet day in camp', as we only had to attend for dental inspection. On Saturday, a kit inspection was ordered, and on it if one of us could not produce such unserviceable articles as the issue razor or hairbrush, or a first-class alibi for its absence, the cost of it was stopped out of our dollar ten later on. By Sunday all were in a state of grouchy discontent because none of us could find out, or nobody would tell us, when we were to sail. There was a good reason for maintaining secrecy on this point, because if it became known we had to spend seven days in Camp No. 9, not less than 95 per cent of the boys would have been A.W.L. (*absent without leave*), for a few days as there is not one of the boys without a home, and his 'home' would naturally be the home of some charming English girl the acquaintance of whose family he has made whilst in hospital or on leave. It would not I think, to be out of place to state in passing that the treatment we Canadian boys received from the English people could not have been more hospitable or generous than it was, and the welcome accorded a Canadian wherever he went in England is something which can always be looked back upon as England's appreciation of the help of her colonial soldiers. To resume: On Monday we had a pay parade when the pay books we handed in at Bramshott were returned to us showing in red ink, the balance of pay due to each one, and each had to sign a form that he was satisfied his credit balance as shown in pay book was correct, and these balances varied from 5 dollars to 750 dollars or more. By Wednesday, we were all fairly well satisfied we would 'pull out for home' the following day and such was the case. On Wednesday evening we were officially notified we would leave next day and we had another early start on Thursday, with reveille at 4.0 am, breakfast at 5.00 am, and lined up on the parade ground – still quite dark at 6.0 am, when we had a final roll call – needless to say all were 'present and correct', and 450 of us left the camp for Abergele Station; where we entrained at 10.0 am for Liverpool and arrived at this great port at 1.0 pm. On the way through Wales and through Liverpool, people 'threw goodbyes' to us and waved handkerchiefs and flags as they knew we were the 'Canadians going home'. We detrained at Lime Street Station, Liverpool, on the identical platform where we entrained some years ago, on our arrival in England – and American Red Cross ladies served us some delicious coffee and cakes. Rumour had it, whilst we were at Rhyl, that we were crossing on the 'Empress of Britain', but this proved erroneous, as we found we were to sail on H.M. Troopship Regina. We went aboard at 3.0 pm, and at 4.0 pm the Regina slipped her moorings to the strains of a brass band of the imperial army playing 'Auld Lang Syne', and 'Good-bye', and the tumultuous cheering of many relatives and friends who had assembled on the wharf to wave us 'bon voyage', and it was clear many of the boys had formed friendships in England that were long and strong. Going down the Mersey, vessels of large and small calibre saluted us with their whistles and sirens, and we got a send-off sufficient to knock all thoughts of sea sickness out of our heads – till later, when many could speak of an 'inner knowledge' of it. Whilst still going down the Mersey all were paraded on deck, assigned lifeboats, rafts etc; in case of any emergency, but with all of Germany's piratical craft safely under lock and key in English ports the probability of an emergency was 'negligible'. The Regina is a new vessel of about 15,000 tons belonging to the White Star Line, and consequently was scrupulously clean, and this trip was her maiden voyage. We slept in hammocks on our deck, and the next deck underneath had for sleeping quarters, tiers of 'ships beds', three-deep, one above the other. The hammocks and blankets were new and clean. The Regina carried slightly over 2,000 troops and each military district in the Dominion, except Toronto, had from 50 to 400 men returning to that area for dispersal. For the first four days out, we wore life-belts whilst on deck, and all the time wore 'flu masks', (the wearing of steel helmets and gas masks was optional). The day after leaving Liverpool each man was paid one pound and most of this sum was soon expended on chocolate, cigarettes and other luxuries, in the canteen on board.

The writer went on to say that eight days after embarking from Liverpool they disembarked at Halifax, Nova Scotia, and received a great welcome there. The men were only 'detained' long enough to hand in their rifles and bayonets, and were given receipts for them. Then west by train, this train made up of those from M. D. Wings 10, 11, 12 and 13. The figures: 50 for Winnipeg; 200 for Saskatchewan; 200 for Alberta and 30 for British Columbia. The writer went then to Quebec, and crossed there what he called, 'the new bridge'. Then a further train journey or two, and he and his comrades, formerly-in-arms, returned to their respective home cities, towns or villages.

As may be gleaned from the above account, that post-Armistice before getting to Kinmel Park Camp, many of the Canadian soldiers eagerly awaiting repatriation had already spent time in at least one or two, other 'staging/transit' camps. Their impatience to be embarking on-board a troopship for home was already present before they even arrived at Kinmel Park Camp – the 'last hurdle' one might say for them to get over before their actually going home aboard a ship became a reality. They were on a moving conveyer belt and woe betide anyone or anything that caused this to stall, let alone stop!

Chapter Three

The serious riots/disturbances of 4/5 March 1919

John Henry Foster Babcock, Canada's last known surviving veteran of the First World War, years later recalled the evening of Armistice Day when he was at Kinmel Park Camp, and remembered a serious altercation between some Canadian soldiers and British soldiers inside the Camp, when the revelries for the end of hostilities got somewhat out of hand: *We were there when the Armistice was signed on November 11 1918. We got into a beef with some British soldiers and they armed themselves with rifles and bayonets. One fellow got a little obstreperous and they stuck a bayonet through his thigh.*

From Armistice Day the war was over and Kinmel Park Camp took on its new role as a staging camp for the thousands of Canadian soldiers, many of them 'war weary' and anxious to get home as soon as possible. From this day, those in charge tried to maintain discipline in the camp as before, but now things had drastically changed and these Canadian soldiers virtually all of whom had been civilians until their enlistment in the C.E.F, were no longer keen 'to play the disciplined soldier', with parades and route marches, for them it was very soon to be their discharge from military service and 'civvy street' beckoned.

A precursor for what occurred later

A number of what can be called 'precursors' to the far more widespread 'mutinous mayhem' of 4/5 March 1919, took place at Kinmel Park Camp between the Armistice and those two dark days in March 1919.

On the evening of 20 November 1918, a quite serious altercation occurred in the camp. It came about because a group of QMAAC's (members of Queen Mary's Army Auxiliary Corps) had invited some Canadian soldiers to a social event in a hut in the camp. However, when they arrived at 'the do' they were brusquely turned away by some British soldiers. They took umbrage to this, feeling slighted that they had only been stopped from attending because they were Canadians. They smashed some windows and at one stage it did look as if this incident was going to turn very nasty indeed. But with the use of rifle butts and clubs by the military police, order was eventually restored.

Probably though the most serious of these precursors occurred on 10 January 1919, and very much to the fore here was a Canadian corporal, one **Holly James Leet**, an example of the part hero, part villain type of soldier who served in the First World War in the Canadian and British expeditionary forces – brave and uncompromising in battle, but indolent away from the Front. A nightmare to deal with for officers, but especially for NCO's.

Holly James Leet was born on 18 December 1896, at Harcourt, Kent County, New Brunswick, Canada. He enlisted at Sussex, New Brunswick, in the C.E.F, and was described as five feet, eight inches tall, of fair complexion, with blue eyes and sandy coloured hair. He arrived in England on 9 November 1915, aboard the S.S. Corsican. When at Bramshott Camp he contracted paratyphoid and was seriously ill for a time, and he spent many weeks in hospital. After recovering, he received further training and kitting out in southern England. Private Holly James Leet, regimental number 445480, was with his unit 55th Battalion (New Brunswick & Prince Edward Island), C.E.F at the

Front in France & Flanders on 17 May 1916. Six weeks later he was given field punishment No.1 for being absent from a working party. On 22 January 1917, he refused to go on a working party; was absent from church parade; and the following day, absent from the commanding officer's parade. Again, he received field punishment No. 1 for these military offences. He also served at the Front with 87th Battalion (Canadian Grenadier Guards).

Yet a few months after these transgressions he was in action at the Front for which he was later to be awarded the Military Medal. Further 'military discipline transgressions' occurred, including one which foretold of later events – his problem with 'the demon drink'. On 8 March 1917, 'on Active Service, Drunk on Parade', as it was put on his military record, more field punishment No. 1 came the way of this obviously 'hard drinking, hard fighting man'.

He was then engaged in fighting in another battle for which he was awarded a bar to his Military Medal – basically he was awarded another Military Medal.

On 10 January 1919, whilst at Kinmel Park Camp awaiting his repatriation, Corporal Holly James Leet was drunk and at the forefront of a group of soldiers attempting to free one of their fellow soldiers from a guard room where he was being held. His military record explains what exactly transpired and note the word 'mutiny' was included in the main charge against him:

In confinement awaiting trial 10/1/1919.
(1) Joining in a mutiny at KPC on 10/1/1919. Joined in a mutiny to secure release of a prisoner confined in the guard room. (2) Striking Superior Officer at KPC. Struck with butt end of rifle Major C. W. Hodgson. Sentenced to be reduced to the ranks & Sentenced to 5 years penal servitude and to be discharged with ignominy from the service – 21/2/1919.

So, now Private Holly James Leet had pushed his luck too far. The fact he had his rifle with him when he went to the guard room, and then used the butt of it to strike a major just shows how drunk and indeed how belligerent he was, and gives us an indication of the attitude of some of the Canadian soldiers in the camp, and remember, this incident took place before the real delays in shipping of the Canadian soldiers back home began. There was a lawlessness and wildness about many of these Canadian soldiers, who when sober did nothing more than grumble and refuse to go on route marches, but in drink, a lot of drink, they lost the plot completely.

Holly James Leet was indeed a lucky man for it was decided that after he had served one year of his five-year prison sentence, the remainder would be remitted, and he returned to Canada.

Holly James Leet, calling himself Wally J. Leet, wrote a letter from his home at Harcourt, Kent County, New Brunswick, dated 19 January 1950, to the Canadian Pension Commission in Ottawa, following a communication he had received from them about his pension. This letter, is as written by him:

Dear Sirs, Inclosed please find life certificate, filled in, is there any way that the board could see their way clear to give me a little more pension. Would you also let me know where my war medals that were not given out are kept. I only got four medals, M.M and Bar and Service Medals. I was recommended for the Victoria Cross three times and did not get it. Another medal I did not get was the Mons Star. Major Black now a baker I believe in Ottawa will tell you all about me. Colonel Donahu and Captain Warng are the officers that recommended me.
Thanking you in advance, I am yours sincerely, Wally J. Leet

He received a prompt and courteous reply dated 13 February 1950, from the director of war service records, who informed him there was no record of any Victoria Cross being awarded to him, and also that he was not entitled to the 1914/1915 Star Medal, also called the Mons Medal, as he had to have been in France before midnight on 31 December 1915 to receive it, whilst he only arrived in France in May of 1916.

Firstly, one could argue having been 'discharged from the service with ignominy' back in 1919, he was rather fortunate to be receiving a military pension at all, despite his heroics at the Front. This 'Jekyll and Hyde' character during the First World War may have thought that he was genuinely entitled to the Victoria Cross, and the 1914/1915 Star, or it could have been the bluster of an 'old sweat'. But I would like to think that he genuinely believed that he was entitled to them. I have come across many cases in the First World War of soldiers being recommended for the Victoria Cross by officers who witnessed their bravery, but the soldiers so recommended, were not actually awarded one. The VC, the so special a military award for 'gallantry in the presence of the enemy' is rarely awarded.

Holly James Leet, known as 'Wally' died on 15 January 1965, aged sixty-eight.

The background to the riots/disturbances of 4/5 March 1919

It is said that the secret of running any staging or transit camp is to keep the people, in this case, Canadian soldiers, flowing through. That way any troublemakers are quickly moved on. That stopped happening at Kinmel Park Camp, which proved to be a 'fatal flaw' in the Canadian military's plans for the repatriation of many thousands of their men.

Bolshevism at this time was very much feared amongst many countries of the world, especially European ones. The revolts in Russia during the First World War, much of it 'the fault' of Germany in their attempts to de-stabilize one of their main foes were proof to many that Bolshevism and Communism were spreading and had to be firmly stamped out. The fact that some of those involved in the riots/disturbances of 4 and 5 March 1919, at Kinmel Park Camp had held aloft a red flag, was in itself a declaration that for some of those involved it was indeed a political struggle, even 'if' this had not really been their avowed intention. These few 'ringleaders' had politicised what in reality was an alcohol fuelled, non-political protest against the poor conditions in the camp, and more importantly the length of time it was taking for them to be gone from the camp and on their way back to their homeland of Canada. Many of those involved very much the worse for the alcohol they had purloined from their looting of canteens and other camp buildings, made them far less open to reason and common sense. Whilst on the other hand, many of the 'defenders' of the camp felt they were protecting what little resources they had in the camp. They were also genuinely outraged that they knew a number of the 'rioters' had not seen action at the Front, and/or were draftees, i.e., not men who had voluntarily enlisted in the C.E.F. As the looters made for the records office at the camp, 'the defenders' also feared that if the personal records were destroyed, it would set back their own dates for their return to Canada.

I have included in this chapter a number of accounts which appeared in Canadian newspapers following the riots/disturbances at Kinmel Park Camp. They are from Canadian soldiers who had not long returned to Canada, having spent themselves weeks in Kinmel Park Camp. Unlike the British newspapers they were not as keen to condemn those involved in the riots/disturbances.

The events of 4/5 March 1919

On the evening of Tuesday, 4 March 1919, at approximately 9.00 pm at Kinmel Park Camp, a large gathering of Canadian soldiers took place. It was neither a military gathering, nor due to any social event that was taking place. The actual number of soldiers was a figure of between 500 and 2,000, depending on what source you take. Many of these soldiers were the worse for alcohol and they decided that they had, had enough of the delays for their sailings back to Canada, and with the 'added bonus' that conditions in the camp, food, heating and a few other things wise, were poor, they went on the rampage. A mob such as this are easily led and seek out persons and/or property on whom or which they can vent their anger. They attacked various buildings including canteens and messes in the camp during the evening, and into the early hours of the following day. Some in the mob felt aggrieved at the prices they were charged for various items, and wrecked the shops, looting their contents. The favourite items for their looting were unsurprisingly, booze, cigarettes and tobacco. They did spare the Salvation Army building, the 'Sally Ann', which they regarded as being a worthy entity.

These disturbances, which I suggest, had not yet reached 'riot' levels, came as a surprise to most of the senior Canadian officers in the camp. They had heard murmurings and were fully aware that a large proportion of those who served under them at the camp were most unhappy at the camp, especially because of their long waits to be repatriated. But such levels of damage and looting they did not expect in the least. They of course were attacking 'their own' camp shops and buildings. By the early hours of the morning, Wednesday, 5 March 1919, the camp's officers led by Colonel Malcolm Alexander Colquhoun had by now a defence strategy. Colonel Colquhoun though was adamant that whatever actions they took to defend the camp it was not to result in bloodshed, he had seen enough of that during the war, and after all, they were dealing with soldiers of their own C.E.F. He also realised that to use force against a drunken mob of soldiers would inevitably result in a pitched battle and that deaths might ensue. Some arrests were made and finally by about 3.30 am things had quietened down.

The damage in the camp was assessed, and it was found that the buildings 'wrecked' consisted of eleven canteens or messes; the eleven privately owned shops in Tin Town, located on land adjacent to the camp; two YMCA huts; and the NACB (Navy and Army Canteen Board) stores for allegedly profiteering at their expense. No 'serious' injuries had been sustained to anyone involved, on either side – yet.

By breakfast time that morning, the senior officers in the camp had gathered together 'defenders' and sent out military police and others in 'mufti' to spy on what was going on, and to identify who were at the core of it. Some violent attempts had been made to free from guardrooms at the camp, some of those arrested, and now detained. Incidents occurred all over the camp, with one group carrying a red flag, who have become known as 'the banner party', and they were hell bent on going on the rampage. Despite being warned not to go to Camp 20, as it was well defended, they did so, and it is here and in the vicinity of here, that the five Canadian soldiers met their violent deaths, by rifle bullets or by the bayonet. It should be said that during the entire riots/disturbances there was a hardcore of soldiers out to cause mayhem at the camp, but others took part in a lukewarm sort of way, and there were plenty of 'hangers-on', really mere spectators to events, but they helped swell the numbers. Both sides were to accuse the other of opening fire first and there is no doubt there was violence on both sides, and 'sheer bloody mindedness' abounded. Camps 15, 19 and 20 had decided they would 'sternly oppose' any attempts of the mob to run riot in their respective camps. Following the shooting by rifle fire, eventually 'some of the mob' raised a white flag and it was over. A number of soldiers were arrested and placed in detention in guardrooms around the various M. D. Wings of the camp.

Five Canadian soldiers were dead, dozens injured, some seriously, fifty or so arrested, and others being sought for arrest. All of the accused would subsequently face a general court martial. Who fired first and indeed who was responsible for the deaths by rifle bullets is still a matter for conjecture, though it was almost certainly the defenders despite their denials. The two killed by bayonet wounds were killed in the struggle between the two opposing sides. Whether the level of intensity of the violence against the defenders warranted men being bayoneted, is only something that those who were there at the time could truly answer.

What is not generally known and I am sure the 'British' authorities would not have wished to become public, was that it was not just soldiers of the C.E.F who were involved in the looting of items during the riots/disturbances. For the military police arrested eight civilians who were caught stealing government owned clothing. Three of them were also stealing food supplies. These eight civilian miscreants were either at the camp working on the infrastructure there, collecting the garbage or delivery men, none would have been Canadian. Some civilians also were mingled in amongst the 'mob' itself.

These accounts taken from returned Canadian soldiers, who had only recently themselves been at Kinmel Park

Camp, appeared very promptly following the riots/disturbances and provide a genuine insight into the causes or perceived causes of them:

The *Edmonton Bulletin*, Alberta, Canada, edition of 10 March 1919:

> Returned Men Not Surprised at Riots in Canadian Camp at Rhyl; Many Causes of Complaints Existed
> Food Served Meagre and Poor in Quality – Grounds Excessively Muddy and Huts Where Men Housed Cold – First Contingent Men Incensed Because Draftees Were Sent Back to Canada First.
> Halifax, March 8 – Many of the veterans of the Canadian forces who returned on the 'Cassandra' said they were not surprised to hear that there had been trouble at Rhyl Camp. They state that a good deal of dissatisfaction exists among the older service men in England. Men of the first contingents are incensed over the fact that 'draftees' are being sent back to Canada first, under the 'units intact' system.
> The conditions at Rhyl Camp are described as bad. The camp is said to be devoid of all organisation, and the sleeping accommodations are 'unfit for human beings.'
> The food was described by many of the men as being unfit to eat. As many as forty-two men were compelled to sleep in one hut, according to one man, and the general conditions at the camp were intolerable.
> Bitterly Cold; Food Poor in Quality
> Montreal, March 8 – The principal complaints heard here about Rhyl Camp are that it is bitterly cold and that the food served there is meagre and poor in quality.
> The bitterest complaints about the camp were made by a number of men who came home on the 'Royal George' and who said that there were no fires in some of the huts.

> Camp Very Uncomfortable.
>
> Toronto, March 8 – Returned Toronto soldiers who were located at Rhyl describe the camp as 'very uncomfortable'.
>
> The ground was excessively muddy, and the huts where they were housed none too warm. Eight weeks ago, when the men interviewed here last night left camp, there was, they said, developing among the troops a spirit of impatience. The soldiers wanted to get home, and Canadians could not understand why they were being held so long. Kinmel Camp is situated about four and one-half or five miles from the town of Rhyl in Wales, and covers about 200 acres on the rising ground at the south western mouth of a valley of which the town is the centre.

An insight into life in and around Kinmel Park Camp for the Canadians by a Canadian soldier who had seen over one and a half years at the Front in France & Flanders. Here is an extract taken from his 'Letter to the Editor' which appeared in the *Edmonton Bulletin*, Alberta, Canada, 15 March 1919 edition:

> ... The riots at Rhyl do not require much investigation. Anyone who has spent more than a few days there will know the conditions of that place. The Camp by the way is not at Rhyl, but at Kinmel Park, which is six miles from Rhyl, three and a half from Abergele, and three miles from Rhuddlan. There is a standard gauge train running from Rhyl to the Camp about ten times a day. But when you arrive from the Reserves, you have to march from Abergele and it is generally after dark, at night. Now if you are an A1 category man you have to carry full marching order. That is to say, rifle, steel helmet, web equipment and kit bag. We entrained at 8.30 am, arrived

at Abergele at 6.30 pm, and had to march nearly four miles. For lunch we had cold beef and a jam sandwich, breakfast had been at 4.30 am.The train running from Rhyl to Kinmel Park was used for taking the troops to Rhyl, at the cost of nine pence return, to the shows etc. Except during the morning when they brought up one train load of provisions to the Camp. When leaving Kinmel Park you have to march that distance also…
(signed) ONE WHO WAS LUCKY

This piece which appeared in the *Armstrong Okangan Commoner*, British Columbia, Canada, edition of Thursday, 27 March 1919, was taken by them from the *British Columbia Veteran's Weekly*. A publication written by soldiers who again had themselves recently, or fairly recently, passed through post-Armistice Kinmel Park Camp.

THE KINMEL PARK AFFAIR
The riots at Kinmel Park will rank amongst the saddest and most depressing events of the war. That men who have done their duty to the limit since the first, should be shot down by their fellows when almost in sight of their long desired embarkation for home, is heart breaking. What a wrench to the already sorely tried feelings of their relatives and friends who were waiting for them on Canada's shore!

The saddest thing of all is that it is the direct result of incompetent management, and of the callous indifference on the part of the responsible authorities. The affair comes as no surprise to the men who have passed through Kinmel Park. The conditions there are as bad as can be, and a spark has only been needed during the past six weeks to produce some such similar conflagration.

The men assembled in the camp have been in a state of inflammatory excitement for weeks past: not merely from lack of shipping, but because of the cruelly hard conditions under which they were expected to exist while waiting.

The food was bad, badly prepared, and quite insufficient. The men literally, have been starved, and maintained themselves in condition, only by buying food in the towns and villages of the district. As numbers of them were financially 'broke' and were unable to obtain their pay on account of some failure on the part of the authorities to make arrangements, many of the men, perforce, had to go hungry.

The sleeping accommodation was unfit for cattle – even cattle are provided straw bedding. But the men who have sacrificed their all for Canada and the world, were not expecting to rest themselves in mid-winter sleeping on the bare floors of draughty and cold huts. Even the poor comfort of wooden sleeping platforms to raise their bodies a few inches above the draughts on the floor was denied, although that was asked for, and there were plenty in store. All that was provided were three dirty, and often times verminous, old blankets.

Can it be wondered at that serious dissatisfaction should arise? As a fact, deaths as a result of the hardships entailed were common, while many other men suffered in health without reporting themselves as ill, for fear they might lose their position in regard to their place on a ship home to Canada.

Then there was the matter of discrimination and the giving of preference to draftees and others less entitled to preference, instead of to the volunteers of three and four years' service. This is a matter of common knowledge, and requires something more than the excuses that have been officially made to give it justification.

The worst feature of all is the attempt that is now being made to put the whole blame on the men. It is said, 'that it is not attempted in the slightest degree to excuse the conduct of the men who took part in the disturbance. Many of the offenders have been placed under arrest, who with others involved will be vigorously dealt with'.

This is simply abominable. These men who have been goaded by cruelty and unfair treatment into a series of reprehensible acts, are to be made scapegoats, while the real culprits, the persons responsible for the conditions that have caused the trouble, are to get off scot free.

Such cannot be the last word in the matter. A military tribunal is now going on; but if a report satisfactory to the men is not forthcoming, a more searching investigation before an impartial tribunal, preferably with a jury, must be demanded. The real culprit must be brought into the light, and that, without fear or favour.

The War Diaries of some of the M.D. Wings at Kinmel Park Camp

These are how some of the M.D. Wings, their full title being Military District Concentration Wings (MDCW's), reported the 'rioting and looting' of 4 and 5 March 1919, and the days that followed in their official War Diaries and appendices reports.

M.D. 13 being located at Camp 15. **M.D. 13's War Diary had an Appendix 'B' included in it:**

CONFIDENTIAL *APPENDIX 'B'.*

M.D. 13,
Kinmel Park Camp,
Rhyl, North Wales, 6th March 1919.

To Headquarters, Canadian Troops, Kinmel Park Camp.
In accordance with your telephoned instruction of today's date the following report of proceedings in this Wing, during recent disturbances is forwarded to you, please.

On receipt of information on the night of the 4th Inst., that certain rioting had broken out in the Area, Picquets were at once detailed. Three parties of 90 men each were formed. Each party was in the charge of an Officer and senior N.C.O.'s.

A small party approached the lines on Tuesday night, but were ordered off and went quietly.

On Wednesday morning, the whole of the Wing where paraded, and the situation explained, and the men in all hands expressed the greatest willingness to resist any intrusion of men from other Wings.

Picquets were posted, and the men ordered to stand-by in their huts ready to fall in immediately on the 'Alarm' being sounded.

Ten Picquets of 60 men each, in the charge of an Officer and three Senior N.C.O.'s where detailed to posts at points controlling access to the Camp from North, and South, at the Guard Room, Record Office and N.A.C.B. Canteen respectively. This gave 300 men on duty, and 300 standing-by continuously. These Picquets were armed upon the arrival of rifles, and bayonets from H.Q. In addition, a party of 25 men were told off under Major Clark, and held back in reserve at Q.M. Stores.

About 11.0 a.m. on Wednesday, a party of about 20 men from other M.D.'s arrived here. They were at once ordered off, and probably because of the party of men who had fallen in on the word being passed around all obeyed promptly, with the exception of one man who hesitated to obey the order, and who was immediately placed under arrest, and put in the Guard Room. Nothing further of any importance occurred.

Upon the commencement of the rioting, the troops of this Unit were confined to Camp, and the Picquets given orders to allow no one out., except on duty. Some of the men eluded the Picquets and went out, but not very many, as when the fall-in was sounded during the day, practically all the men were present. The spirit of the men seemed to be excellent, and expressions of disapproval of the conduct of the rioters was very general. The Officers of the Wing rendered very good service and stayed constantly with the men. In this connection I would particularly draw your attention to Lieutenants Postans and Metler, the Company Commanders who performed most meritorious service. They always had their men well in hand and the result of the discipline they have previously maintained was very evident.

No looted articles of any kind were seen being brought into these Lines. No damage of any kind was caused.
*H. Hon******, Major,*
O.C., M.D. 13 Wing,
Kinmel Park Camp.

The two lieutenants Postans and Metler named in the above, were soon to be promoted, and they were Captain Thomas Grierson Postans and Captain Orland Leo Metler.

The War Diary entries for the following three days, 7, 8 and 9 March 1919, merely mentioned the weather and mundane everyday matters. However, the War Diary entry for 10 March 1919, was one of expecting further rioting within Kinmel Park Camp:

10th March 1919 – Wet and very windy. 7 Officers and 286 Other Ranks dispatched to Canada, sailing on the 'S.S. Celtic'. There was a meeting of Wing Commanders at H.Q. Command, Kinmel Park Camp, at night, at 20.30. On return of the C.O. a meeting of all the Officers in the Wing was called and it was explained that another and more organised riot might take place. Picquets were immediately sent out and Scouts sent out.

11th March 1919 – Heavy rain, turning to sleet and snow later. The night passed quietly. 3 Officers taken on strength from M.D. No. 11.

The War Diary of M.D. 6 – Camp 19

The references to Private David Gillan I have taken out and are shown in the following chapter.

5th March 1919 – Cold cloudy day with rain.
11.00 Commanding Officer called a Parade of all Officers and other ranks, and asked for their support if this Camp was attacked by the rioters.
13.15 Rioters reached Camp 20 carrying red flags. Parade called and all the men told off in the Platoon under Officers and placed in defensive positions.
13.45 Fight started between Rioters and Camps 19 and 20. Rifles and live ammunition used by rioters.
7 Prisoners taken by Camp 19.
15 Prisoners taken by Camp 20. 4 Rioters killed.
14.00 All Prisoners sent away under strong escort in lorries to Camp Headquarters.
All men stood to in Camp all night, but everything was quiet.

6th March 1919 – Fine bright day in the morning, but cloudy in afternoon.
11.00 General Turner V.C., and Colonel Colquhoun, G.O.C. Kinmel Park Camp visited camp and talked to the men on parade re disturbances in Camps, and congratulated the men of this District on their behaviour.

7th March 1919 – 8 men proceeded on Pass for 6 days for good conduct in the Rioting.

8 and 9 March 1919 – Everyday matters only put in War Diary.

10th March 1919 – Cloudy day with high wind and rain.
15.00 Conference at Headquarters for all Wing Commanders.
19.00 Concert in canteen by Artillery Concert Party.

The last entry shows of course that despite the rioting and looting, the deaths of five soldiers from the camp, including 'their own' Private David Gillan, life went on pretty much as normal. That I suppose is what war does to human beings. Many of those at the camp had been in the trenches at the Front, and been in bloody battles, and stared death squarely in the face on a daily basis.

M.D. 3 War Diary

Kinmel Park 4-3-19. Serious rioting occurred in this Wing. The rioting commenced at approximately 9.15 pm, in No. 7 Canteen which was wrecked and looted. The merry rioters then proceeded to No. 6 Canteen which shared the same fate of its predecessor. The Sergeant's Mess next claimed the attention of the mob who then proceeded to the N.A.C.B. Stores in Camp 7. It seems that almost simultaneously the shops in 'Tintown' were sacked. The mob had by now grown to great proportions, perhaps the greater portion of whom were not active participants in the riot, but merely onlookers enjoying the spectacle and indulging in small indulgences made safe for them by the general confusion. All were more or less under the influence of alcohol. All night the most remarkable and disorderly scenes were witnessed. The fact that the N.A.C.B. and Tobacco stores are looted in camps occupied by this Wing, causing it to be a storm center to which all the disorderly spirits in the area flooded.

Many attempts to curb the disturbances were made but without success owing to the size and temper of the mob.

Kinmel Park 5-3-19. Rioting continues and many disorderly scenes are witnessed.

Kinmel Park 6-3-19. Riots have apparently subsided and comparative quiet prevails.

Arrests of a number of ringleaders of the rioters are made. One at least ex-Sergeant of this Unit who is regarded as being responsible for much of the damage done in this camp.

Kinmel Park 7-3-19. It is learned today that the reports in the newspapers to the effect that the rioters entered the quarters of the N.A.C.B. girls and took from them their clothing while the girls were in bed, is totally without foundation. The girl's overalls worn by the rioters were secured when the N.A.C.B Stores were looted.

Kinmel Park 8-3-19. Brigadier-General McBride, C.B, C.M.G, D.S.O., arrives on tour of inspection of the damage caused in the recent riots.

Kinmel Park 9-3-19. The camp has now resumed its normal aspect. Pioneers are engaged in the work of repair to damaged buildings and are rapidly putting things to rights.

M.D. 7 War Diary

Kinmel Park Camp: March 5 1919 – In the Disturbances that occurred in this Area on March 5th, the following casualties were reported by this Wing:
Killed – 326914 Gnr Hickman J.S. & 438680 Corporal Young,

J. Wounded – 793998 Spr. Robins, G.A.; 274182 Pte Bryson, J.; 445037 Spr Walsh, W.P.

M.D. 10 War Diary

5th March – Rioting continued throughout the day.

6th March – Lieut. General Sir R E.W. Turner, V.C., K.C.B., K.C.M.G., D.S.O, CD visited this Wing at 11.0'clock on this date and addressed the men. He fully explained the situation regarding the delay in despatching the men from this camp. The address and explanation given was listened to with keen interest, and the men appeared quite satisfied that everything possible was being done in their interests.

7th March 1919 – Normal conditions restored in camp today. Routine work as usual.

M.D. 11 War Diary – Camp 17

Kinmel Park Camp – 4th March 1919. Everyday details, but at the end of this entry a note.
Note: N.A.C.B. Canteen was raided and looted by troops this date. Sgt's Mess ditto.

5-3-19 – Rioting continued during the morning and afternoon in the Area. This Wing was not affected.

A strong permanent armed camp guard was formed.

No. 2137797 Pte Golden, J of this Wing was placed in the Guard Room for rioting and looting.

All pay records were removed to a place of safety.

No. 102032 Pte Bisloud, B; No. 64527 Pte Williams, H.B. and Pte Scott of this Wing removed from this area under escort from M.D. 6 Guard Room charged with rioting and looting.

6-3-19 – (Details of hospital admissions and discharges given) No. 2137797 Pte Golden, J was taken under escort to Guard Room M.D.1 prior to removal to London.

No. 2140663 A/Cpl Morrison, J.B. placed in Guard Room and taken under escort to Guard Room M.D. 1 prior to removal to London, on charge of rioting and looting.

M.D. 5 War Diary

Strangely, the War Diary of M.D. 5 has no references to any 'disturbances' in Kinmel Park Camp, but only includes in entries every day, mundane matters. Obviously, they were not at all or to any extent affected by the riots/disturbances.

M.D. 4 War Diary

Again, no mention of the 'disturbances' of 4 and 5 March 1919, in their War Diary entries. Again, we can assume they were not affected.

Chapter Four

The five soldiers killed during the riots/disturbances

1. David Gillan – born in Scotland

David Gillan was born on 2 December 1898, in Lanarkshire, Scotland, to John Gillan, a Scottish coal miner who was born in 1868, and wife Emily Gillan, nee Gray, born in 1875. This Gillan family were living in Drygate Street, Larkhall, Lanarkshire, when, seeking a better life on 25 April 1903 they emigrated to Canada. They left the Port of Glasgow aboard the S.S. Mongolian bound for Halifax, Nova Scotia, Canada. At this time David Gillan was a child of four and his elder brother John (junior) was six.

At the outbreak of the First World War, David Gillan was like his father and elder brother John, a coal miner at Sydney Mines, Nova Scotia. Sydney Mines being a community and town which was then a great centre of coal production. John Gillan (junior) decided to volunteer and enlisted in February 1916, in 185th Battalion (Cape Breton Highlanders). The following month David Gillan volunteered and enlisted at Sydney Mines on 13 March 1916 in 85th Battalion (Nova Scotia Highlanders), an infantry battalion and part of the C.E.F. He was given the regimental number of 877467, and on his attestation papers he gave his next of kin as being his father, John Gillan of Florence, Cape Breton, Nova Scotia. On enlistment David Gillan still only seventeen was five feet five inches tall and gave his religion as being Presbyterian. By this time the Gillan's had had two further children, Robert Gillan born on 22 January 1907 and Emily Gillan born on 15 April 1912.

Sadly, Emily died aged but four months in August of 1912.

After some initial military training in Canada, Private David Gillan embarked on 13 October 1916 for Britain and the ongoing war on the Western Front aboard the S.S. Olympia, arriving at the Port of Liverpool on 19 October 1916. Due to his young age, David Gillan spent some time at the Witley Camp, Surrey, England, rather than going to the Front in France and Flanders. He was at this military training camp until 23 February 1918, when he was transferred for a short period to the Bramshott Camp, Hampshire, from where on 28 March 1918, he left for the Front.

David Gillan survived his time at the Front, and post-Armistice found himself one of the thousands of Canadian troops at the Kinmel Park Camp, North Wales. He arrived here on 25 February 1919 from the Ripon Camp, and he was placed on M.D. Wing No. 6.

The No. 9 Canadian Military Hospital Kinmel Park Camp hospital report upon David Gillan was as follows:

877667 Pte. Gillan, David
85th Btn; M. D. 6; Camp 19
The body of a well-developed young man, age estimated at 29, was dead on arrival at hospital. No particulars thus available.
Identified as Pte. Gillan. Badges on tunic of 85th Btn. C.E.F.
Has an old scar from operation for appendicitis.
Entrance wound evidently of a bullet over scapular area at shoulder; wound overall less than half inch in diameter.
Exit wound one inch in diameter; in front of neck immediately to rt of thyroid
A cut on chin caused by the passage of same missile.
Cause of death – Bullet wound to neck.
H.W. Kerfoot, Captain.

The M.D. 6 Wing, War Diary entry for 5 March 1919, included a piece on David Gillan – 'one of their own' from this Wing:

Kinmel Park Camp 19 – March 5th.
No. 877467 Pte Gillan, D, killed in action against rioters.

The M.D. 6 Wing, War Diary entry for 10 March 1919, included this:

10.00 Funeral of No. 877467, Pte Gillan, D, who was killed on the 5th inst. against rioters. Service was held in Canteen where the body was lying, and final service was held in Bodelwyddan Church.

A funeral service in the Wing's canteen in the morning for David Gillan and a few hours later in the same canteen a 'jolly concert' was held.

Private David Gillan was buried at St Margaret's Churchyard, St Margaret's Church, Bodelwyddan (The Marble Church), in grave reference 506.

David Gillan was almost certainly one of the 'defenders' of Camp 20, and was facing the 'attacking mob' when he was accidentally hit by a rifle bullet from behind, fired by a fellow 'defender'.

2. William Lyle Haney – born in the United States

William Lyle Haney, known as Lyle, was born on 12 July 1896, at Benson County, North Dakota, United States, to Edward Eugene Haney, a farmer born in 1858, and Mary Frances Haney, nee McGowan who was born in 1869. The 1910 Census shows the Haney family residing in Normania Township, Benson County, North Dakota. In 1913, this Haney family emigrated to Alberta, Canada, and are shown on the 1916 Census as residing at Battle River, Alberta. Here seven children are shown to be living with the Haney's, Lyle being elsewhere.

Lyle Haney enlisted in the C.E.F on 4 February 1918, at Calgary, Alberta, in 78th Depot Battery, giving his occupation as rancher, and his next of kin being his father Edward now of Talbot, Alberta, who was also a rancher. Lyle was now Gunner William Lyle Haney, regimental number 1251417. He was tall for those days at five feet, eleven inches. Described as having a dark complexion, with brown eyes and dark brown hair. Whilst training at Calgary, Canada, on 15 February 1918, a horse at the 78th depot horse barns 'stomped' on his right foot and the big toe nail of this foot had to be removed at a military hospital. Whilst on active service he contracted diphtheria, a serious bacterial infection and spent time hospitalised in early Summer 1918. He was a signaller with 78th Battalion (Winnipeg Grenadiers).

Post-Armistice, Lyle Haney moved from Witley Camp, Surrey, England, to Kinmel Park Camp on 21 February 1919, and was placed on M.D. Wing No. 13, to await his embarkation on a troop transport ship back to Canada.

The medical examination and completion of the official 'Medical Case Sheet' at No. 9 Canadian General Military Hospital at Kinmel Park Camp were again carried out by Captain Herbert Wilfred Kerfoot. He made out two 'Medical Case Sheets' for William Lyle Haney. The first when he was brought in alive, but in a poor medical condition and the second after he had died. About the only real difference between the two records was that on the first one he had put: G.S.W. Head – accidental. This is the second and later one:

1251417 Signaller Haney, W.L.
Unit, Age and Service not known at this time.
Gunshot Wound Head.
This man was brought in to hospital about 2.30 pm, March 5th
Unconscious when admitted.
Died 7 o'clock same day.
Entrance wound of bullet on left side of face below eye.
Exit wound over left ear causing an extensive fracture of parietal bone of skull & disintegration of brain tissue which exuded.
Blood also exuded from mouth & nose, for a fracture of base of skull.
No other injury found on the body.
Cause of death directly due to the penetration of head by bullet.
H.W. Kerfoot, Captain, C.A.M.C.

Gunner N. J. McLeod, regimental number 1251433, who knew Lyle Haney well, was sent over to the hospital where his body was lying to make a formal identification. He was Gunner Norman James McLeod, born on 22 October 1892, at Montreal, Quebec, Canada, a son of G.H. McLeod, a prominent Alberta legislator and his wife, Ella McLeod. Gunner McLeod also served in 78th Battery of the C.E.F. On 3 May 1919, he embarked from Liverpool for his return to Canada, disembarking at Halifax, Nova Scotia, on 14 May 1919.

William Lyle Haney is buried in St Margaret's Churchyard, St Margaret's Church, Bodelwyddan (The Marble Church), in grave reference 503.

Records show that his mother Mary Frances Haney received the plaque, scroll and medals for her late son Lyle. She would also later have received a Canadian memorial cross.

William Lyle Haney does appear to have been amongst the group of soldiers who attacked Camp 20, and was killed by a bullet fired from a rifle by one of the 'defenders.'

The *Edmonton Bulletin*, Alberta, Canada, edition of 11 March 1919, had this in relation to William Lyle Haney. It contains the error in spelling of the name of 'Haney' as 'Hinney', but is an interesting insight into 'matters', so soon after his death during the riots/disturbances:

> Alberta Soldier, killed at Rhyl, Wales, had seen long service
>
> Calgary, March 10 – Private W. H. Clarke, late of the 89th battalion, and the son of the late Commissioner, S. J. Clarke, superintendent of the Banff National Park, and Private P. O'Reilly, of the 56th battalion, who arrived back home the other day, fully confirm the statement as to the cause of trouble at Kinmel Park Camp, Rhyl. It's just a matter of the men becoming impatient owing to promises not being carried out in connection with transportation. Both these men also state that much of the blame attaches to those in charge of the official papers: it is quite a common thing for these by some means or other to be mislaid or lost and this is much resented by the soldiers. Another feature in connection with the trouble is that men who have never been to France have been given the preference over those who have been in the trenches for four years or more.
>
> Private Clarke and Private O'Reilly knew Gunner William Hinney, who is reported one of the casualties in the riot, quite well. They state that Hinney was a fine type of man and had seen long service in France. Like others, he was naturally anxious to get back here. He was one of the cases, they state, where papers were lost.
>
> It would appear from what these men state that there is a complete absence of system at Kinmel Park. Whether this arose through sheer lack of ability, or whether much

of it was done purposely, they are not prepared to state, but from what they say, there would appear to be a little of both. In monotonous fashion the men are called out on parade and expectations rise high that they will be included in a 'sailing' company: but that sort of thing merely goes on from day to day without the men getting any further than Rhyl.

Another thing that the Canadian soldiers resent is the alleged preference that is being given to Americans, who, it is stated, are being sent home in a satisfactory manner. Not a little of the discontent is caused by the poor condition of the huts at Kinmel Park. Some of these it is stated are quite unsuitable for the purpose for which they are intended.

3. John Frederick Hickman

John Frederick Hickman, known as Jack, was born on 12 December 1897, at Dorchester, Westmorland County, New Brunswick, Canada. His parents were John Howard Hickman, born on 26 October 1858 at Dorchester, who owned and ran the local hardware and general store, grew vegetables commercially and operated a lumber (timber) business, and Theresa Hickman, nee Hay, who was born on 9 June 1871 at Dartmouth, Nova Scotia, Canada.

Theresa Hickman died on 7 February 1917, aged but forty-five whilst her son John Frederick Hickman was serving in France with the C.E.F (Canadian Expeditionary Force).

Gunner John Frederick Hickman, regimental number 326194, was five feet, ten inches tall, of medium complexion, with blue eyes and light-coloured hair, and arrived in England with the C.E.F on 22 September 1916, aboard the S.S. Metagama. After some further military training at Canadian camps in the south of England and kitting out, he went to serve at the Front in France & Flanders with 58th Battery, Canadian Royal Artillery (CRA).

Post-Armistice he found himself at Kinmel Park Camp, the final step before he would be given a place on a specific ship, leaving on a named date.

This is the medical case sheet for Gunner John Frederick Hickman at No. 9 Canadian General Hospital, Kinmel Park Camp:

326194 Pte Hickman, J.
C.R.A. Age 21.
Body of a young man brought to Hospital morgue about 5.30 p.m. on March 5th 1919.
The only mark of violence on body was a wound in centre of praecordia. This was fully an inch in diameter, with uneven edges. Two ribs were broken.
Profuse bleeding had occurred. Heart was penetrated.
This wound had the appearance of one caused by a bullet having turned in its course or by a ricochet.
No exit wound.
Cause of death – Penetrating wound of heart, probably by a bullet.
H. W. Kerfoot, Capt. C.A.M.C.

The newspapers local to Dorchester, New Brunswick, not surprisingly. covered the funeral of 'one of their own', when after demands by the Hickman family, the body of Jack Hickman was disinterred from the St Margaret's Churchyard (The Marble Church) at Bodelwyddan, and returned to Dorchester for a family burial. This account appeared:

THE FUNERAL OF GUNNER HICKMAN

May 29, Dorchester, N.B.

A large attendance and deeply solemn service was held in Dorchester. The Reverend W. E. Best paid a fitting tribute to a Dead Hero. Reverend Best said, 'It is not the usual custom of the church that the performance of the office for a burial of the dead should be made an occasion for preaching. But the present occasion seems to call for a slight deviation from the order, and just a brief word may not be out of place. The large congregation assembled here today is I take it, a tribute of respect to the memory of one who went forth from our midst, as did so many others, of the very flower of youth of our land, at the call of King and Country. And who having done his duty, having nobly and well played his part in the great struggle for right, was safely preserved through all the perils of the battlefield, only to be stricken down under such tragic and regrettable circumstances. Had he been killed in action, his death would have been a blow to his relatives, and a loss to his native place, where he was such a general favourite. The blow is rendered doubly sad, in that it was not so, how he met his death. There would be no good purpose served by entering into the details of the occurrences at Kinmel Camp on March 5th. But it is only right and fair to the memory of the brave lad, and the gallant soldier, that mention should be made of the fact that Jack Hickman was in no way whatsoever to blame for any share in those disturbances, which led up to his death. On the day upon which he was killed he was doing his duty. At the time when he was struck by a stray bullet he was where he had a right to be, and his death humanly speaking was purely accidental, and in no sense whatsoever his own fault. Of this we have abundant testimony, both from the evidence of those who were present in the camp at the time of the riot, and also from an official communication, lately received from the military authorities after enquiry into the circumstances. It is doing him bare justice that this should be said, because unfortunately, owing to the form in which the newspaper reports were received, there appeared to be for some time no very clear information as to whether Gunner Hickman was amongst the rioters or an innocent victim of a disturbance for which he was not to blame, and in which he was in no way involved. It is a matter concerning which, I believe no very definite statement has appeared in the Canadian press. Indeed, it was for some time a source of distress to his friends that from the press reports, there seemed to be at least reason for question on this point, and it was a great relief to have the matter officially set at rest, and the name of a brave soldier cleared of any suspicion even of indiscipline or unruly conduct'. Reverend Best then made reference to the death of Gunner Jack Hickman's mother, who had sadly passed away whilst he was serving in France. He now thought of the beloved mother and the child of her prayers, now reunited in Paradise.

Trinity Church was crowded to its utmost capacity with a very representative body of people from Moncton, Shediac, Memramcook, Sackville, Port Elgin and Amherst, being largely represented. Flags were half-masted on every flagpole in town. The public schools were closed for the afternoon. Every place of business was closed, and every office was closed to do honor to the fair name of the dead hero. The funeral procession was led by a detachment of Khaki clad soldiers, numbering thirty. The following returned soldiers performed the duties of pallbearers: Major H R Emmerson, Lieut H G Palmer, Lieut Willard

> Hutchinson, Sergeant Edgar Cole, Pte James Walker and Pte Ernest Getson. The casket was covered with the Empire's standard, and a rich profusion of flowers.

It was said that following the funeral service, at the burial itself at the Dorchester Rural Cemetery, that Gunner Jack Hickman's father, John Howard Hickman, now a widower aged sixty, 'stood ramrod straight in grief's dark silence, as the earth took the body of his son in'. John Howard Hickman died two years later, on 10 May 1921, aged sixty-two.

Gunner John Frederick Hickman there is no doubt was a totally innocent bystander killed by a stray rifle bullet, fired by one of the 'defenders' of Camp 20. At the coroner's inquest a Private Jack Norritt gave evidence that he and 'Jack Hickman' had gone out of mere curiosity to see what was happening, and they had been watching the events unfold for about three minutes when Jack Hickman was shot. When asked if he saw anyone take steady aim, he replied, 'I saw both sides taking very steady aim'. But he added that in the first attack as he called it, he saw the rioters with only one rifle and it was a broken one. When shown on a table in the room a bundle of coloured flags, he said they were being carried by one of the rioters who was very drunk.

4. William Tarasevich – born in the Russian Empire

William Tarasevich, incorrectly shown on some documents relating to him as Tarasevish or similar, was born on 22 February 1889, at probably Grodno, now in Belarus and formerly in the Russian Empire. He was a single man, a labourer, residing at 272, Cadieux Street, Montreal, Quebec, Canada, when on 3 January 1917, at Montreal, he enlisted in the C.E.F. He was living in a poor quarter of the city at the time and being an immigrant, he may well have chosen to enlist like many others did for financial reasons.

The Canadian army pay was not great, but at a basic one dollar and ten cents per day, it compared favourably to poorly paid labouring work, or of course of no work at all. He was described as being five feet, nine inches tall, of sallow complexion, with light blue eyes and brown hair. He signed his military papers 'W. Tarasevich', gave his religion as Greek Orthodox and his next of kin as being his mother, Mary Tarasevich who was living at probably Polotsk, now in Belarus, but formerly part of the Russian Empire. Sapper William Tarasevich, regimental number 1057297, embarked from Halifax, Nova Scotia, on HMT Justicia on 3 May 1917, disembarking at Liverpool, England, on 14 May 1917. He was at several Canadian military camps in England, until he went to France & Flanders from Purfleet Camp, Essex, with 4th Battalion, Canadian Railway Troops from 17 April 1918.

Sapper William Tarasevich arrived at Kinmel Park Camp, on or around 22 February 1919, to await his return by ship to Canada. On the afternoon of Wednesday, 5 March 1919 he was alleged to have been one of the leaders of the mob who made their way to Camp 20 to cause serious trouble there. Many of their number intent on continuing their wrecking and looting of the buildings in the camp. But despite being warned they would face stern opposition here, they still went to attack Camp 20. Shots were fired and violence broke out. Sapper William Tarasevich received what was certainly a bayonet thrusted into his abdomen, causing him not surprisingly to collapse. A number of different entries in his military record have the same explanation as to why he died: *Accidentally killed during disturbance at Kinmel Park.*

The medical case sheet for his death and cause of death was completed by Captain H. W. Kerfoot, Canadian Army Medical Corps., and was as follows:

No. 9 Canadian General Hospital, Kinmel Park Camp
Year 1919
1057297 Pte Tarasevich, William
23 Canadian Reserve Battalion, Age 30
Body of this man brought to Hospital morgue about 3.30 pm, March 5th.
The only mark of violence on the body was a wound through abdominal wall in the centre just below umbilicus. Wound an inch in diameter, a loop of intestine protruding. No haemorrhage. Wound had the appearance of a bayonet thrust.
Cause of death: Penetrating wound to abdomen by an instrument of the nature of a bayonet.

Sapper William Tarasevich was buried at St Margaret's Churchyard, St Margaret's Church (The Marble Church), Bodelwyddan, grave reference 505.

5. Joseph Young – born in Scotland

Joseph Young was born on 30 September 1882, at Glasgow, Scotland. In 1901 he was working in Glasgow as a confectioner's packer. He emigrated to Canada, and was thirty-two years of age, and a labourer, when on 29 April 1915, he volunteered and enlisted in the C.E.F at Port Arthur, Ontario, Canada. He gave his next of kin as being a sister, Miss M. Young of Pacific Street, Central Falls, Rhode Island, the United States. Joseph Young was described as being five feet, ten inches tall, of fair complexion, with blue eyes and brown hair. He became Private Young, regimental number 438680. After undergoing some military training and being kitted out in Canada, he arrived in England on 3 December 1915. After undergoing further military training in the South of England, he went to the Front in France & Flanders with 52nd Battalion (New Ontario), a C.E.F infantry battalion. Private Joseph Young must have shown a degree of aptitude for leadership, for in July 1916, he was first made lance-corporal and then promoted to corporal. In February 1917 he was taken ill with pyrexia, trench fever, and it was serious enough for him to have to spend some weeks in hospitals in England. He did not return again to the Front due to a medical condition.

Post-Armistice he found himself at Kinmel Park Camp on 9 December 1918, and was placed on M. D. 7 Wing awaiting repatriation. He showed his dislike of the camp, or the delay in his repatriation, or perhaps for some other reason, when he was severely reprimanded at a hearing on 31 January 1919, for having overstayed his permitted leave from the camp from 24.00 hours on 3 January 1919 to 12 January 1919, and forfeited nine days pay. Mind you he certainly was not the only one to do this. Pre-Armistice this offence of going AWOL (absent without leave), would have been dealt with by a more severe military punishment.

On the afternoon of Wednesday, 5 March 1919, Corporal Joseph Young was with a party of rioters in the camp who decided to attack Camp 20, even after they had received prior warning that this camp would offer them stern resistance to their wrecking and looting of buildings in the camp. In the melee which ensued between the attackers and the defending party, shots were fired, violent blows were struck and Corporal Joseph Young was struck in the face and neck by a 'sharp instrument' which no doubt was a bayonet. This occurred at about 3.30 pm, and he was removed still alive to the military hospital at the camp, where he was pronounced dead at 5.45 pm.

The medical case sheet for his death and cause of death, was completed by Captain H. W. Kerfoot, Canadian Army Medical Corps and this is what he wrote:

No. 9 Canadian General Hospital, Kinmel Park Camp
No. 2630 in Admission and Discharge Book – Year 1919
430600 Cpl Young, Joseph
52nd Battalion, M. D. 7
Wound of face
This man (particulars as yet unobtainable except those given above)
He is not yet identified.
Admitted to Hospital at about 3.30 pm, March 5th. Taken to operation room.
Died about 5.45 pm after return to ward.
This body is that of a heavily and powerfully built man, apparently of 35 years of age or more. Wound of face is seen which looks like one caused by a bayonet or sabre. This entered just below and outside left eye causing an opening an inch in diameter. This opening extended down towards front of neck fracturing part of solar bone; destroying whole of right side of base of tongue from which there had been very free haemorrhage, and ended opposite thyroid cartilage. Here, a large haematoma had formed which had been removed by operation. Tracheotomy had also been done.
Cause of death: A wound of head and neck by a sharp instrument, fracture by a bayonet.
This man has since been identified.

Corporal Joseph Young was buried at St Margaret's Churchyard, St Margaret's Church (The Marble Church), Bodelwyddan, in grave reference 504.

The *North Wales Chronicle* of 28 March 1919, reported upon the verdict reached by the coroner's inquest into the five deaths:

THE KINMEL CAMP RIOTS
JURY RETURN OPEN VERDICT
An open verdict was returned at the inquest at Rhyl yesterday on the five Canadians who lost their lives in the disturbance at Kinmel Camp.

The Coroner said that as all efforts to identify any individuals as being directly responsible for any of the deaths had failed, he felt it was useless to prolong the inquiry. The Home Office agreed with his view.

Captain H.W. Kerfoot who made the examinations and completed the medical reports on all five of the Canadian soldiers who suffered violent deaths on 5 March 1919, was **Captain Herbert Wilfred Kerfoot**, born on 25 March 1882, at Smiths Falls, Eastern Ontario, Canada. He was a physician and surgeon who had already served five years with Canadian military units when he enlisted for the C.E.F in early 1915, and served with the C.A.M.C. (Canadian Army Medical Corps) overseas, firstly in the Dardanelles and then in Salonika. After a period at Canadian military hospitals in England, on 4 January 1919, he was attached to No. 9 Canadian General Military Hospital at Kinmel Park Camp. He was present in the camp during the riots/disturbances of 4 and 5 March 1919. He left Kinmel Park Camp on 9 July 1919, finally sailing back to Canada on 12 September 1919.

Dr Herbert Wilfred Kerfoot died on 28 February 1974, aged ninety-one.

Chapter Five

Some of those soldiers found guilty of serious offences

1. Robert Archie – First Nations Canadian

Robert Archie was a Chippewa Indian, also known as Ojibwa of the First Nations, born in Morson, Ontario, Canada, on 3 December 1895. He was a fisherman who stood five feet, six inches tall, of dark complexion, with brown eyes and black hair. He was a single man when he enlisted in the C.E.F at Rainy River, Ontario, on 6 March 1916. He became Private Robert Archie, regimental number 820363. On his papers he gave his next of kin as being his mother, Maggie Archie, his father was Edward Archie. Private Robert Archie served in France & Flanders with 44th Battalion (Manitoba). On 2 March 1918, his military record shows that he had been granted a 'good conduct in the field badge'. Then on 27 September 1918, he was wounded in action, but remained on duty. Like so many other Canadian soldiers he suffered a bout of influenza. His in late November 1918, from which he recovered well, unlike so many at Kinmel Park Camp, and indeed around the world who did not.

He then found himself at Kinmel Park Camp, to await being returned to Canada. Private Robert Archie was accused of having taken an active part in the riots/disturbances, of 4/5 March 1919, at the camp. As a result of which he was arrested on 5 March 1919, and placed in military detention to await a court martial.

This extract is taken from the *Denbighshire Free Press* edition of 2 May 1915:

A RED INDIAN'S STORY

Private Robert Archie, full blooded Red Indian, of the 44th Battalion, appeared before the court martial on Monday charged with mutiny and with not using his best endeavours to suppress the riots. Captain Weir recognised Archie as one of the several men who were in the front of the main body of rioters. Lieut J. A. Gauthier identified prisoner as being one of the men, and also deposed to having seen him about 2.00 pm, when he was one of the men in front of the flag bearers in the party of rioters by the N.A.C.B. bakery stores. When witness warned them not to go near Camp 20, Archie said, 'Come on boys, come on, let's go', waving his arms. Lieut H. Perry said that about 3.00 pm on March 5th accused was leading a band of rioters from the direction of Camp 18, waving his arm and beckoning to the others to advance, and using abusive language. It was decided that the Camp 20 pickets should rush the rioters, and Archie was arrested. Archie, who was not sworn, made a statement in which he said his mother and father were Chippewa Indians. He enlisted in March 1916, went to France in June 1917, fought in many engagements, and came to Kinmel Park on March 1st. On the day of the riots he was told by a man whom he took to be a sergeant to go to the canteen and stand at the door with a rifle and bayonet. The place was attacked by such numbers that it was no use trying to defend it, and he hid his rifle. In trying to get away he was mixed up with the rioters. Major Weyman submitted that a man of the accused's antecedents could hardly be one of the rioters, nor, with his limited knowledge of English, could he have been a leader of white men in the mutiny as alleged. His story was quite consistent. A stranger to the camp, he got

> mixed up with the rioters in trying to get away from the canteen. As an Indian he was entitled to more consideration than the ordinary Canadian. The court adjourned to consider the case, and called for evidence of character. Sentence will be promulgated.

So, like others accused of being involved in the attack on 5 March 1919 upon Camp 20 and its defenders, he faced two main charges, namely, First Charge: 'Joining in a mutiny in Forces belonging to His Majesty's Military Forces, in that he at Kinmel Park Camp, on or about the 5th day of March 1919, joined in a mutiny by combining among themselves with then soldiers of the Canadian Expeditionary Force to resist their superior officers and to attack Camp 20, Kinmel Park Camp'. Second Charge (a lesser charge): 'Being present and not using their utmost endeavours to suppress a mutiny in Forces belonging to His Majesty's Military Forces. In that they at Kinmel Park Camp on or about the 5th day of March 1919, were present when soldiers belonging to the Canadian Expeditionary Forces combined together to resist their superior officers and to attack Camp 20, Kinmel Park Camp, and did not use their utmost endeavours to prevent same'.

His defence counsel Major Weyman played the 'race card' here by suggesting at the court martial that his client, Private Robert Archie was entitled to more consideration than the ordinary Canadian soldier. He of course was quite wrong in doing this, for Robert Archie was entitled to 'the same consideration' as the ordinary Canadian soldier, no more and no less. Being of First Nations (the indigenous people of Canada) appearance, he was always more likely to be identified by any witnesses. As it was, three Canadian officers had given evidence which totally contradicted Private Robert Archie's own account of what had transpired that afternoon. So, in the event it was not surprising that on the first more serious charge he was found guilty, though on the second, the lesser charge, he was found not guilty. He was sentenced to 23 months imprisonment with hard labour. This sentence promulgated at Grace Road Barracks, Liverpool, on 21 May 1919. That day he was not returned to further detention at M.D. 10, Kinmel Park Camp where he had been held since his arrest, but was committed to Walton Gaol, Liverpool to serve his sentence in a civilian prison.

However, much of his sentence was remitted, for on 22 October 1919, at Southampton, England, he embarked for Halifax Port, Nova Scotia, on his way back home.

2. John Patrick Brennan – born in England

John Patrick Brennan was born at Liverpool, England, on 3 June 1897, though one military record shows that he was born in Ireland. He was living in Huntley, eastern Ontario, when he enlisted in the C.E.F at Ottawa, Ontario, on 18 March 1916. He was described as being just a tad over five feet, three inches tall, of dark complexion, with brown eyes and hair. He gave his next of kin as his mother, Mrs Bridget Brennan, of 41, Victoria Square, Liverpool, England. At this time, he was a farmer and gave his religion as Roman Catholic. He embarked from the port of Halifax, Nova Scotia, aboard the iconic RMS Mauretania, arriving in England on 31 October 1916.

The RMS Mauretania was a true luxury liner, built for Cunard's in 1906, by the Swan Hunter Shipyard, Wallsend, Tyneside, England. During the First World War it became for a time a hospital ship, then a troop-carrying ship for Canadian soldiers, and then later in the war for American soldiers. For military use in the First World War it was painted in a most striking blue and white diamond pattern, which was one of the so called 'dazzle camouflage designs', used to outwit enemy U-Boats. But it was not just this camouflage that ensured the RMS Mauretania was not sunk by the enemy, but also its speed. For many years this fine ship was the holder of the 'Blue Riband' for the fastest crossing of the Atlantic. It was also, until in 1911 the S.S. Olympic was built, the world's largest ship. Post-First World War after much 'refurbishment' it returned to being a luxury cruise liner, until it was retired from service in 1935. Sadly, and much to the chagrin of many who had cruised and sailed on her, including American President, Franklin D. Roosevelt, who wrote a private letter against the scrapping, the RMS Mauretania was scrapped in 1937, with her fine fittings and furnishings auctioned off in lots.

Private John Patrick Brennan, regimental number 633885 had initially been with 154th Battalion, but when at the Front in France & Flanders he served with 21st Battalion (Eastern Ontario), C.E.F, except when on three occasions he was sent to England for hospitalisation, and on these three occasions he was temporarily with a reserve battalion. On or around 14 May 1917, he sustained a shell related wound to his nose, no doubt from shell fragments. Then back at the Front on 4 March 1918, he sustained a gunshot wound (a GSW) to his left hand. The medical report on this injury stated: *He has sustained a comminuted fracture of the 4th metacarpal at distal end. A few minute particles of detached bone in the region.* There is to be found in his military file a copy of the x-ray taken of this hand injury to Private Brennan. Back again at the Front, on or around 13 October 1918, he sustained a shell gunshot wound to his left arm, described as being a flesh wound. Having survived the trenches and three times being 'wounded in action', post-Armistice he ended up at Kinmel Park Camp on 8 January 1919, and was placed on M. D. 3 Wing, to await his return to Canada.

Following the riots/disturbances at the camp, he faced two serious charges. This is an account which appeared in the *North Wales Chronicle*, edition of 25 April 1919:

RAID ON CANTEEN

At Saturday's sitting of the court 63385 (actually 633885) Private John Patrick Brennan, of the 6th Canadian Reserve Battalion, was charged with having joined in a mutiny, and been guilty of conduct prejudicial to good order and military discipline. Provost-Sergeant Scott deposed that on the night of March 4th Brennan was the leader of a large crowd of men who raided the 'wet' canteens of Camp 7. He directed the taking down of the counter and the rolling out of the barrels of beer. Cross-examined by Captain Black, witness said that news of an intended raid to be 'pulled-off' at the canteen reached the sergeant's mess in the afternoon. He went down with four military policemen to protect the place. They had about twenty other men at the canteen ready to help them, but these men who were all privates, were under no orders. They were merely casual customers, whom witness had asked to help him out. Witness added that there were two young ladies serving at the counter. He had them removed into the dry canteen adjoining, so that they would be out of harm's way. Driver Percy Charlton of the Canadian Field Artillery said that when the door of the canteen was burst open, Brennan, who was one of the first to enter, threw missiles inside. Private George Murray also spoke of Brennan as one of the leaders of the canteen raid. The accused Brennan read a prepared statement denying completely that he had taken part in the canteen raid or incited others, or thrown stones. After the luncheon adjournment the court received evidence of character and considered the verdict.

With considerable eye witness evidence against him it was not surprising that John Patrick Brennan at his general court martial held on 19 April 1919, was found guilty and sentenced to one years' imprisonment with hard labour. However, as in all these cases he was not to serve his full sentence. He was moved to Wandsworth Detention Barracks, London, prior to him having the remainder of his sentence remitted and he was on his way back to Canada by mid-October 1919. On his discharge certificate in red ink is written for reason for discharge: Misconduct. But this is crossed out and replaced with the word: Demobilisation.

3. Fred Peter Clement

Fred Peter Clement was born on 25 December 1893, or on 25 December 1894, depending upon which record one believes, at Saint Joseph, Gloucester County, New Brunswick, Canada. When enlisting in the C.E.F he gave his home address and also that of his next of kin, his father Peter Clement, as being Bathurst, Gloucester County, New Brunswick. His mother was Marie Mary Clement. Fred Peter Clement enlisted at Bathurst on 7 January 1916. He was described as being just over five feet, four inches tall, of medium complexion, with blue eyes and brown hair.

As Private Clement, regimental number 793535, he served with 42nd Battalion (Royal Highlanders of Canada), C.E.F for over one year in France & Flanders. On the Western Front at Vimy Ridge on 10 January 1917, he sustained a wound to his back. Then on 2 November 1917, during the Battle of Passchendaele (31 July 1917 to 10 November 1917), he was wounded in his left arm by shrapnel. He suffered a fracture of the middle of the radius, which resulted in his spending twenty-eight days in hospital. His military records show that during his time at the Front, he was gassed and had shell shock.

It was on or just before 19 December 1918, that Fred Peter Clement arrived at Kinmel Park Camp from Bramshott Camp, Hampshire, England, to await his return to Canada. Here he was placed on M.D. Wing 7. Following the riots/disturbances of 4/5 March 1919, he was charged with having 'Joined in a mutiny', and with being involved in an attack upon a canteen, and trying to enter the sergeant's mess. At his court martial on 18 April 1919, some of his court martial proceedings were reported in the *North Wales Chronicle* of 25 April 1919:

> 793535 Private F. Clement, Canadian Black Watch, was charged with mutiny and with attempting to enter the sergeant's mess. Sergeant J. D. Irving said that on the morning of the 5th he took his staff from the record office to defend the dry canteen, in front of which was a jeering crowd. The accused, who was at the front of the crowd asked the witness, 'What the h.... they thought they were going to do'. Someone threw a brick and knocked over a corporal standing beside him.
>
> There was at that time a miniature 'No Man's Land' between the parties. A number of the crowd rushed the door of the wet canteen, and the record office staff took them in the flank. Then they rushed through the ladies' quarters to the interior of the wet canteen, where they found the commanding officer and the adjutant. As they entered, the doors were smashed by a prop torn from the ground and used as a battering ram. The officers tried to pacify the rioters, who, however grew violent, and bricks came flying from every direction. 'We tumbled over tables', continued the witness, 'and tore the legs off them, and roared to the officers to let them (the rioters) come on. The officers let in four or five men at a time, and as they came in, we knocked them over. There seemed no

> real head of things, and councils of war were being held all over the place'. The accused in evidence, contradicted the foregoing statements, and Private Lorette, whose case was heard the previous day, gave corroborative evidence.

Private Fred Peter Clement was found guilty of having 'joined in a mutiny' and received a prison sentence of eighteen months with hard labour. This sentence was confirmed on 6 May 1919. However, it was officially recorded in London on 5 November 1919, that the unserved portion of his sentence was remitted. A good job really, for on this day he was already sailing back to Canada aboard HMT Tunisian.

4. Vladimir Costughko – born in the Russian Empire

Vladimir Costughko was born on 1 May 1897, in the then Russian Empire. He was a labourer, a single man, when on 3 November 1915, at Welland, Ontario, Canada, he enlisted in the C.E.F. He was described as being five feet, eight inches tall, and gave his next of kin as being his mother, Tafilo Costughko. He sailed from Halifax, Nova Scotia, aboard the S.S. Lapland, disembarking in England on 25 July 1916.

He went to France & Flanders and served at the Front with 20th Battalion (Central Ontario), C.E.F as Private Vladimir Costughko, regimental number 210203. On 10 April 1917, at Vimy Ridge, during The Battle of Vimy Ridge (9 April to 12 April 1917), he suffered a gunshot wound to his right shoulder and was initially treated at No. 2 Australian General Hospital, Wimereux, near Boulogne, France. Then in England at a military hospital he refused an operation on the wounded right shoulder, and after forty-five days of hospitalisation he left hospital. After that he was at the Shorncliffe and West Sandling camps.

I believe that he only arrived at Kinmel Park camp on 22

February 1919, and following the riots/disturbances of 4/5 March 1919, he found himself in detention awaiting a court martial. On 24 April 1919, he appeared at his court martial charged with (1) Joining in a mutiny, and (2) Being present and not endeavouring to suppress a mutiny. He was found not guilty of the former charge, but guilty of the latter. It must have been because of his previous service, which included being wounded during The Battle of Vimy Ridge, that he received the lenient sentence of ninety days detention, especially as he was a 'foreigner' and they fared badly at these court martial proceedings.

Vladimir Costughko served his detention at the Wandsworth Detention Barracks, London, and embarked at Glasgow for Montreal on 25 July 1919, aboard the S.S. Saturnia.

5. Russell Henry Edmondson

Russell Henry Edmondson (some military records incorrectly show him as Edmundson), was born at Spanish River, Ontario, Canada, on 1 April 1895. He enlisted in the C.E.F and when doing so gave his next of kin as being his brother, Harold Edmondson, of the same address as himself, 71, Shaw Street, Toronto, Canada. Russell Henry Edmondson was on enlistment a single man, standing a tad over five feet, seven inches tall, with blue eyes, dark hair and of fair complexion. Private Edmondson, regimental number 3037026 only arrived in England aboard the S.S Bellerophon on 16 August 1918, less than three months before the end of the war. But at that time, it was believed that the war could go on indefinitely, though by late August 1918, it had finally turned very much in favour of Britain and its Allies, especially after the initially successful, but subsequently catastrophic failure of the German Spring Offensive of 1918.

Private Edmondson found himself at Kinmel Park Camp and following the riots/disturbances of 4/5 March 1919, he faced two serious charges, one of joining in a mutiny, and the lesser, failing to act to assist in stopping such. But Private Edmondson had something else which only a few other accused had, a bullet wound to his head. For Private Edmondson was one of the eight soldiers who received bullet wounds in the Camp 20 violence, but survived, unlike others. The bullet wound to his scalp resulted in nine days in No. 9 Canadian General Hospital, Kinmel Park Camp. He was shot 'allegedly' when he was prominent in the ranks of the attackers upon Camp 20. Despite his bullet wound, he did not receive any kind of sympathy at his court martial, for he was found guilty and sentenced to five years penal servitude, which he initially served at H.M. Prison Walton, Liverpool, and later at H.M. Prison Portland, Dorset, where on 27 November 1919, his sentence was commuted to one of two years detention. Then on 27 December 1919, this reduced sentence was quashed and the 'unserved portion of his sentence was to be remitted'.

On 3 January 1920, Private Russell Henry Edmondson left London bound for Canada, a free man soon to be discharged from the military once he was on Canadian soil.

6. Mervon English – born in the United States

Mervon English was in fact American, as he was born on 25 October 1893, in Chicago, Illinois, United States. He was a 'marine man' and gave his home address when enlisting in the C.E.F at Port Arthur, Ontario, Canada, on 22 September 1917, the same one as his next of kin, his grandmother Mrs Mary English, namely, Campbell Street, Midland, Simcoe County, Ontario. On enlistment he was five feet, six and a half inches tall, and arrived in England with the C.E.F on 14 December 1917, aboard the S.S Metagama. He served with the Canadian 10th Forestry & Railway Construction Company as Sapper Mervon English, regimental number 2502989. He served from 18 January 1918 to 18 January 1919 in France & Flanders. Returning to the British mainland he was initially posted to Witley Camp, then Ripon Camp and then on 21 February 1919, to Kinmel Park Camp, where he was placed on M.D. 2 to await his turn to be transported back to Canada. During his time when serving in France & Flanders he had the misfortune to have suffered from scabies. Scabies is not an infection but is an infestation of tiny mites who lay their eggs inside 'their victims' skin, causing the unfortunate person to have a rash and constantly feeling very itchy. Many soldiers especially those who spent long periods in the trenches got scabies.

The *Brandon Daily Sun* newspaper, Brandon, Manitoba, Canada, had this in their edition of 28 April 1919:

> Sapper M. English of The Canadian Railway Troops pleaded not guilty to the charge of Mutiny. Lieutenant Gauthier gave evidence that English had encouraged others to advance. That English had cursed the picket defending them and threw stones at them. Lt. Gauthier said he estimated 250 to 300 rioters, but the pickets rushed them and he arrested English. Captain Black defending called Private Walker and Sergeant Murdock as witnesses for the defence. They both swore on oath that Lt. Gauthier had told English that he had had nothing to do with his arrest.

The outcome of this court martial for Sapper Mervon English was that on 7 June 1919, he was found guilty of being present at, and not using his utmost to suppress a mutiny. He was handed for this lesser charge than 'joining in a mutiny' itself, 120 days detention. However, only some two months later, Sapper Mervon English on 13 August 1919, set sail for Canada from Liverpool aboard the S.S. Belgic. He was officially demobilised from the Canadian military on 25 August 1919, at Toronto, Canada.

7. Walbray Hamelin

Walbray Hamelin's is I believe one of the most intriguing 'stories' that came out of the riots/disturbances. The defence put forward at his court martial was that he should be cleared of all charges due to his insanity. *The North Wales Chronicle* of 23 May 1919, had this article which led me to follow up the story of Walbray Hamelin:

> KINMEL PARK COURT MARTIAL
> A PLEA OF INSANITY
> At the General Court Martial inquiring at Liverpool into cases in connection with the Kinmel Park Camp Mutiny, a plea of insanity was put forward on Wednesday on behalf of Private Walbray Hamelin, Canadian Medical Corps, who was stated to have been in the front line of the rioters, holding one of the poles supporting the 'Red Flag'. A doctor expressed the opinion that the prisoner was unfitted for an ordinary soldier's life, and that under such conditions as existed at the time of the riots, he would have been incapable of knowing the difference between right and wrong.

Private Walbray Hamelin when one studies his full military record with the C.E.F, cannot I suggest, for a host of reasons, be regarded as a suitable person for military duties especially at the Front.

Walbray Hamelin was born at Three Rivers (Trois-Rivieres), Quebec, Canada. On enlistment at Montreal,

Canada, on 27 January 1916, he gave his next of kin as being his father, Charles Hamelin. Walbray Hamelin was a single man, aged twenty-nine years and nine months of age, and initially was enlisted into 69th Battalion (Canadien-Francais), C.E.F, and given the regimental number 847261. He was a bricklayer and possessed a qualification in bricklaying. On 27 August 1916, he was in France with the C.E.F. After an 'incident' in the field in France in early January 1917, he was on 18 January 1917 in confinement awaiting trial. He was tried and convicted by a Field General Court Martial of three serious military offences, when on active service: *(1) Disobeying a command by his superior officer; (2) Using threatening language to his superior officer; and (3) Conduct to the prejudice of good order and military discipline; viz: When asked by Lieutenant J. Brillant why he was not on parade, answered, 'It is none of your Christly business', or words to that effect.*

Private Hamelin was found guilty of all three offences and sentenced to 'penal servitude for life, yes for life, for these kinds of offences where always treated far more seriously when committed at the Front, and not back behind the lines or in a military training camp. This sentence was confirmed by Brigadier-General A. H. Macdonald, G.O.C, 5th Canadian Infantry Brigade, who then 'mitigated the sentence' to three years penal servitude. Private Hamelin was taken to serve his sentence at No. 3 Military Prison, Le Havre, France. His sentence was then reduced to two years with hard labour, and then on 30 June 1917 he was released from prison and the remainder of his sentence was suspended. He re-joined his unit in the field on 7 July 1917. He then suffered 'alleged' bouts of bronchitis. I write alleged because he was examined by doctors who could find nothing physically wrong with him. But entries on his military record do show that he was suffering from '*nervousness, poor control of himself, runs out of patience at the slightest provocation, is very irritable, is tremulous, sleeps poorly and dreams a great deal*'. The doctor who wrote this diagnosis also stated: '*His Family History Has a History of Nervous Trouble. Father and Mother, living and well. Has two brothers and one sister, all well*'. It surely must have been obvious to those around him that Private Walbray Hamelin was 'mentally unwell' and extremely unsuited to the military life, and would he not be a liability to comrades in the face of the enemy? Some sense did prevail as he was returned to England and was an orderly in 4th General Canadian Hospital, Basingstoke, Hampshire. Here he was said to have suffered a mental breakdown. Perhaps it was now, or later at his court martial that it became known that Private Hamelin prior to his enlistment had suffered with depression and had shown suicidal tendencies.

Following stints in other military camps in Britain, on 26 February 1919, Private Hamelin was now at Kinmel Park Camp, on M.D. 4 Wing. Following the riots/disturbances, Private Walbray Hamelin was arrested and faced two charges: One of joining in a mutiny at the camp on 5 March 1919, and an alternative lesser charge of, 'conduct to the prejudice of good order and military discipline, in that he at Kinmel Park on 5 March 1919, was concerned in marching on Camp 20 carrying a red flag, and thereby provoking a disturbance in said camp'. Hamelin through his defence counsel pleaded not guilty to both charges, and the plea of insanity was put forward. Hamelin though found not guilty of the first charge of mutiny, was found guilty of the alternative charge and was sentenced to five years penal servitude. It was noted on his military record that he had been in military detention from 6 March 1919 until 20 May 1919, his court martial being held on 21 May 1919 at the

Grace Road Barracks, Walton, Liverpool. Private Hamelin was taken away to serve his prison sentence at H.M. Prison Walton, Liverpool. On 3 November 1919, he was removed to the Wandsworth Military Detention Barracks, London, with his sentence having been commuted to two years in a detention barracks, not a civilian prison. On 20 November 1919, 'officially' the unexpired portion of his sentence was remitted, though he had already sailed for home on 5 November 1919, aboard HMT Tunisian. He was discharged from the military on his arrival at Quebec for 'misconduct'.

I believe that Walbray Hamelin died on 30 December 1969.

8. Roy Edward Henley – born in England

Roy Edward Henley was to say the very least, something of an enigma as a soldier and indeed as a man. A real character, whom it would not I believe be unfair to call a real 'Walter Mitty' type character. However, if not adhering to the old adage that 'you should not speak ill of the dead', then you might call him 'an inveterate liar'. He had a tremendous propensity for failing to tell the truth, something which may well I suspect emanate from an obviously difficult childhood. Roy Edward Henley whatever story he spun to others was actually born in the December Quarter of 1901 in the Romney Marsh Registration District, Kent, England. His mother was Eliza Avery Henley, who was born in 1881, and died in 1949. She was I am certain unmarried at the time that she had Roy in late 1901, aged about twenty, and earlier in that year she was a barmaid at the Apollonian Hotel, Margate, Kent. Her own parents were Alfred Henley, a shoemaker, and wife, Eliza Henley, nee Wilds. In 1904, his mother had a daughter, his half-sister by another man whom she named Stella Mary Henley (born 1904 – died 1978).

Eliza Avery Henley on 24 November 1910, married at Kingston Register Office, Surrey, England, one Charles Heydon (born 1876 died 1943).

Roy Edward Henley was either not wanted by his mother, or because she was now married, he may have become 'an impediment' to her new life, and, he became a 'Barnardo's Boy'. Roy aged nine in 1910, along with hundreds of other 'Barnardo's Boys' was aboard the S.S. Sicilian bound for Canada, where these boys – orphans or unwanted children were placed in rural farming communities all over Canada. There are stories of many of these boys having a terrible time with their new 'families', some of whom were said to treat them like slaves. Whilst others, the lucky ones, had a reasonable time of it. Roy was placed with the Misner family of Gainsboro, Lincoln, Ontario, and was described by them as being a lodger. We do not know of Roy Edward Henley's time with the Misner's but we do know that when in 1914 enlisting in the Canadian Expeditionary Force his deceit and tall tales began in earnest.

When first enlisting in the C.E.F he told them that he had been born in 1897, at Kilmarnock, Scotland. He gave his address as the Red Triangle Hut, Dominion Square, Montreal, a YMCA establishment. He was probably homeless, and he then enlisted on a number of occasions, too involved to fully go into here, without having a whole chapter on this man. Suffice to say he would provide different personal details, including that he was born at London, Ontario, on 29 September 1898, and was a teamster. He was knocked back on at least a couple of occasions as he looked under-age. He managed to get to England with the C.E F in 1916, but only saw the inside of military camps and their hospitals, suffering from such ailments as tonsillitis. He was returned to Canada as being underage and after a time got back to England with a different battalion. His military record runs to an amazing 258 pages, when even 'real war heroes' records, for three or more years of service at the Front run to less than a third that number of pages.

Roy Edward Henley's very extensive military record shows he was not in France & Flanders until August 1918, where in fairness to him, with 42nd Battalion he did suffer a wound to the face and neck. But the rest of his military service consisted of deserting, going AWOL (absent without leave) and being unwell with a variety of ailments. Amongst several regimental numbers he received, 670194 and 514204, are amongst them.

Roy Edward Henley eventually arrived at Kinmel Park Camp awaiting his return to Canada and was placed on MD. 2. Following the riots/disturbances of 4/5 March 1919, he faced a number of charges including that of having 'joined in a mutiny'. At his court martial he was found guilty and sentenced to three years imprisonment. Like all of the others found guilty, after a time in prison his sentence was remitted and he was returned to Canada.

Not long back in Canada, despite his obvious loathing of the military, especially officers, which he was later to freely espouse when providing quotes for a number of First World War books, he joined-up again on 4 November 1919, as Gunner Henley, with No. 2 Company, R.C.G.A, Halifax, Nova Scotia, regimental number 4217, only to desert a couple of months later taking with him a lot of military equipment that was not his.

On 12 October 1925, at Esquimalt, British Columbia, he enlisted in another Canadian military force, using a different date and place of birth. For this one he said he was a 'former aero pilot.' I believe he was discharged from this one for being unfit for the service.

Over the years Roy Edward Henley regularly crossed the border from Canada into the United States and back again. For what purpose(s) we do not know, but he used different variations of his full name, false addresses and differing dates of birth, each time he did so. He seemed to keep this up all his life, for on his marriage certificate when he married Bertha Littlewood of York, Ontario on 15 March 1920, he is shown as being born at Kilmarnock, Scotland. He liked to pretend he was Scottish born and always had plenty to say, most of it sadly was not the truth.

Roy Edward Henley, 'the old sweat', truly enjoyed the limelight in his latter years when people came calling for him to tell them of his First World War experiences. He would leave out his sentence of three years imprisonment for his part in the Kinmel Park Camp riots/disturbances, and his deserting on several occasions, but loved to 'bad mouth' the officers under whom he served. Despite the fact, that as a soldier his military record clearly shows he was something of a disaster. CBC, the Canadian Broadcasting Corporation took him as an 'old sweat' to Vimy Ridge and filmed him speaking of his experiences as he walked over the ground at Vimy Ridge, Vimy, France, that so iconic for the Canadians location of the 'Battle of Vimy Ridge' (9 April – 12 April 1917). But there is a major problem with this, for he was not there, in fact on 2 April 1917, he was in Toronto undergoing another enlistment.

Roy Edward Henley died on 27 January 1998, aged ninety-six, at Sydney, British Columbia.

9. John Hiba – born in Russia

John Hiba was born on 6 January 1887, in Russia. When he enlisted for the C.E.F at Edmonton, Alberta, Canada, on 10 April 1916, he was living and working in Edmonton, and was described as being five feet, nine inches tall, of dark complexion, with grey eyes and brown hair. He stated he was a labourer and gave his next of kin and to whom separation allowance should be paid as his wife Mari Dmitrievna Hiba, who with their five-year-old son, Mikly Hiba, were still living in Russia. He initially enlisted in 218th (Edmonton) Battalion, C.E.F. From Halifax, Nova Scotia, on 16 February 1917, he embarked for Liverpool, England, arriving there on 27 February 1917. He was now placed in 8th Battalion, the Canadian Railway Troops, as Sapper John Hiba, regimental number 279502. He served in France & Flanders with this battalion.

He was sent to Kinmel Park Camp on 26 February 1919, and placed on M.D. 2 Wing. Only a few days later he got involved in the riots/disturbances at the camp, as a result of which on 5 March 1919, he received a 'lacerated wound to the scalp', which required him being hospitalised in the camp's military hospital for a total of seventeen days. When discharged from hospital on 22 March 1919, he was formally arrested on serious charges and placed in military detention until 27 May 1919, to await a court martial. He appeared on 28 May 1919, at The Grace Road Barracks, Liverpool, to face three charges. The first, (1) was the 'usual' charge of having joined in a mutiny at the camp with others, but added was, 'and improperly to enter Camp 20'. The second charge, (2) was in two parts as follows: 'Offering violence to his Superior Officer being in the execution of his office, in that he, at Kinmel Park Camp on or about the 5th day of March 1919, attempted to strike with a club Lieutenant A. M. Edward, 15th Reserve Battalion, who was at the time endeavouring to quell certain disturbances in said Kinmel Park Camp.' The third charge, (3) was: 'Offering violence to his Superior Officer, being in execution of his office, in that he at Kinmel Park Camp on or about the 5th March 1919, attempted to strike with a club Lieutenant-

Colonel J. P. French, who was endeavouring to suppress certain disturbances in the said camp.'

Sapper John Hiba pleaded not guilty to these serious charges, vehemently protesting his innocence, and a fellow Russian born soldier gave witness evidence in his favour. But John Hiba was found guilty and sentenced to seven years' penal servitude. Bear in mind that unlike many other of his fellow accused, he was married and had a young child to support. His imprisonment would have had serious financial implications for his wife who had been receiving his 'separation allowance'.

Separation Allowance consisted of the soldier allotting a portion of his soldier's pay, which was normally matched by the Canadian Government, to dependent's, to ensure that they did not become destitute without his income when at home with them. It also applied to unmarried soldiers who could prove that either before the war began, of before their enlistment, they financially assisted dependant's such as a father, mother, sister, or other member of the family. The amount varied according to a soldier's particular rank. Later in the war it was increased to be fifty per cent of the soldier's pay.

After a period in H.M. Portland Prison, Dorset, a civilian prison, he had his sentence firstly reduced to two years imprisonment with hard labour, then to one of military detention for the same period. When at the Wandsworth Military Detention Barracks, London, the remainder of his sentence was remitted, and on 23 December 1919, he was on his way back to Canada, where he gave his discharge office the information that he would be residing at 113, Queen Street, Toronto, Canada. Again, for John Hiba, his discharge certificate originally had typed upon it, discharged for 'misconduct', but this word was struck out and replaced with 'demobilization'.

10. George A. Lorette

George A. Lorette was born on 14 October 1888, at Middle Sackville, Westmorland County, New Brunswick, Canada. He stood five feet, six inches tall, when on 5 June 1915, he enlisted in the C.E.F at Fredericton, New Brunswick. He stated that he was a shoemaker by trade and gave his next of kin as being his wife, Christine Lorette, of Charlotte, Fredericton. He enlisted in 7th Brigade of the Canadian Field Artillery and Gunner George A. Lorette, regimental number 90256 served in France & Flanders from 18 January 1916, until January 1919.

He arrived at Kinmel Park Camp on 17 February 1919, and was placed on M.D. 7 Wing. Following the riots/disturbances of 4/5 March, he faced two charges at his court martial, at which a number of witnesses gave evidence against him. The main charge was joining in a mutiny, and also the lesser charge of failing to do his utmost to prevent a mutiny. Sergeant-Major Gilbert Smith alleged that Gunner Lorette was one of four or five men acting disorderly in the camp and waving a red flag, and that Lorette was amongst a group of men who threw stones at some cavalrymen on horseback who were at the main gate of the camp. Though he admitted he had not actually witnessed Lorette throwing stones himself. He also claimed that earlier in the day he had seen but not heard what was said, when Lorette addressed a group of men whilst standing on a soap-box. This part of his evidence was strongly refuted by the defence who claimed that Lorette was appealing to the men not to act disorderly. A Sergeant then gave similar evidence against Lorette, especially the part that he was one of those waving the red flag about.

Gunner George A. Lorette was found guilty at his court martial of the lesser charge. and as a result he received a sentence of three months detention to be served at the

Wandsworth Military Detention Barracks, London. However, on 9 August 1919, he was sailing back to Canada from Liverpool on designated Sailing No. 101, aboard the HMT Caronia. During his military service his wife moved to Saint John, New Brunswick.

11. Valentina Miculka – born in the Austro-Hungarian Empire

Valentina Miculka shown sometimes incorrectly as Valentine Miculka, was born on 6 May 1896 at Ostrava, now in the Czech-Republic. Valentina Miculka was a butcher by profession and on his enlistment papers he gave his next of kin as being his mother, Barbara Miculka, now remarried and Barbara Lipk, who lived in Schulenburg, Texas, United States. This small city in Texas is noted today for its German culture. He enlisted for the C.E.F at Windsor, Ontario, Canada, on 1 May 1917, and was five feet, six inches tall. He arrived at Liverpool, England, on 23 August 1917, aboard the S.S. Grampian. He was part of a 'Forestry Draft' sent to 21st Reserve Battalion and was Private Valentina Miculka, regimental number 243315. He only saw service in Canada, England and fatefully for him in Wales

Valentina Miculka arrived at Kinmel Park Camp on or around, 7 February 1919. His 'alleged' involvement in some of the more serious events of the riots/disturbances meant that when he was brought from military detention to his court martial on 28 May 1919, he faced several charges including the most serious one, that of 'joining in a mutiny', but also of offences relating to the smashing up and looting of the canteen at Camp 8. He pleaded not guilty to all charges, but was found guilty of them. His sentence was an eye watering ten years of imprisonment. He was taken away from the Grace Road Barracks, Liverpool, to nearby H.M. Walton Prison to begin his sentence. By late November

1919 his sentence was reduced to one of two years, then in December 1919 the remainder of his sentence was remitted.

I am sure Vladimir Miculka was a mightily relieved man when on 2 January 1920, at Saint John, New Brunswick he was discharged for 'misconduct' from the Canadian military. Later, as in virtually all of the cases, on his military record the word misconduct was struck out and replaced by demobilisation.

12. James Bert Morrison

James Bert Morrison was born at Toronto, Ontario, Canada, on 13 December 1895. On enlistment in the C.E.F on 5 August 1918, he gave his address as 'General Delivery', Seattle, Washington, the United States. He gave his mother, Mrs Nellie Morrison of 107, King Street, Centralia, Lewis County, Washington, as his next of kin. He was described as being six feet tall, of dark complexion, with brown eyes and hair. A Methodist by religion, he gave his occupation as musician. He now was Private Morrison, regimental number 2140663. He served only in Canada, England and Wales. On 9 February 1919, he was with 1st Reserve Battalion at Kinmel Park Camp.

He is referred to in the War Diary entry for M.D. 4 & 5 Wings which were at Camp 16, on 6 March 1919:

Kinmel Park. 6-3-19. No. 2140663, A/Cpl Morrison, J. B. placed in Guard Room and taken under escort to Guard Room M. D. 1, prior to his removal to London, on charges of rioting and looting.

At his court martial he was found guilty of the most serious of the charges against him, that of 'joining in a mutiny', and he was sentenced to five years imprisonment, and taken off to nearby H.M. Prison, Walton, Liverpool. On 25

November 1919 this sentence was commuted to two years of military detention, and then the unexpired portion of his two years of detention was remitted, and he was weeks later embarking for Canada. On his discharge certificate at Saint John, New Brunswick, Canada, dated 10 January 1920, this typed document states, 'and is now discharged from the service by reason of demobilization', the word 'misconduct' having been typed through with x's.

13. William Robert Sampson

William Robert Sampson was born on 12 August 1886, at Napanee, Ontario, Canada. On his enlistment on 11 November 1915, he was a single man, who worked as a piano mover, and was described as five feet, nine and-a-half inches tall. He gave his next of kin as his mother, Sarah Sampson. At this time he was living at McGee & Wellington Street, Winnipeg, Manitoba. He sailed to England from Halifax, Nova Scotia, on 31 May 1916, aboard the S.S. Olympic. He served in the C.E.F with 78th Battalion, and 26th Battalion Canadian Forestry Corps. He served in France and Flanders as Private Sampson, regimental number 187154.

On 22 February 1919, Private Sampson was at Kinmel Park Camp on M. D. 3 Wing. On 5 March 1919, he was admitted to the camp's military hospital having sustained a blow to his skull. He was concussed and had a laceration wound to his head. He had apparently been clubbed unconscious by Canadian Military Police when caught 'red handed' wrecking the quartermaster's store on the evening of 4 March 1919. Those who had arrested him 'claimed' that his injuries had been caused when he had accidentally struck his head when resisting arrest. When discharged from hospital on 12 March 1919, he was formally arrested and placed in military detention to await his court martial. On 12

May 1919, at Orrell Park, Liverpool, he faced a number of charges including the most serious one of 'joining in a mutiny'. At least one witness at his court martial deposed that Private Sampson's head injuries had not been the result of an accident, far from it in fact, but that they had witnessed him being beaten unconscious by some military police soldiers. One can only conclude, that though found guilty of serious offences, he received only thirty days of detention, due to the 'violent circumstances' of his initial arrest, and the serious injuries he had sustained as a result. Private William Robert Sampson embarked at Liverpool for Canada on 5 July 1919, aboard the S.S. Carmania.

14. Joseph Schmidt

Joseph Schmidt was born at St Louis, a village in Saskatchewan, Canada, on 4 March 1898. When he enlisted on 3 May 1916, at Wakaw, Saskatchewan, for the C.E.F, he was described as being five feet, nine and a half inches tall, of dark complexion, with brown eyes and black hair. He stated he was a farmer, a single man, of the Roman Catholic religion. He initially was in 214th (Saskatchewan) Battalion, as Private Schmidt, regimental number 267960.

In France & Flanders he saw service with 28th (Northwest) Battalion of the C.E.F, but his military record is one of on several occasions going 'awol' (absent without leave) for days on end.

Post-Armistice on 27 December 1918, he found himself at Kinmel Park Camp and he went absent without leave again, this time for a total of eighteen days – no wonder he was not on his way back to Canada quickly! Following the riots/disturbances it was alleged by a number of witnesses at his court martial that he had led the mob on the Tuesday evening who had broken into the canteen at Camp 4, and looted it. Then he was alleged on the following day,

Wednesday 5 March 1919, to have urged the mob to go to Camp 20 and attack it. This attack on Camp 20 was of course to result in the five deaths that afternoon. Lieutenant Gauthier gave damning evidence against Joseph Schmidt, as did Major St George, the assistant provost-marshal at Kinmel Park Camp. Two sergeants from the Camp 20 'defenders' provided corroborative evidence against Schmidt. Schmidt did not testify in his own defence, neither did he offer any witnesses to support his pleas of not guilty to all four charges he faced – had he been badly advised, or did he decide this course of action himself? In the event it was not surprising that he was found guilty of 'being present and not trying his utmost to suppress a mutiny in His Majesty's Forces'. He was not as far as I can ascertain found guilty of the more serious offence of 'joining in a mutiny' or the two charges of offering violence to a superior officer, and only received a sentence of twenty-two months detention, not a prison sentence. I believe that in his case there was too much evidence against him, including that he was alleged to have been causing trouble in the camp in two places at the same time on the Wednesday. It came out also that Joseph Schmidt was particularly poorly regarded as a soldier, and looking at his military record it is hard not to disagree.

Private Joseph Schmidt served his detention at Wandsworth Detention Barracks, London, and the remainder of his sentence was subsequently remitted and he was back home in Canada, arriving from Glasgow, at Halifax, Nova Scotia on 30 November 1919.

15. Fred Sherstabetoff – born in the Russian Empire

Fred Sherstabetoff, though this was no doubt not his actual name, but one he 'went by' in the Canadian military, was born on 1 May 1895 at Petrograd (through recent history also known as Saint Petersburg and as Leningrad), Russia,

Russia's second largest city after Moscow. Sherstabetoff enlisted for the C.E.F on 2 July 1916, at North Battleford, Saskatchewan, Canada. Military records show that he was five feet, nine inches tall, and his religion was recorded as being the Greek Catholic Church. He gave as his next of kin, his mother, Mrs Agatha Sherstabetoff of Blaine Lake, Saskatchewan. He arrived with his contingent of the C.E.F at Liverpool, England, aboard the S.S. Northland on 29 April 1917. He had originally enlisted in 232nd (Saskatchewan) Battalion, but on 9 June 1917, it had been absorbed into 15th Reserve Battalion. Following further military training in England, Private Sherstabetoff, regimental number 1018617, served in France with 11th Company, Canadian Forestry Corps.

Post-Armistice, when still in France, he was on 20 December 1918, laid-up with influenza at Boulogne. If it was the same strain of influenza known as the Spanish Flu which killed millions around the world that he had, then he was one of the fortunate ones to recover from it. He was then sent to Kinmel Park Camp, arriving here on 19 February 1919, placed in M.D. 13, to await being returned to Canada. For his alleged part in the riots/disturbances of 4/5 March 1919, Sherstabetoff faced two specific charges. One was one of the 'usual two', that he had 'joined in a mutiny'. But the second one he faced was a different one to most others, for he was also charged with 'striking a superior officer'. An offence in the military if committed at the Front may well have resulted in him being summarily executed. At his court martial, Private Sherstabetoff pleaded not guilty to both serious charges, and his defence counsel, Major Weyman used as part of the defence the highly unflattering claim: '*But he is only an ignorant foreigner*'. I am sure this was done with the best of motives, but Sherstabetoff was no such entity. For he was a Doukhobor, spiritual Christian people of

Russian origin who after being heavily repressed in 'Mother Russia' by the Russian authorities, fled their homeland and accepted the Canadian Government's offer to settle as a large group in Canada, this huge but sparsely populated country. So, some 7,000 Doukhobors including a four-year old Fred Sherstabetoff began a new life in Canada in some of the harshest areas it 'has to offer'. Some 200 of them including his family settled in the Blaine Lake area of Saskatchewan. Being hardy and resourceful people, they adapted well in this harsh environment. Doukhobors are known as being very capable at many practical things, but perhaps soldiering and having to work under strict military discipline was not to Sherstabetoff's liking, mind you this was true of thousands of other soldiers who took part in the First World War, conscripted men and even many who had voluntarily enlisted. Doukhobor means 'Spirit Warrior or Spirit Wrestler', and in Russia they were in serious disagreement with the Russian Orthodox Church, as they rejected the Russian Orthodox priesthood, and loathed their use of icons and what they thought was their over-elaborate church ritual. They were in effect what we call dissenters.

The defence 'ploy' failed and Private Sherstabetoff was found guilty, and sentenced to two years of imprisonment with hard labour. He was removed from the court martial directly to a civilian prison. However, like so many other 'convicted men' he did not have to serve out his sentence. For on 29 December 1919, he was removed from prison in Liverpool and taken to Wandsworth Detention Barracks, London. This was part of Wandsworth (Civilian) Prison which was used by the British military, particularly when they dealt with conscientious objectors. Whilst here the remainder of his sentence was remitted, and by late March of 1920, he was back home in Canada.

16. Rufus Simon (aka Rufus Samson) – born in the United States

Rufus Simon is something of a mystery man for when he enlisted for the C.E.F at Toronto, Canada, on 23 February 1918, he did so as Rufus Samson, and signed this name to this effect on his enlistment form. He later in England on 24 September 1918, made a statutory declaration that his real name was Rufus Simon. Whichever was the real one, he claimed to have been born on 7 January 1885, at Chicago, Illinois, the United States. He stated he was a tailor, of the Jewish religion, and described as five feet, three and a half inches tall, of dark complexion, with brown eyes and hair. He enlisted in 1st Battalion (Ontario Regiment), C.E.F and arrived in England on 19 April 1918, aboard HMT Tunisian, regimental number 3232279. He did not go to France & Flanders and was for a time at Bramshott Camp. Rufus Simon, as I shall refer to him, arrived at Kinmel Park Camp on 19 February 1919 and was placed on M.D. 2 Wing.

Following the riots/disturbances of 4/5 March 1919, he was arrested at Sykes' Café in Rhyl, North Wales, and was held in detention until his court martial. He stood accused of 'joining in a mutiny' and the lesser charge of 'failing to do his utmost to suppress the same'. He was alleged to have been actively involved in the stoning of the cavalry troops by the main gate of the camp, and perhaps more damning for him, he was overhead loudly telling all who would listen in this Rhyl café that if things did not improve at the camp there would be further trouble there. Two main witnesses gave evidence against him at his court martial. He in turn produced two soldier witnesses and claimed he had wrongly been identified as one of the leading rabble rousers in the mob. Rufus Simon was found guilty of the 'joining in a mutiny' charge and received a sentence of five years imprisonment. He was taken away from the Grace Road Barracks to begin his prison term at nearby H.M. Prison, Walton.

As in all of those convicted at these court martials, he was to firstly have his sentence reduced and then have the remainder of it remitted. On 8 January 1920 aboard the S.S. Scotian he arrived on Canadian soil and was discharged from military service.

17. Everett Winfield Smith

Everett Winfield Smith was born on 12 October 1894 at Stonehaven, Gloucester County, New Brunswick, Canada. He enlisted in the C.E.F on 1 December 1916, at Fredericton, New Brunswick, in 236th Battalion (New Brunswick Kilties), also known as 'Sir Sam's Own', and as 'The McLean Kilties of America', for in the Spring of 1916, the battalion not only recruited throughout Canada, but also in the New England region of the United States. In March 1918 on the Western Front it was absorbed into 20th Battalion (Central Ontario), C.E.F. Everett Winfield Smith became Private Smith, regimental number 1030348. He gave his next of kin as being his father, John J. Smith.

Private Everett Winfield Smith arrived in England on 19 November 1917, aboard the S.S Canada. He arrived in France for duty at the Front on 7 March 1918. He served with 20th Battalion and saw plenty of action, and on 9 August 1918, he sustained a gunshot wound, described as being a superficial one to his left thigh, as a result he was invalided back to England. After spells at the Bramshott and Ripon camps he found himself at Kinmel Park Camp on 27 February 1919. Only a few days later he found himself well and truly in trouble. For during the riots/disturbances he was alleged to have been one of the carriers of the 'notorious' red flag (banner) when the rioters roamed in numbers around the camp. As a result, he faced serious charges, especially the one of 'joining in a mutiny'. He pleaded not guilty to the charges, but was found guilty at his court martial and was sentenced to three years of imprisonment.

As was the norm for these convicted soldiers, he was not to serve out the majority of his sentence. Private Everett Winfield Smith sailed for home from London on 5 November 1919, aboard HMT Tunisian.

Chapter Six

Some of those found not guilty or acquitted of serious offences

1. Battista Giovanni Bertucci

The *Morning Bulletin* newspaper, Edmonton, Alberta, Canada, edition of 26 May 1919, had an account in it, in relation to the ongoing court martials at Grace Road Barracks, Liverpool, into the riots/disturbances of 4/5 March 1919. The newspaper referred incorrectly to him throughout as Bertucco, which I have amended here:

> KINMEL CAMP RIOTER EARNED HONORS IN WAR
>
> Soldier Who Stood Trial for Aiding in Uprising is Acquitted
>
> LONDON, May 25 (Reuter's). 'He was one of the first who volunteered to go out and put up a double apron fence 30 yards in front of our firing line', said Sergeant-Major Lister, describing a trench incident of early in 1916, giving evidence on Saturday before the Kinmel court-martial on behalf of Private Battista Bertucci of Victoria, British Columbia, who pleaded not guilty to the charge of joining in the mutiny. The case arose from the disturbances at Camp 20, when three men were killed. Pte Bertucci was identified as among the rioters.
>
> He was arrested on the edge of a trench were a man was lying fatally wounded.
>
> The defence was that accused was drunk at the time and did not arrive on the scene until the disturbance was over, when he went to the trench out of drunken

curiosity. He described earlier adventures in the mess, where a sergeant was giving out free beer. 'He was hilariously drunk and the whole world was a joke, said the witness, who declared that the accused even tried to persuade a major to have a drink. Pte Bertucci was found not guilty.

Battista Giovanni Bertucci, regimental number 102032, was according to his military records born on 9 January 1884, at Victoria, British Columbia. He was a sailor and gave his next of kin as being his wife, Maria Bertucci. When he enlisted on 1 September 1915, he was described as of dark complexion, with brown eyes, black hair, and five feet, ten inches tall. In France & Flanders he served in several battalions of the C.E.F including 67th Battalion (Western Scots). Post-Armistice he was as a married man at the Canadian Discharge Depot (CDD), Buxton, Derbyshire, England, prior to him being at Kinmel Park Camp.

Due to his 'enforced' late availability to be returned home due to his court martial, he finally embarked for Halifax, Nova Scotia, and home, on 2 July 1919.

Battista Giovanni Bertucci died on 4 August 1950.

2. Wilburt Burton – born in England

Wilburt Burton was born on 15 November 1885, at Hull, Yorkshire, England. A miner by occupation, he emigrated I believe firstly to the United States, then during the First World War decided to throw his hand in by crossing the border into Canada and enlisting in the C.E.F to fight overseas. He stood six feet tall, enlisted at Camp St Charles, Winnipeg, Manitoba, giving his next of kin as not any relation of his, but a friend, Harold Montgomery of Grasston, Minnesota, United States.

After some initial military training in Canada, Private

Wilburt Burton, regimental number 2173509, arrived in England on 7 December 1917, aboard the S.S. Megantic. He served in France & Flanders in 27th Battalion (City of Winnipeg), and on 22 August 1918, when at the Front he sustained a GSW (gunshot wound) to his right knee, which required him to be hospitalised.

Post-Armistice Private Wilburt Burton arrived at Kinmel Park Camp from Seaford Camp on 5 January 1919, but things most certainly did not go smoothly for him whilst he waited here to be sent back over the Atlantic. For only a few days after arriving at Kinmel Park Camp on 10 January 1919, he was found guilty of drunkenness and received the punishment of twenty-eight days field punishment No. 2. However, less than a month later at the camp he found himself in a great deal more trouble, indeed in very serious trouble that if found guilty it would mean a number of years of imprisonment. For, following the riots/disturbances of 4/5 March 1919, he was charged with having joined in a mutiny at the camp, and also in his case, with, 'having used violence to a superior officer, in that he held the arms of Regimental Sergeant-Major Brierley, who was endeavouring to suppress the disturbances.

At Private Wilburt Burton's subsequent court martial, Sergeant-Major Brierley gave evidence that on the afternoon of 5 March 1919, he saw the accused Burton at the head of a group of rioters entering the camp's parade ground. He stated that he said to Burton, 'Get these men back'. In reply he stated that Burton waving his arms in the air turned around to the crowd of men behind him and shouted, 'Come on'. Later after the canteen had been broken into, RSM Brierley stated he was surrounded by about half-a-dozen men who were armed with clubs. He alleged that they wrenched his R.S.M pace stick from him and held his arms so that he was unable to do anything. He tried to reason with one or two of these men, and that Burton then said to him, 'I can get these men to do anything for me'. Even more seriously RSM Brierley then alleged that Burton said that they were going to Abergele to burn it. An incendiary threat in more ways than one. The President of this court martial, Major-General Sir H. E. Burstall then stated, 'I prefer that no statements be made with regard to future proposed crimes.' RSM Brierley continued his evidence that he then asked Burton if he had any control of the men. Burton he alleged, answered in the affirmative, whereupon he ordered Burton to take the men away. He said Burton refused, stating that they had a grievance, and that he had led strikes in the States and on the coast. In the opinion of R.S.M Brierley, Burton was not under the influence of liquor, but in fact he was perfectly sober, an opinion which was later to be very much called into question. Private Wilburt Burton then gave evidence in his own defence. He denied taking part in the rioting and recounted his endeavours to get assistance to pacify the rioters. He claimed the first he had seen of the rioters was when he saw them going in the direction of the records office. They were shouting that they were going to get their own papers; as they had been at Kinmel Park Camp long enough; and they would burn them up. Burton claimed to have mixed with the crowd, telling the men involved that if they broke into the records office they would never get back to Canada. Burton went on to say that these men then started off across the parade ground, and he met a Major. Burton averred that he urged this senior officer to get himself on top of a hut to address the crowd, and use moral persuasion with them to stop their wrecking. Burton admitted to having drunk a quart of gin on that day. Major W. E. Kidd, senior chaplain to the Canadian Forces at the camp then gave his testimony which greatly contrasted with that of RSM Brierley's. For Major Kidd, a highly respected man, a Military Cross winner, stated that he found the accused Private Burton standing outside a canteen which was in the possession of the rioters. He confirmed that Private Burton had asked him to go inside to stop the destruction, but he chose not to do so, fearing for his own safety. Major Kidd described Private Burton as being 'quite drunk' at this time. He also did not consider Private Burton to be one of the rioters, but thought that in his drunken condition, 'Burton was not a wise man to have in a crowd', as he put it. Two sergeants then gave evidence of Private Burton's desire to stop the looting and wrecking, and both agreed to the fact that Private Burton was indeed in an inebriated condition on the afternoon of 5th March. On the following day this court martial resumed, and defence counsel Major Weyman recalled Private Burton to give evidence. Burton denied that he had ever been connected with strike or strike-breakers in the United States or elsewhere, nor had he any recollection whatsoever of having in any way physically seized RSM Brierley. After a short deliberation this court martial produced not guilty verdicts on both the serious charges with which Private Wilburt Burton had been charged and acquitted him. Whereupon he was released of his escort and was permitted to leave the court unattended. An amazing result bearing in mind RSM Brierley's sworn evidence to this court martial.

Chaplain Major Kidd's testimony had been believed over that of RSM Brierley's. On this occasion it had proved to be that 'the clerical collar was mightier than the pace stick.'.

3. George Alexander Lorne McLeod

George Alexander Lorne McLeod was born on 20 September 1899, at Saint Mary's, New Brunswick, Canada.

He stated when he enlisted in the C.E.F on 24 April 1918, that he was a student, and gave his next of kin as his father, Alexander Daniel McLeod. George McLeod according to military records was five feet, ten inches tall, and was given the regimental number 336308. He arrived in England from Canada on 25 September 1918, on board the 'Themistocles'. He never saw active service, for the Armistice came on 11 November 1918, and he was still undergoing the required military training in England.

He was transferred in early October 1918 to Kinmel Park Camp, and placed on M.D No. 7 Wing, to await a sailing to return him to Canada. He was made an acting corporal and was responsible for sanitary matters on his Wing. He was hospitalised with influenza at the Kinmel Park Military Hospital (it had not yet become No. 9 Canadian General Hospital, Kinmel Park Camp) from 10 October to 15 October 1918. He was one of those who spent many months awaiting his turn to sail home to Canada.

Acting Corporal McLeod either 'got mixed-up in', or 'was involved in' the serious riots/disturbances at the camp of 4 and 5 March 1919. For on 5 March 1919, he was arrested and remanded in military custody to await a general court martial on two charges: one, that of joining in a mutiny, and two, that of failing to use his utmost endeavours to suppress the mutiny. He pleaded not guilty to both of the charges.

His court martial extended over three days at the conclusion of which The Judge Advocate stated: *By saying the utmost endeavour did not necessarily mean the utmost of which a man was capable, but such endeavour as a man might reasonably and fairly be expected to make'*. On such semantics legal cases are often to be won or lost. George Alexander McLeod was 'acquitted on all charges', as it was put, and soon finally on his way back to Canada.

4. Wilmont Burchell Nason

Wilmont Burchell Nason, shown on some records as Wilmot, or William (he signed his attestation papers as William B. Nason), was born on 16 February 1896, at Tracy Station, Sunbury County, New Brunswick, Canada, to Ezekiel McLeod Nason, and wife, Arminta Olive Nason, nee Boone. He was described as being six feet tall, of fair complexion, with blue eyes and brown hair, when he enlisted at Sussex, Kings County, New Brunswick, on 25 October 1915, in 104th Battalion of the C.E.F. He gave his next of kin to be his mother, Mrs Arminta Morgan, now remarried to a Wesley Morgan. Private Wilmont Burchell Nason, regimental number 709240 after undergoing some military training in Canada, arrived in England on 6 July 1916, from Halifax Port, Nova Scotia, on board the RMS Olympic. After further military training and kitting out, he landed in France on 29 November 1916, and now served with 5th Battalion, the Canadian Mounted Rifles, though despite the name it was now very much, due to prolonged trench warfare, an infantry battalion. To say he had an 'eventful' time at the Front in France & Flanders is truly an understatement. On 30 October 1917, he was reported as 'missing in action', and when found alive and not a prisoner of war, he had a shotgun wound to his left hand, which resulted in him being treated at a military hospital in Etaples. France.

On 26 August 1918, when in action during The Battle of the Scarpe (26 August to 30 August 1918), he sustained a shotgun wound, again to his left hand. This battle took place during what is called 'The Hundred Days Offensive' by the Allies. Here at Monchy-le-Preux, France, the Canadian corps including 5th Battalion C.M.R, as part of 3rd Canadian Infantry Division advanced over five kilometres, pushing back the Germans and in doing so captured the French towns of Monchy-le-Preux and Wancourt.

Wilmont B. Nason

On 26 August 1918, during this Battle of the Scarpe, Lieutenant Charles Smith Rutherford of 5th Battalion, C.M.R captured a German group of forty-five soldiers, including two German officers, seized three enemy machine-guns, and then with the support of his men and a lewis gun went on to capture a German pill-box with another thirty-five German soldiers and their guns. For this action Lieutenant Rutherford, born on 9 February 1892, at Haldimand Township, Colborne, Ontario, was to receive the Victoria Cross (VC). Lieutenant Rutherford had begun the war as a private. As a sergeant he had already been awarded a Military Medal, then after being commissioned he was awarded a Military Cross. This amazing soldier survived the war and he died in Ottawa on 11 June 1989, aged ninety-seven.

Wilmont Burchell Nason post-Armistice arrived at Kinmel Park Camp on 22 February 1919, to await repatriation. However, following the riots/disturbances of 4/5 March 1919 at the camp, he was facing serious charges. Whether the following action by him was his own idea or someone else's, I do not know, but he put forward that: 'he was not likely to receive a fair hearing at his court martial', and surprisingly all charges were dropped against him. Perhaps there was poor evidence against him, and one of those who did give evidence against him was Lieutenant J A. Gauthier, who featured 'perhaps a little too prominently' in a number of these court martials. But it may also have been that his previous considerable service at the Front 'in 'battles', could have counted very much in his favour.

He was 'struck off strength' of the C.E.F on 16 July 1919, at New Brunswick. On the 1921 Canadian census he is shown as a labourer, residing with his mother Arminta Morgan at Gladstone, Fredericton, New Brunswick.

Wilmont Burchell Nason, known by family and friends as 'Bill', lived in New Brunswick all of his life. He was married I believe twice, and had several children. He died on 21 October 1987, at the age of ninety-one. He was buried at the Tracy Cemetery, Sunbury County, New Brunswick. At some time, a rectangular shaped piece of stone has been placed to mark his resting place. Upon it is written:

PTE WILMONT B NASON
1896 – 1987
104 BATTN CEF
LEST WE FORGET

It is a shame that this stone does not instead have 5th Battalion, CMR, upon it. For it was with this battalion of course that he fought in battles at the Front and was wounded on two occasions.

Much to my personal chagrin about a year ago, I saw too late, that on an auction site First World War items which had belonged to Wilmont Burchell Nason had been up for auction. The collection included his British and Victory war medals, both engraved '709240 Pte W. B. Nason 5-CMR', with original ribbons. Plus, his CEF dog tag (identification tag), and 5th Battalion CMR badge with pin. All said to be in the 'original box'. I hope they went to a person or an organisation who will appreciate them.

I wondered exactly what kind of man and soldier the main defence counsel, **Major Edward Colpitts Weyman** was who featured so prominently in the court martials. He was born on 27 August 1882, at Studholm, Kings County, New Brunswick. He was a barrister on his enlistment on 28 May 1915, and described as being five feet, nine and a half inches tall, a Baptist by religion. He sailed from Montreal to England with the C.E.F on 30 October 1915, aboard the S.S. Corsican. He fought in France & Flanders with 42nd Battalion (Royal Highlanders of Canada). On 29 April 1917, during The Battle of Arras (9 April – 16 May 1917) he was seriously wounded in battle, receiving gunshot wounds to both legs. His right leg had to be amputated from four and a half inches below the knee. After a great deal of hospital treatment and convalescence he went to Queen Mary's Hospital, Roehampton, and there was fitted with a prosthetic limb. Major Weyman stayed with the C.E.F and was a key figure in the Kinmel Park Camp court martials.

Major Edward Colpitts Weyman, O.B.E., K.C., returned to Canada and continued as a barrister. He died on 3 February 1936, aged fifty-four, and was buried at Saint Paul's Anglican Church Cemetery, Hampton, Kings County, New Brunswick. His widow, Jean Blacklock Peacock Weyman who died in 1981, aged ninety-five, was buried in the same grave.

Chapter Seven

Some of the Canadian soldiers who died whilst at the camp

For the period September 1918 to July 1919, when Canadian soldiers and Canadian nursing sisters were at Kinmel Park Camp, I have found that of the total of eighty-five who died there, eighty-four of them are buried in the nearby St Margaret's Churchyard, St Margaret's Church, Bodelwyddan, North Wales. This church and its churchyard better known to many as 'The Marble Church'.

The eighty-four buried there consist of eighty-three male soldiers and one nursing sister. Though all eighty-four were at the camp serving with the C.E.F, the Canadian Expeditionary Force, amongst their number are soldiers who were actually born in England, Scotland, Ireland, the United States, and even one in Costa Rica, Central America. I have researched and found the following figures:

Died of influenza/bronchial pneumonia – the Spanish Flu as it was named: 73
Killed during the riots/disturbances of 4/5 March 1919: 4
Committed suicide: 2
Died of heart disease/failure: 2
Died from diabetes/a diabetic coma: 1
Died from tubercular meningitis: 1
Died from an intestinal obstruction: 1

Forty-five of these eighty-four deaths occurred during 1918, and a number of these were 'draftees', ones conscripted into the C.E.F, and had only recently, some very recently, arrived in Britain from Canada. Once it was seen that the war was looking likely to end quite soon, many were transferred to Kinmel Park Camp from Canadian camps in England, with thoughts of promptly shipping them home. Of course, if it had looked like in August and September of 1918, that the war would drag on for at least a year or two, then these soldiers would have almost certainly soon found themselves on the Western Front and not at a staging camp in North Wales.

The thirty-nine deaths which occurred in 1919, have a higher proportion of those soldiers who had seen 'action' on the Western Front.

The total 'death toll' includes one nursing sister, Rebecca MacIntosh, who died from influenza and pneumonia on 7 March 1919.

The total figure buried at St Margaret's Church would have been one more, but the family of Gunner John Frederick Hickman, accidentally killed during the riots/ disturbances on 5 March 1919, a mere innocent bystander, demanded that his

'Marble Church', Bodelwyddan

body be returned to Canada for burial there. The family got their way and the body of John Frederick Hickman was disinterred from the St Margaret's Churchyard and shipped to Canada, where some ten weeks later in late May 1919, he was buried in his hometown of Dorchester, New Brunswick, following a moving and very well attended funeral service.

Why so many deaths, of so many young men and one woman at Kinmel Park Camp from one cause – Influenza/Bronchial Pneumonia? Well, as a disease it killed worldwide an estimated 50 to 100 million people. That is between approximately 3% and 5% of the then world's population. This H1N1 influenza virus which first appeared in a number of countries, including the United States back in 1917, then mutated to become deadlier by October 1918 around the world. Kinmel Park Camp was hit by this second wave of the more deadly strain, and with the 'general conditions' at the camp being as they were, it truly is a wonder how the death toll though shocking as it was, was not far higher bearing in mind that thousands of military personnel, many physically weakened from their time in the trenches at the Front, or from various military camps perfect places for germs to spread, had ended up at a wooden hutted, windswept, short of coal and of decent food, camp in North Wales – Kinmel Park Camp. For recent investigations have shown that in 'normal times' the death toll would not have been so high. But it struck during a bitter world war, with malnourished people, poor hygiene generally, but with virtually nil hygiene for hundreds of thousands of soldiers in and around the trenches at the Front. Everywhere was overcrowded – hospitals, military camps, trains, ships etc., where the virus could spread more easily.

To get matters in relation to this 'pandemic' of

1918–1919 into worldwide perspective: Some 228,000 deaths occurred in Britain; between 30,000 to 50,000 died in the then quite sparsely populated Canada; some 675,000 deaths in the highly populated United States, with a population around this period of thirteen times more than Canada's; and Japan is said to have had 23 million who were affected by it, with 390,000 of them dying. It truly was the greatest global pandemic to hit the world since The Black Death, also known as The Great Plague, of the 14th Century. Whilst the total numbers who died in this 14th Century pandemic were a lot less, it should be remembered that at that time the world's population was a small one in comparison to the First World War period.

1. William Albany – First Nations Canadian

William Albany was born on 3 August 1894, at New Liskeard, (after the amalgamation of New Liskeard and two other towns is now named Temiskaming Shores), north-eastern Ontario, Canada. He was brought up as an Algonquin 'Indian' of what we now call The First Nations, Canada. He was the son of Algonquin hunter and trapper Peter Albany who was born in 1876, and his wife, Philomena Albany, nee Wabanicenabe, who was a Chippewa, better known today as an Ojibwa.

William Albany enlisted in the C.E.F, unable to read or write in English. Aboard the S.S. Missanabie he disembarked in England on 7 April 1917. He was Sapper William Albany, regimental number 1007062, placed in 256th Battalion, Canadian Railway Troops. When in France & Flanders this battalion became 10th Battalion, Canadian Railway Troops. This battalion on the Western Front was involved in work on the existing standard gauge railways, constructing new light, narrow gauge railways and the building of bridges. Still in France post-Armistice, William

Albany had influenza, no doubt the Spanish Flu strain, and on 7 December 1918 was treated at a military hospital in Boulogne. Said to be seriously ill he was then at Bordon Camp, Hampshire, on 16 December 1918. Why he was then moved when seriously ill to No. 9 Canadian General Hospital, Kinmel Park Camp, on 6 February 1919, I cannot really fathom.

Sapper William Albany, aged twenty-four, died at the camp's military hospital at 3.40 am on 10 February 1919. He was buried in the St Margaret Churchyard, St Margaret's Church (The Marble Church), Bodelwyddan, grave reference 485.

2. Lieutenant Robert Brown – born in Scotland

Robert Brown was born on 20 October 1889, at Renton, Scotland. He was a clerk in accountancy at Niagara, Southern Ontario, Canada, when he attested on 10 June 1915 for the C.E.F. He was described as being five feet, six and a half inches tall, of fair complexion, with grey eyes and fair hair. He gave his religion as being Presbyterian.

Following some initial military training in Canada, Private Robert Brown, regimental number 408566, embarked from Halifax, Nova Scotia, aboard the S.S. Lapland on 27 November 1915, disembarking in England, on 11 December 1915. Whilst undergoing further training and being kitted out at Bramshott Canadian Camp, Hampshire, he was promoted to the rank of corporal on 13 December 1915, to acting sergeant on 7 June 1916, and then whilst at Dibgate Camp, Folkestone, a staging camp for the C.E.F for their soldiers going to the Western Front, he was made on 25 August 1916, a temporary lieutenant.

Lieutenant Robert Brown served in France & Flanders from the end of August 1916, until May of 1917. Whilst in France he was admitted to 14th General Hospital,

Boulogne, suffering from the nasty pyorrhoea, a serious form of gum disease. In its early stages it is called gingivitis, but if allowed to develop often goes into the more serious periodontitis. With this the gums can move-way from the teeth, bone can be lost and teeth start to fall out. Soldiers at the Front, especially those in the trenches had far more pressing things to worry about than oral hygiene, until struck with this, which due to so many soldiers at the Front having got it was often called 'trench mouth'. He was treated in hospital for this and then given an extended leave. I strongly believe that during his time at the Front he was gassed, and in addition suffered some level of shell shock, often referred to in medical terms as neurasthenia.

On 2 June 1919, he was at Kinmel Park Camp awaiting repatriation to Canada. However, on 5 September 1919 at the camp, now no longer 'officially' occupied by the C.E.F, he committed suicide. We can surmise that it was due to his physical and mental health difficulties. He was buried in grave reference, 523, in the St Margaret Churchyard, St Margaret's Church (The Marble Church), Bodelwyddan, aged twenty-nine.

3. Alfred Selwyn Basil Jones – born in Wales

Alfred Selwyn Basil Jones was born at Lanfair Dyffryn Clwyd, near Ruthin, Denbighshire, North Wales, on 28 March 1881. He was working in British Columbia, Canada as a land surveyor, when on 14 October 1915, at Vancouver, British Columbia, he enlisted in 1st Canadian Pioneer Battalion. He gave his next of kin as his father, Canon Basil M. Jones, the Vicar of Llanfair Dyffryn, residing at the vicarage there. Alfred Selwyn Basil Jones was a single man, five feet, nine inches tall, of fair complexion, grey eyes and brown hair.

As Private Alfred Selwyn Basil Jones, regimental number

154592, he arrived in England from Canada on 30 November 1915. He was then in France & Flanders with 1st Canadian Pioneer Battalion. He received quick promotions to lance-corporal, corporal, then sergeant, until on 11 July 1916, he was commissioned as a temporary lieutenant. Then only some nineteen days later, when at the Front on 30 July 1916, he was wounded when an enemy high explosive shell exploded close to him, embedding bits of metal in his right upper arm and right thigh. He was initially treated in France and then convalesced at Miss Pollock's Hospital, 50, Weymouth Street, London. Recovered, he was seconded for a time to The Light Railways Directorate due to his abilities as a land surveyor. Back at the Front in France & Flanders in July 1917, he was hospitalised for a few days at 14th Canadian General Hospital, Wimereux, France, with influenza.

Post-Armistice he found himself at Kinmel Park Camp with 9th Battalion Canadian Railway Troops, a location only seventeen miles away from his family and family home near Ruthin. On 3 February 1919, Lieutenant Alfred Selwyn Basil Jones was in Kinmel Park Camp's own military hospital suffering from influenza. He died there on 9 February 1919, aged thirty-seven, and was buried at St Mary's Churchyard, Llanfair Dyffryn Clwyd, near Ruthin, North Wales.

4. Heber Percival Lett

Heber Percival Lett was born on 15 September 1893, at Merrickville, eastern Ontario, Canada. He was working as a salesman when drafted (conscripted) and placed in the Canadian Field Artillery, C.E.F, as a gunner and signaller, regimental number 2022937. He disembarked at London on 25 September 1918, and found himself being moved around, firstly at Witley Camp, Surrey, then Bordon Camp,

Hampshire, and ending up at Kinmel Park Camp when it was still designated as a segregation camp.

Here on 20th October 1918, he became most unwell. The medical report upon him I place below, for those who were struck down at the camp with influenza, the Spanish Flu, would have sadly gone through a similar progression, and died once bronchial pneumonia set in:

Medical Report on the death of:
2022937, Pte Lett, Heber
134 Draft Canadians
Age 25. Service 6/12
The above-named man was admitted to Military Hospital, Kinmel Park on 20/10/18, complaining of severe headaches – general aching to limbs – severe cough which caused considerable pain in chest – diagnosed influenza.

On 22/10/18 his respirations became more rapid – pulse quickened – cough increased – no expectoration.

Examination of chest revealed moist rales all over upper part of chest – gradually, fine crepitations developed at bases of both lungs and on 25/10/18 dullness on percussion was present.

From this date the pulse began to fail – become rapid and thread – he perspired freely – respiration became rapid and shallow, and he was markedly cyanotic. He died of heart failure at 03.30 on 3/11/18.

The cause of death was Broncho-Pneumonia, complicating Influenza, due to exposure to infection while on military training during the present war.

5/11/18 – (signature), Major, O.i/c, Medical Division, Military Hospital, Kinmel Park.

Gunner Heber Percival Lett died on 3 November 1918, and was buried at St. Margaret's Churchyard (The Marble Church), Bodelwyddan, in grave reference 463.

5. Andrew Neville

The *Lancashire Evening Post* edition of Monday, 10 February 1919, reported upon a rather sad story:

> Soldier's Delusion
> Private Andrew Neville, Canadian forces, was found in a quarry near Kinmel Camp, Rhyl, hacking at his throat with a clasp knife, when the weapon was taken away.

This Canadian soldier was Andrew Neville, born on 1 January 1882, at Cobden, Ontario, Canada. He was working as a drug clerk and residing with his wife Ethel May Neville when he was drafted under the Canadian Military Service Act of 1917. He was passed as medically fit and called up in January 1918 to serve with 11th Reserve Battalion, Canadian Infantry (Manitoba Regiment), as Private Andrew Neville, regimental number 2383381.

He arrived in England and underwent military training, including at Seaford Camp. On 21 December 1918, he was moved to Kinmel Park Camp. It was on 5 February 1919, that he was found hacking at his throat with a clasp knife. Sadly, he did not survive, being pronounced 'dead on arrival' at No. 9 Canadian General Hospital, Kinmel Park Camp. The report upon his death stated: *Died, 5 February 1919, self-inflicted wound to throat – Suicide.*

Private Andrew Neville was buried at the nearby St. Margaret's Churchyard, Bodelwyddan (The Marble Church), grave reference I.5.

His widow Ethel May Neville in 1920, was now living in Toronto, Ontario.

6. Sigurjon Paulson

Sigurjon Paulson was born at Winnipeg, Manitoba, Canada,

on 18 May 1892, to Iceland born parents, Sigfus Paulson, a teamster, and, wife, Sarah Paulson. This Paulson family had emigrated to Canada in 1887 to begin a new life. The family during the First World War resided at 488, Toronto Street, Winnipeg.

Sigurjon Paulson was a teamster like his father, and at Winnipeg on 19 February 1916, he enlisted in the C.E.F. He was described as being five feet, six inches tall, of fair complexion, with grey eyes and fair hair. He gave his religion as Lutheran and his father as his next of kin. He disembarked from HMT Scandinavian at Liverpool, England, on 6 February 1917, having embarked from Halifax, Nova Scotia. He arrived in France on 22 April 1917, and what can be said about his military service in Europe was that it was most certainly ups and downs. He was wounded in France & Flanders on 15 August 1917 when serving with 107th Battalion (Winnipeg), but remained on duty. He received at least in 'the field', three periods of field punishment No.1, for going AWOL (absent without leave). He also served in France & Flanders in several Canadian units and seemed to be constantly moved around. Also, on one occasion at least he was found drunk, again receiving official army punishment and his military record was endorsed to that effect. Back in 1916 he had been made a lance-corporal, then promoted to corporal, but was then reduced to the rank again of private, though the reason for this I cannot exactly ascertain.

What is known is that he arrived post-Armistice from Seaford Camp, East Sussex, England, at Kinmel Park Camp on 12 April 1919, to await his repatriation. His medical records show that he had been falling ill and complaining of feeling weak for a few months before he arrived at the camp. He had a number of medical tests carried out upon him from when he was admitted to No. 9 Canadian General

Hospital on 24 April 1919. It was reported on 24 May 1919, that he was now dangerously ill in this military hospital and was in a diabetic coma.

Private Sigurjon Paulson died at 3.00 pm on 24 May 1919 of 'diabetes'. He is buried in the St Margaret's Churchyard, St Margaret's Church (The Marble Church), Bodelwyddan, North Wales, in grave 519.

7. Israel Sands – First Nations Canadian

Almost certainly the youngest of the Canadian soldiers to be buried here is Israel Sands. On his enlistment papers in 1917, he gave his date of birth as being 14 May 1898, and almost two years later when undergoing a routine medical examination his date of birth is shown as 14 May 1900, but after research I believe his true date of birth was in fact 14 May 1901, and is to some extent supported by a medical report, the details of which I include in this piece. Also, when persons lie about their age, they usually keep the same day and month, just changing the year.

Israel Sands was born at Walpole Island, south western Ontario, Canada, situated on the border between the Canadian province of Ontario and the United States state of Michigan. Walpole Island is a First Nations reserve and Israel was of the Ojibwa-Chippewa/Potawatomi people from here.

So, I believe that when on 5 May 1917, he enlisted for the C.E.F at Toronto, he was still only fifteen-years of age, and told them he was a lumberman. He was described as being of dark complexion, with brown eyes and black hair, and five feet, four inches tall. He embarked from Halifax, Nova Scotia, on 28 June 1917, aboard the S.S. Justicia, disembarking at Liverpool on 5 July 1917. He was now Sapper Israel Sands, regimental number 2250586, of 60 Company, Canadian Forestry Corps, their nickname was 'the Sawdust Fusiliers'. At Smith's Lawn, Sunningdale, Berkshire, Israel Sands was medically examined before being sent to France & Flanders. Written on his medical notes by a doctor was: *Underdeveloped – Looks younger than age stated. Not sufficiently developed for full duty. Classified as B1.'* Sapper Israel Sands arrived in France on 30 July 1917, and I do not believe that at any time he served at the Front. Recruitment posters for the Canadian Forestry Corps, included they were looking to recruit, 'lumber men, bushmen and sawmill hand's'. Perhaps, due to his immaturity, and, hopefully not for an any more 'sinister' reason, he got into trouble on at least two occasions, after all he was still 'just a kid'. On the first in August 1917, he was docked twenty-eight days of pay for insolence to an N.C.O, and in August 1918, he was docked a week's pay for 'neglect of duty'.

Post-Armistice via Sunningdale Camp, he arrived on 12 March 1919, at Kinmel Park Camp, to await repatriation. Only six days later, on 18 March 1919, he was admitted to the camp's military hospital with what was diagnosed as influenza. As this strain known as Spanish Flu particularly took a heavy toll on younger people, he went through a most difficult time trying to fight against it, but on 29 March 1919, at 2.40 am he succumbed and died, aged but still seventeen.

Sapper Israel Sands was buried in the St Margaret's Churchyard, St Margaret's Church (The Marble Church), Bodelwyddan, North Wales, in grave reference 513.

8. William Herbert Stow

The *North Wales Chronicle* of 25 October 1918, reported upon the Spanish influenza cases locally:

CASES ON THE INCREASE

All reports show that the influenza epidemic is striking

> harder and its roots are more widespread. Several medical authorities including Dr Spilsbury, the well-known pathologist, urge that warm clothing and plenty of good nourishing food are the best preventatives. The lack of doctors is being severely commented upon, but in view of the calls to the Front, it is all but impossible to make up the shortage. In many districts, also undertakers are unable to cope with the increased demands, and one undertaker at St Pancras Military Tribunal, who said he was phenomenally busy, got four months exemption. There is a serious outbreak at Kinmel Camp, near Rhyl.

Sadly, one of the victims of this reported 'serious outbreak' of the Spanish Flu at Kinmel Park Camp was William Herbert Stow, known as Herb. Herb Stow was born on 29 July 1894, at Hamilton, Ontario, Canada, to Thomas Stow and Clarissa Stow, nee Dawson. Herb Stow was a labourer, who then became a brass moulder. He was latterly employed as a blacksmith on the T.H. and B. Railway (the Toronto, Hamilton and Buffalo Railway which ran from 1894 until 1987). This Stow family resided for many years in Dundurn Street, Hamilton, Ontario.

On 10 October 1917, Herb Stow married Elizabeth Ann Tilson, known as Beth, at St Joseph's Church, Hamilton, and they set up their married home at 409, Main Street West, Hamilton. Only some three weeks later on 3 November 1917, Herb Stow enlisted for the war and underwent military training with 2nd Depot Battalion, 2nd COR. In September 1918, after a short period of leave at home, Herb Stow left Canada aboard the HMT Themistocles. bound for Britain where he arrived on 25 September 1918.

He found himself at Kinmel Park Camp, then being used as a segregation camp for incoming drafts of Canadian soldiers. But just two weeks later on 11 October 1918, Herb Stow was reported to be 'deathly sick with influenza'. Nine days later, on Monday, 20 October 1918, Herb Stow, aged twenty-four, died in the Kinmel Park Military Hospital, from bronchial pneumonia brought on by the influenza. Herb Stow was buried in the St Margaret Churchyard, (The Marble Church), Bodelwyddan, grave reference 430.

The *Hamilton Spectator* edition of a few days later, carried an obituary piece about him. The war ended a few weeks later, and it was said, the only possession of Herb Stow's returned to his family in Canada was a brass locket which contained two small photographs – one of Herb Stow in his army uniform and one of his young wife Beth. Some eight months after his death, Beth gave birth to their son, she named Herbert Gerard Stow. Herbert after his father, whom he would never see or know. Beth subsequently remarried and moved to live in Detroit, the United States.

Tragedy again struck this Stow family years later, when Herbert Gerard Stow who had enlisted in 1941 for the Second World War, came home unscathed, only to be killed in a car accident in Detroit, having only recently married wife Verna – history repeating itself for father and son – young lives snuffed out and marriages cut short.

Chapter Eight

First Nations Canadian soldiers at the camp

I am sure like myself, many if not most, non-First Nations Canadians or Native American Indians, had realised or indeed given any thought to the involvement of these indigenous/aboriginal peoples in the two great world wars of the 20th Century. Then along came in 2002, the John Woo film, '*Windtalkers*', starring Nicholas Cage and Adam Beach (a Canadian actor with much of his ancestry being First Nations Canadian). It was a dramatization based on the real Navajo 'Indian' code talkers of the Second World War. These Navajo (also, some Comanche, Lakota and Meskwaki) Native American Indians with the United States Marines, used their 'native languages' to communicate vital military messages, and outwitted the otherwise very able Japanese cryptographers in the South Pacific. This film started me off on a quest to find out more on this matter. I found that this was not a new military phenomenon, for during the First World War, Cherokee and Choctaw Native American Indians had already pioneered such 'code talking' to fine effect at the Front against the German enemy.

Here in this chapter I seek to show the important part Canadian First Nations soldiers played in the First World War with the C.E.F. Due to their innate abilities many of these First Nations soldiers became snipers and scouts, two of the riskiest of roles to take on in and around the trenches on the Western Front. Many were adept in the use of camouflage, and at wrangling, the latter very useful with horses and mules playing vital roles in the war. It is estimated, that about 4,000 First Nations Canadians served in the First World War, a number of them were killed, many wounded, and a good proportion were awarded military honours for bravery in battle – some of whom in late 1918 into 1919, were at Kinmel Park Camp.

Enos Williams, MM, First Nations Canadian

What first drew my attention to Enos Williams was when I found this entry in the War Diary of M.D. 3 Wing for 11 March 1919, less than one week after the riots/disturbances occurred at the camp:

Kinmel Park. 11-3-19. Presentation of the military medal was made today to Private E. Williams, No. 739294. In spite of the heavy rain which fell, the ceremony passed off smoothly and Pte Williams was cheered by the troops formed up on the parade ground as the medal was presented by the G.O.C., while the Area Band played appropriate selections.

This was the awarding of the Military Medal, a military decoration awarded to personnel in the British Army, or other arms of the armed forces, or as in the case of Enos Williams, to personnel of the Dominion countries below the rank of a commissioned officer. It was awarded for bravery on land for 'acts of gallantry and devotion to duty under fire'. Many of the 'old sweats' from the 'other ranks' were unhappy at the introduction of this new decoration in 1916, for they felt strongly that it was only introduced in order to avoid awarding the higher Distinguished Conduct Medal (DCM) to more of the 'other ranks.' The DCM itself being ranked just below the Victoria Cross (VC). Officers received the equivalent award, known as the Military Cross (MC), which I proffer sounds as if it has more importance, and indeed the Military Cross was also a finer looking medal than the much plainer Military Medal. In 1993, the Military

Medal was discontinued, the Military Cross to be awarded now for all ranks – commissioned officers and other ranks. – a more equitable decision.

Enos Williams was no ordinary Canadian soldier, for he was a member of the Six Nations, who back in 'less enlightened days' would have been referred to as an 'Indian or Red Indian'. Enos Williams was born on 15 May 1886, at The Six Nations Tuscarora Township, near Brantford, Brant County, Ontario. There was much debate, indeed rancour early in the First World War concerning 'Canadian Indians' being allowed to enlist in the Canadian military. There was a suggestion put forward that they could be allowed to join 'Indian only' battalions, under white officers. It was also put forward, and I suggest that this did have some merit – that should a 'Canadian Indian' be made a prisoner of war by the German's or their Allies, that he would not be treated as decently (to put it mildly) as a white Canadian soldier. The German's during the First World War did indeed discriminate shockingly against certain ethnic groups of prisoners of war, such as Slavs and Poles, something of course they were to repeat on a far more hideous scale during the Second World War.

Enos Williams decided like many of his Six Nations people to volunteer to fight in the Canadian military. On 23 March 1916, when residing at New Credit, Ontario, as a member of the Mississauga Ojibwa First Nation, he enlisted at Ohsweken, near Brantford, Ontario. At this time he was a farm labourer, described as being five feet, four inches tall, of dark complexion, with brown eyes and black hair. He gave his religion as being Baptist, and his next of kin as his father, Chancy Williams of Sixty-Nine Corners, Ohsweken, a Six Nations village of The Grand River First Nation Reserve, near Brantford, Ontario. He was now Private Enos Williams, regimental number 739294 in 114th (Haldimand) Battalion, also known as 'Brock's Rangers, a recently formed infantry battalion of the C.E.F.

He was actually with 1st Canadian Infantry Battalion in France & Flanders from 17 May 1917. Records show that he was for at least some of the time in this battalion's 'B' Company. Private Enos Williams fought with his battalion at the 'Hell that was Passchendaele', taking an active part in The Second Battle of Passchendaele (26 October to 10 November 1917), very active in fact, for it was as a result of his actions here on 6 November 1917, that he was subsequently awarded the Military Medal. His citation:

> *London Gazette, Number 30573*
> *Dated March 13, 1919*
> *Enos Williams (739294), 1st Battalion*
> *At Passchendaele, November 6, 1917, this man assisted materially in the capture of an enemy machine-gun which was immediately brought into action against the enemy. On two occasions his gun was buried and both times he promptly recovered it and kept it in action. Under heavy shelling he returned back over captured ground to bring up ammunition for the gun.*

He appears to have come out of The Battle of Passchendaele unscathed, at least physically. However, with his battalion around Arras, northern France, on 30 August 1918, he was seriously wounded in action during The Battle of The Scarpe (26 August to 30 August 1918), which was a part of The Second Battle of Arras (26 August to 3 September 1918). Private Enos Williams suffered a shell wound to his left leg, which was first treated at No. 2 Canadian General Hospital, Le Treport, France, and then at two hospitals in England. Firstly, thirty-three days, from 6 September 1918 to 9 October 1918, at No.10 Canadian General Hospital, Brighton (formerly known as The Kitchener Hospital, Brighton). He was then for a further thirty-three days from 9 October 1918 to 11 November 1918, Armistice Day itself, at Princess Patricia's Canadian Red Cross Hospital, Bexhill, Sussex. He then spent some time at Witley Camp, Surrey, until on or around 3 March 1919, he was at Kinmel Park Camp, and placed on M.D. 3, awaiting his repatriation to Canada. It was here of course on 11 March 1919, as appears at the beginning of this piece, that he was 'officially' presented with his well-deserved Military Medal. On 23 March 1919, at the camp, he was medically and dentally examined, before his repatriation.

Life back home for Enos Williams in the post-First World War years does not appear to have been easy for him, the same of course could be said for many, many thousands of ex-service personnel after their wartime experiences. In early 1921 when farming, he 'defaulted on his settlement loan' and the property he had been running was taken off him by the DIA (Department of Indian Affairs) and given to another member of the Six Nations.

Enos Williams died at the General Hospital, Brantford, Ontario, on 6 July 1957, aged seventy-one, leaving a widow Winnifred. Enos Williams was buried at Mount Hope Cemetery, Brantford, Ontario.

First Nations 'Brothers in Arms'

Also, at Kinmel Park Camp post-Armistice was the equally most highly decorated First Nations Canadian soldier of the First World War, namely Charles Denton Smith. The other most equally decorated was … his older brother, Alexander George Edwin Smith (junior). Both were at different times, in different battles, the worthy recipients of the Military Cross. Alexander was the father of 'Tonto', and Charles was an uncle of 'Tonto's' – the explanation of which is revealed below.

Charles Denton Smith, the younger brother, was born on 2 October 1883, at The Six Nations Reserve, Tuscarora Township, Brant County, Ontario, to Six Nations Cayuga Chief, Alexander George Smith (senior), who was born on 15 April 1849, and, his wife, Mary Smith, nee Wedge, who was born on 15 August 1848.

The Six Nations of the Grand River was founded in 1784, on land granted to Mohawk chief, Joseph Brant (Thayendanegea), after whom a number of places in the area are named in his honour. This granting of land in Canada followed the American War of Independence, when the Mohawks under Joseph Brant had fought on the English side against the Americans. This land was a new home for the members of the Iroquois, who set up the Six Nations Confederacy, consisting of Mohawk, Oneida, Onondaga, Cayuga, Seneca and Tuscarora. A fine achievement since some of the six were on opposite sides in bloody warfare during the American War of Independence.

Charles Denton Smith, MC

Pre-First World War, Charles Denton Smith was a carpenter and local militia member, who was married to Mary Stella Smith. He volunteered and enlisted in the C.E.F at Hartford, Ontario, in 114th Battalion (Haldimand), also known as 'Brock's Rangers'. He was described as five feet, five and a half inches tall, of dark complexion, with brown eyes and black hair. He was given the regimental number of 739177, and after undergoing some military training in Canada, he left behind a wife and one-year-old son, to fight in Europe. He arrived at Liverpool Port and for a few months he underwent officer training in southern England, until he was sent as a lieutenant to France & Flanders with 20th Battalion (Central Ontario). He was then transferred to 18th Battalion (Western Ontario). He had influenza in January 1917, and was hospitalised. He returned to the Front and it was on 9 November 1918, two days before the Armistice, the combatants on the ground were not of course aware of it being in the offing, that he was in a military action which was to result in his being awarded the Military Cross. This is the citation for it, which appeared in the London Gazette, Issue 31266, of 2 April 1919:

> *Military Cross*
> *Smith, Charles Denton (Lieutenant)*
> *For conspicuous gallantry and determination at Framieres on 9th November 1918. He led his platoon forward with such rapidity that he surprised a party of sappers preparing to blow up a road mine. Rushing forward, he shot the man who was in the act of igniting the fuse. The same evening, he personally captured a machine-gun, disposing of the crew.*

Post-Armistice, Lieutenant Charles Denton Smith was granted 'the usual' two weeks leave in Britain, and following a time at Witley Military Camp, Surrey, he on 1 April 1919, found himself in the wooden hutted, windswept camp, that was Kinmel Park Camp. He was at the camp until on 7 May 1919, when he sailed back to Canada.

In the Autumn of 1919, the Heir to the Throne, David, Prince of Wales made an official and extensive visit to Canada, largely to thank the Canadian people of 'all races, creeds and colours' for their wonderful efforts during the war. He visited on 17 October 1919, Brantford, Ontario, and there in an official ceremony presented Lieutenant Charles Denton Smith, MC, with his Military Cross, along with medals to eight other 'local' Canadian soldiers and one Canadian widow. Whilst in the area, the Prince of Wales, later to become the 'controversial' King Edward VIII, visited 'The Mohawk Chapel' at Brantford. It is the oldest surviving church building in Ontario. This, the first Anglican church in Upper Canada was constructed in 1785, and originally named St Paul's. It was a gift of the British Crown to the Mohawk people, led by Joseph Brant, for their support during the American War of Independence, also known as the American Revolutionary War. The chapel, one of only three 'Chapels Royal' in the whole of Canada is officially entitled today, 'Her Majesty's Royal Chapel of the Mohawks'.

Charles Denton Smith's older brother was **Alexander George Edwin Smith (junior)**, born on 14 August 1879, at The Six Nations Reserve, Brant County, Ontario. He had served in 37th Regiment (Haldimand Rifles), a Canadian militia for some eighteen years and held the rank of major with them when the war began. At this time, he was a contractor, residing with his wife, Mabel Phoebe Smith, at Sixty-Nine Corners, Ontario. He promptly volunteered and enlisted in the C.E.F at Cayuga, Ontario, on 13 November 1914. Due to his considerable previous experience in the military, he was made a lieutenant in the C.E.F, and on enlistment described as five feet, ten and a half inches tall, of dark complexion, with brown eyes and black hair.

He arrived at the Front in France & Flanders, and served with 20th Battalion (Central Ontario). At The Somme, France, on 16 September 1916, he was blown-up by an enemy high explosive shell, and in the aftermath, he suffered shell shock and a profound loss of hearing. For his actions during the battle when commanding 'C' Company, he was awarded the Military Cross. The citation for which appeared in the London Gazette, Issue 29824 of 14 November 1916, and reads:

> *Lieutenant Alexander George Edwin Smith*
> *20th Battalion, C.E.F.*
> *For conspicuous gallantry in action. He proceeded with a party of bombers and captured an enemy trench and fifty prisoners, displaying the greatest courage throughout. He was twice buried by shells, but stuck to his post.*

Rather badly injured he was treated at several military hospitals including for a time at the Canadian Officers' Convalescent Hospital, Matlock Bath, Derbyshire, England. Whilst in hospital in England he wrote a number of letters to his father back at The Six Nations Reserve. An extract taken from one of them:

> *You may tell Mabel that I was awarded the military cross for bravery and gallantry in the field of the greatest battle the world has ever known. Don't forget to tell Donnie and Harold what God has enabled me, their papa, to go through and do.*

The 'Harold' mentioned in the letter was young son, Harold Preston Smith (born 26 May 1912 – died 5 March 1980), better known to 'those of a certain age' by his stage name of Jay Silverheels, the Mohawk Canadian actor, stuntman, and fine athlete, who starred as 'Tonto', alongside fellow actor Clayton Moore in the one might say 'quite iconic' American television series 'The Lone Ranger', which ran from 1949 to

1957, and often repeated for many years afterwards. In 2013, 'The Lone Ranger', a film directed by Gore Verbinski, and starring Johnny Depp as Tonto was released. Unlike, Jay Silverheels/Harold Preston Smith, Johnny Depp is not of the First Nations of Canada or a Native American Indian.

Now promoted to the rank of captain, Alexander George Edwin Smith due to his wounds and serious hearing impairment was sent back to Canada, but not to be idle. He became the assistant adjutant-general for the training of 'The Blue Army' as they were called. A Polish Army of nearly 23,000 encamped at Niagara-on-the-Lake, Ontario, undergoing military training. This 'Blue Army' under the auspices of the Canadian military later fought on the Western Front with the Allies. For his valued service to the 'Blue Army', Captain A. G. E. Smith received the 'Order of the Black Star of Poland', only one of five Canadians awarded this honour.

Captain A. G. E. Smith post-war went back to being a contractor and followed in the footsteps of his father when he became the Chief of his people. He died of a heart attack on 22 October 1954 at a veteran's hospital in Buffalo, New York, the United States, aged seventy-five, survived by his widow, Mabel Phoebe Smith.

Amongst other First Nations Canadian soldiers who spent time at Kinmel Park Camp post-Armistice were four with the surname of 'Brant', all born and raised in Ontario, Canada:

Brant Brant, regimental number 637076; **Charles Clinton Brant**, regimental number 220324; **John Henry Brant**, regimental number 2499291; and, **Matthew Brant**, regimental number 455599.

Fred Gaffen, a military historian at the Canadian War Museum in Ottawa, Ontario, Canada, in his fine and authoritative 1985 book, *Forgotten Soldiers*, states in relation to the First World War:

> *Of all the Indians in Canada, Ontario Indians enlisted in the largest numbers. Most came from the Six Nations Reserve, near Brantford, and the Tyendinaga Reserve, near Deseronto on the Bay of Quinte. The record of the Mississauga Indians, near Peterborough, is also noteworthy.*

Also, at Kinmel Park Camp was a First Nations Canadian who was to become quite famous, partly because of his brave exploits in battle during the First World War, and partly because through his writings and lectures, he brought about a greater understanding of First Nations peoples to others. He was the wonderfully named **Mike Mountain Horse** (Miistatisomitai), born on 1 November 1887, at The Blood Reserve, Macleod (now named Fort Macleod), Alberta, Canada. Mike Mountain Horse was a carpenter, married to Mary and living a quiet sort of life until the death occurred of one of his brothers, Albert Mountain Horse, born

Mike Mountain Horse

on 25 December 1893, who had served in France & Flanders as a driver with the Canadian Army Service Corps, regimental number 30396, and had died in Canada after being invalided back from Europe suffering from bronchial pneumonia. He died on 19 November 1915, aged but twenty-one, and brother Mike believing that Albert's exposure to German poison gas had caused his death, joined the C.E.F seeking one might say – revenge. Mike Mountain Horse enlisted on 23 May 1916, at Macleod. He was six feet and a half inch tall, and given the regimental number 89504. He fought at the Front in France & Flanders with 50th Battalion (Calgary), and was involved in some of the main battles which the C.E.F were involved in during the war. On 25 August 1917, he was at 7th Casualty Clearing Station 'dangerously wounded', his military record shows. For a few days earlier during The Battle of Hill 70, (The Canadian Corps against the German 6th Army, 15 August to 25 August 1917), at Lens, France, he had been involved in hand to hand fighting and suffered a bayonet wound to the abdomen. It occurred when he and his unit were clearing the enemy, house by house at Lens. During this month of August 1917, he had been involved in a number of skirmishes with the enemy, and had killed at least three of the enemy using what he called, 'his war knife'.

During, The Battle of Amiens (8 August–11 August 1918), Mike Mountain Horse painted Blackfoot victory signs all over a captured German field gun. The First World War though a decidedly European war of empire served to provide First Nations Canadians such as the Blackfoot soldiers a chance to be warriors again. To be able to return home with stories of fighting and victory, just as their own fathers and forefathers had. Indeed, back home on the reserves their deeds in the First World War were painted onto robes, hides and even tepees.

Mike Mountain Horse, post-Armistice was at Kinmel Park Camp, and placed on M.D. 13. From here he embarked for Canada on 2 May 1919, aboard the S.S. Cassandra. He was later to say, '*The war proved that the fighting spirit of my tribe was not squelched through reservation life. When duty called, we were there, and when we were called forth to fight for the cause of civilization, our people showed all the bravery of our warriors of old*'.

Mike Mountain Horse had orally received the story of his father, Mountain Horse and an uncle, Bull Shield, fighting in 'the last great battle on Canadian soil between First Nations peoples' – The Battle of the Belly River, which took place on 25 October 1870, between his Blood Tribe, the Blackfoot and Peigan (the Blackfoot Confederacy), against their longstanding enemy, the Cree (the Iron Confederacy). The Cree were beaten in a bloody battle, with around three hundred of their warriors killed. About a year later a lasting peace between the two warring confederacies was agreed. The Belly River location today is within the city of Lethbridge, Alberta.

Mike Mountain Horse over the years worked as an interpreter for his people with The Royal North West Mounted Police and then as a labourer in the workshops of the Canadian Pacific Railway, where his fellow workers affectionately called him 'Chief'. In his later years he turned his hand to journalism with the *Lethbridge Herald* newspaper, Lethbridge, Alberta, which is still going strong today. His writings and lectures were of 'handed down stories' of his Blood Tribe, the Kainai, and their traditional ways.

He died on 31 January 1964, at Cardston, Alberta, aged seventy-seven. He was buried at the Blood Band Cemetery, Cardston, and his grave is marked by a fine marble gravestone which reads:

MIKE
MOUNTAIN HORSE
PRIVATE
50 BATTN CEF
31 JAN 1964
AGE 81

I believe the age shown on it is incorrect, but apart from that, for me it is 'perfect'. Mike Mountain Horse has gone, but is certainly not forgotten, because of his writings, photographs of him in later life wearing a fine Blood Tribe headdress, and he is honoured by the local school at West Lethbridge being proudly named, 'The Mike Mountain Horse Elementary School'.

Another First Nations Canadian 'war hero' who was at Kinmel Park Camp was **Joseph Crow Chief**, known as 'Joe'. He was also from the Blood Reserve, Macleod, Alberta, and was born in August 1894. He was five feet, nine inches tall and arrived in England with the C.E.F on 7 April 1917, aboard the RMS Regina.

Joe Crow Chief was in the trenches at the Front in France & Flanders with 50th Battalion (Calgary), regimental number 895282. On the first day of The Battle of Canal du Nord (27 September – 1 October 1918), Private Joe Crow Chief was wounded attacking the enemy. This battle was a particularly vital part of the Allies, Hundred Days Offensive, which led to ultimate victory. During this five-day battle, in which Private Joe Crow Chief received 'a machine-gun bullet to the left forearm, fracturing the ulna', no less than a total of twelve Victoria Crosses were awarded. Joe was quite seriously wounded and after treatment at a casualty clearing station, he was at two hospitals in England. Joe Crow Chief recovered well, and was at Kinmel Park

Camp post-Armistice. He arrived back in Canada on 22 March 1919, and was discharged from military service on 4 April 1919, at Medicine Hat, south-east Alberta. In his latter years he did suffer breathing problems from having inhaled mustard gas during the war, but it was said that did not stop him enjoying life to the full.

An elder brother of his, who chose to go by the name of **Nicholas King**, born at the Blood Reserve on 12 November 1885, was a miner, six feet tall, when he enlisted for the C.E.F. Private Nicholas King, regimental number 895178, served at the Front in France & Flanders with 50th Battalion (Calgary), and was wounded in late 1918 on two separate occasions, suffering gunshot wounds to the right hand and to the forehead. He survived the war and returned to his wife, Little Painted Woman King, to whom he had been sending his separation allowance whilst serving in the C.E.F. Nick King as he was generally called, became known for having gone to war in Europe with his fine, full length one horn headdress. Apparently, he did not return to Canada with it, as someone in Europe 'took a fancy to it'. Whether it was stolen from him or he sold it I am unable to ascertain. Nicholas King died on 15 June 1957, aged seventy-one.

Samuel Glode, DCM, known as Sam, was a Mi'kmaq from Nova Scotia. He was born on 20 April 1878, and when he enlisted in the C.E.F he was a lumberjack and part-time guide for hunters and fishermen. He served in France & Flanders, regimental number 469762, with a tunnelling company, and then with the Canadian Engineers. For his outstanding work in the clearing of enemy mines and demolition charges at the Front he was awarded the Distinguished Conduct Medal (DCM). The citation for which stated, '*He showed great devotion to duty and an utter disregard of personal danger, and successfully removed 450 charges.*'

Sergeant Samuel Glode managed to survive such deadly work and was for a time at Kinmel Park Camp. Post-war, looking back at his time at the Front he said: '*I'll never forget the first night. I stayed out most of the night watching the flares go up and over no man's land, like fireworks, and hearing the cannons and bursts of rifle and machine gun fire*'.

Samuel Glode

Back home, Samuel Glode who never liked any form of indoor work, lived alone in a shack on his own land in the woods outside the Potanoc Settlement, Queens County, Nova Scotia, and continued acting as a guide to fishermen and hunters who visited the area. He joined the Canadian Legion at Liverpool, Nova Scotia, and often went there to reminisce about wartime experiences with fellow veterans, whilst enjoying a few drinks of beer or rum. Samuel Glode, DCM, died on 25 October 1957, in the Camp Hill Veterans' Hospital, Halifax, Nova Scotia, aged seventy-nine.

Two sons of Chief Redsky, Ojibwa from Shoal Lake, Ontario, were both at different times at Kinmel Park Camp. **James Redsky**, born in 1898 served with 52nd Battalion (New Ontario), regimental number 820872, and was a victim of poison gas in France & Flanders. Older brother,

Edward Redsky, born on 10 June 1891, also served with 52nd Battalion, regimental number 820905. He too was gassed at the Front, as a result of which he spent three months in military hospitals.

Two of the best known of the First Nations Canadian soldiers were both deadly snipers, a role which in the stalemate of trench warfare proved a vital asset. One was Private **Henry Louis Norwest**, nicknamed 'Ducky', regimental number 435684, a former ranch hand and rodeo rider was a Metis, of some Cree ancestry from Alberta. He was a prolific sniper and was 'credited' (a strange term when one considers each success was a life, albeit of an enemy soldier), with a verified total of 115 hits, it is reliably said that he actually had many more 'hits' than this figure, and he was awarded the Military Medal and Bar. He was killed by a German sniper on 18 August 1918, at the Somme.

The other was **Francis Pegahmagabow**, nicknamed for ease of address as 'Peggy', regimental number 6846. He was an Ojibwa of the Parry Island Band, Ontario. He was a distinguished sniper, believed to have been 'the most prolific' in the entire war on either side. He is credited with 378 'hits', though quite a number of these were officially discounted for he did not always have a 'sniper's observer' with him. Francis Pegahmagabow was awarded the Military Medal and two Bars. He survived the war and became an activist for his First Nations people.

The above two may well be the best publicly known today of the First World War's, First Nations soldiers, but many more of them were awarded military honours, those from 52nd Battalion (New Ontario), one of the so called 'Bull Moose Battalions' included:

Leo Bouchard, regimental number 3327611, from Lake

Nipigon, Ontario, Distinguished Conduct Medal (DCM); **David Kejick** (sometimes shown as Kisek), 821017, from Shoal Lake Reserve, Ontario, DCM; **Augustine (Gus) Belanger**, 439699, from Fort William Reserves, Ontario, Military Medal (MM); **Joseph DeLaronde**, 439776, an Ojibwa from Lake Nipigon, Ontario, MM;

Some from other battalions:
George McLean, regimental number 688302, from the Head of the Lake Band, Okanagan, British Columbia, Distinguished Conduct Medal (DCM); **Edwin Victor Cook** (also Cooke), 703323, Nimpkish/Namgis Band of Alert Bay, Vancouver Island, British Columbia, DCM; **Thomas Godchere**, 199199, an Ojibwa of the Long Lake Band, Longlac, Ontario, Military Medal (MM).

It must have been a tremendous culture shock for many of the First Nations Canadian soldiers when they had to assimilate into the military life, a military conducted in the English language, and consisting of 'the white man's' idea of uniforms and discipline. Then there was Europe – different again, far more cosmopolitan than any place they would have ever visited before. Yet they surmounted these obstacles. I have seen that a number went to the bright lights of Paris on their leaves' (furloughs) from duty, a real eye-opener for any Canadian soldier, let alone those who had come from peaceful reserves, working on the land, or as trappers, hunters or fishermen.

Elsewhere in his book, *Forgotten Soldiers,* Fred Gaffen states this of First Nations Canadian soldiers as we refer to them today, then referred to generally as Members of Indian Bands or Tribes:

... Indians who enlisted, probably those from remote areas during the First World War, had to face a severe culture shock, as they adapted to military life. For some, proper military dress and deportment were very foreign to their way of life. But once in the services and acclimatized, the Indians generally proved to be the ones who complained the least.

Chapter Nine

Black Canadian soldiers and the 'Black Battalion' at the camp

Benjamin Randolph Hagin – a black Canadian soldier

Benjamin Randolph Hagin was not the 'usual' Canadian soldier to be found at Kinmel Park Camp post-Armistice, for he was a black soldier.

Benjamin Randolph Hagin was born on 5 March 1893, at Lockport, Shelburne County, Nova Scotia, Canada. He was directly descended from slaves, who had years earlier been relocated in Nova Scotia by the British, whom they had supported in two wars against America (the United States).

A number of his direct descendants I have come to know personally. These include a son of his, John Twist Hagin, now retired, who for many years ran his own building company, building houses in the Kinmel Bay, Prestatyn and Talacre areas of North Wales. Another is a lovely lady named Julie Parry, one of John's daughters and a granddaughter of Benjamin Hagin. Julie has kindly assisted me with an account of her grandfather Benjamin, and provided me with a photograph of him.

Benjamin R. Hagin

Benjamin Randolph Hagin was a fisherman, single, and drafted (conscripted) under The Military Service Act 1917, to join the C.E.F and fight overseas. Benjamin Hagin may well have previously tried, like many other black Canadians to enlist, but had been turned down for blatantly racial reasons. It was 'interesting', that due to the shortage of volunteers for the C.E.F, depleted due to their ever-increasing casualties at the Front, that suddenly black Canadians 'of all people' should be drafted/conscripted under this act. Little wonder then that many black Canadians were said to have been resentful about now 'being good enough to be forced by law to enlist', yet when they had made earnest attempts to voluntarily enlist earlier in the war, they were insulted and told to go away as they were not wanted, with recorded comments from white enlistment personnel such as, 'go home, this is a white man's war'.

Benjamin Hagin initially was enlisted into 1st Depot Battalion, the Nova Scotia Regiment. On his enlistment papers he was shown as five feet, six and a half inches tall, of 'colored complexion' as it was put, with black eyes and hair. He gave his next of kin as being his mother, Ann Samuels, formerly Hagin, who had married Henry Samuels, a ship's rigger, who had been born in Montserrat, a Caribbean island in the Leeward Islands. Private Benjamin Hagin, regimental number 3188816, sailed from Canada on 3 August 1918, with 62nd Draft of 1st Battalion, Nova Scotia Regiment, arriving in England on 15 August 1918. He was initially sent for further military training to Bramshott Camp and then transferred to the Canadian Forestry Corps.

It was virtually impossible for a black Canadian soldier to serve in an infantry regiment at the Front during the First World War, though a few did manage it, when all of the officers and other ranks in the regiment would be white or of white appearance. That is how it was in the First World War, a time of incredibly different views and attitudes to race and colour than is the norm today. Private Hagin was then sent to Sunningdale Camp, and post-Armistice on 14 December 1918, to Kinmel Park Camp. Here he was placed on M.D. 4. But Private Benjamin Randolph Hagin was not to return to his native Nova Scotia, Canada, for whilst at the camp he met Elizabeth Twist of nearby Rhyl, North Wales. She was a single, white young woman. Private Hagin was at the camp during the riots/disturbances, and on 26 May 1919, he was granted permission by the military authorities to marry Elizabeth Twist. On 22 June 1919, prior to his being formally discharged from the military at Kinmel Park Camp, he was given the standard medical examination and dental examination. Unlike so many of his Canadian soldier counterparts who married British women and took their wives back to Canada with them, Benjamin Hagin on 8 July 1919 was 'Discharged in the British Isles' and gave his proposed future residence as 7, Brickfield Terrace, Rhyl, where he was going to live with new wife Elizabeth and her parents, John Twist and Elizabeth Twist, nee Roberts. For a number of years after the First World War, Benjamin Hagin worked at a slaughterhouse in Ffordd Las, Rhyl, North Wales. When I suggested to his family members that it was not a very nice job to do, they replied that during the 1920's and early 1930's, 'the Depression Era', it was the perfect job. For Benjamin and his wife had nine children, plus two children of one of their daughters to look after, and working at the slaughterhouse he was allowed to go home with plenty of the offal. So, this large Hagin family of thirteen in total did not lack for food. Though son John Twist Hagin informs me that since then he has never liked offal, especially not liver!

The family also inform me that Benjamin Hagin on a very regular basis, come rain or shine, would cycle from his home in Rhyl to the churchyard at 'The Marble Church', Bodelwyddan, to visit and pay his respects to six former Kinmel Park Camp Canadian soldier comrades who are buried there. Sadly, with the passing of time, they are unable to tell me exactly who the six he 'visited' were, only that they had all died of illness at the camp.

It has been a pleasure, indeed an honour to have met his direct descendants who not only reside today in the Rhyl area, but also around different parts of England. Today, one part of the family runs a successful sea angling business 'Jensen's' which owns two boats, one on the North Wales Coast and the other at Liverpool Port – fishermen just like Benjamin Randolph Hagin when he was back in Nova Scotia pre-First World War.

Benjamin Hagin, though a black man, and married to a white woman in Rhyl, an area overwhelmingly a 'white one' is said to have had little or no problem. Perhaps this was due in part at least to his affable nature and him being a genuine sort of individual. Benjamin Randolph Hagin died in 1947, aged fifty-four, and he and wife Elizabeth 'founded' a Hagin/Twist dynasty which now has many descendants, none of whom who would exist today but for Benjamin Hagin from far off Nova Scotia being at Kinmel Park Camp awaiting his repatriation to Canada. His wife, Elizabeth Hagin, nee Twist, known as 'Betsy', a 'Canadian War Bride' back in 1919, died in 1970, aged seventy.

Black Canadians and the First World War

Black Canadians were no different to any other Canadians in that some wished to go to fight, for what I would say was 'Country and King', and some were not so keen to do so. But for black men born in Canada, who did wish to enlist in the C.E.F, there was an added ingredient, a very potent one – they felt strongly that it was their fundamental right to go to fight, especially when 'their country' was calling for volunteers. But these black men who did try to enlist in the C.E.F in a 'regular battalion' faced virtually insurmountable barriers in order to do so. Those in charge of the Canadian military and especially recruitment openly questioned whether black Canadians should serve at all, and if they did, that they must not be allowed anywhere near the Front to fight, but if they had to be allowed to enlist, then they should only be 'workers' behind the lines. Sadly, for many of these, the days of black people cotton picking as slaves had well and truly passed!

Major-General Willoughby Garnons Gwatkin, the British born, public school educated chief of the general-staff in Ottawa for the Canadian forces during the First World War sent a memorandum in April 1916, which stated this: *The civilised Negro is vain and imitative, in Canada he is not impelled to enlist by a high sense of duty; in the trenches he is not likely to make a good fighter, and the average white man will not associate with him on terms of equality'*. How widely this memorandum was circulated I do not know, but it clearly gives us an insight into the mindset of one such as Gwatkin – highly regarded as a military organiser, but as far as my research has found 'he was not one who during his long and well rewarded with military honours career, actually did any fighting himself' – a man who was very much of his time, who was an advocate of what we would call today 'institutional racism'.

Other leading white commanders expounded their overt racist views, with one New Brunswick commanding officer writing to his superiors in Halifax declaring that, *'his white soldiers should not have to mingle with negroes'*. On quite a number of enlistment records which I have found for black Canadian men in 'regular Canadian battalions' the man is enlisted, but within a couple of weeks he is discharged and written upon the official military record is 'UNDESIRABLE'. Other Canadian battalions who having enlisted black recruits, chose to get 'shot of them' by putting down on their military records the more subtle, 'DECLINED'. One particular battalion very much in need of recruits had enlisted twenty 'apparently, fit and suitable' black men, but then discharged all of them for no longer being required. These twenty were of course eminently suitable apart from one thing – the colour of their skin!

A few black Canadians in the First World War did manage to overcome barriers to enlist and remain in otherwise totally white soldier battalions, but these were indeed, very few and far between. One was the now quite legendary **Jeremiah Alvin Jones**, known as Jerry, who was born on 30 March 1858, at East Mountain, Colchester County, Nova Scotia. He was a teamster on his enlistment with 106th Battalion (Nova Scotia Rifles), regimental number 716221. He was described on his enlistment form for complexion as 'negro', and he lied as to his actual age, for he was fifty-eight years of age, and off to fight in the C.E.F. Private Jeremiah Alvin Jones served at the Front in France & Flanders with The Royal Canadian Regiment (The RCR), an infantry regiment. On 9 April 1917, during The Battle of Vimy Ridge (9 April – 12 April 1917) at Vimy, France, part of The Battle Second Battle of Arras (1917), he showed great bravery and initiative in the heat of battle. Here he received a gunshot wound (a GSW) and was 'reportedly' recommended by an officer to receive the high military award of the Distinguished Conduct Medal (DCM), but never received any such medal. Several veterans later came forward to confirm that 'Jerry' had been recommended for the DCM. If this is correct, then surely he should at least have been awarded a Military Medal? Today, we can only surmise as to why he received nothing, well, he would have received exactly the same war medals that were post-war awarded to soldiers who never saw more than the inside of a military camp in Canada, England or Wales!

Private Jeremiah Alvin Jones was treated for his wounds, and on 6 November 1917, he embarked on his return to Canada, 'officially' no longer fit for service. The doctors who treated his wounds realised that he was actually now nearly fifty-nine years of age, and suffering from a painful hernia, which was operated on a few weeks later at the Camp Hill Military Hospital, Halifax, Nova Scotia. Private 'Jerry' Jones was a black man who had seen more action in battle in his months at the Front in 1917, than Major-General Willoughby Garnons Gwatkin had seen in forty-years of 'staff officer type soldiering'.

Jeremiah (Jerry) Alvin Jones after a long and full life, died on 23 November 1950, aged ninety-two.

The 'Black Battalion' in the Canadian Expeditionary Force

A quite momentous thing happened at Pictou, Nova Scotia, on 5 July 1916, when No. 2 Construction Battalion was formed. No, it was not an infantry battalion of the C.E.F, but a definite breakthrough of sorts, for it was the first black military unit of any size in Canadian history, certainly one that left Canadian shores. Just over six hundred black recruits, many from Nova Scotia, but also some from Ontario, New

No. 2 Construction Btn. cap badge

COLORED MEN!

Your KING and COUNTRY Need YOU!

NOW is the time to show your Patriotism ; Loyalty

Your Brothers of the Colonies have rallied to the Flag and are distinguishing themselves at the Front. ¶ Here also is your opportunity to be identified in the Greatest War of History, where the Fate of Nations who stand for Liberty is at stake. Your fortunes are equally at stake as those of your white brethren

LT. COL. D. H. SUTHERLAND
C. O. No. 2 Construction Battalion

Will you heed the call and do your share?

NO. 2 CONSTRUCTION BATTALION

Now being Organized All Over the Dominion Summons You. **WILL YOU SERVE?**

The British and their Allies are now engaged in a great forward movement. Roads, Bridges and Railways must be made to carry the Victors forward. The need of the day is Pioneers, Construction Companies and Railway Construction Companies. No. 1 Construction Company has been recruited. No. 2 Construction Company is now called for.

Lt. Col. D. H. Sutherland is in charge of the Company's Headquarters at Pictou; at Halifax applications may be made at the Parade Recruiting Station; elsewhere to any Recruiting Officer, or by letter to—

MAJOR C. B. CUTTEN, *Chief Recruiting Officer, Halifax, N. S.*

Royal Print & Litho Limited, Halifax N. S.

No. 2 Construction Btn. (photo of many of them)

Brunswick, about twenty-five per cent from across the border in the United States, and a number originally from the West Indies, were recruited. It's formation to a great extent was due to the efforts of the black Baptist minister, Reverend William Andrew White, who was the very first black man to be commissioned as an officer into the Canadian or British armies, though he would be called an 'Honorary Captain', to please 'certain sensibilities'.

The Atlantic Advocate, Halifax, Nova Scotia, was the first African/Black Nova Scotian newspaper to ever be published which was created and edited by, and for, black Nova Scotians. Some members of No. 2 Construction Battalion were involved with the writing and production of this newspaper. One of them **Wilfred Adolphus DeCosta**, born in Jamaica, British West Indies, on 20 March 1885, was I believe the publisher of this newspaper. He was regimental number 931353, and though some historians have him as a sergeant-major in No. 2. Construction Battalion, I can only find that he enlisted, trained and then went over to England with them. But did not go to France with No. 2, instead he was in Canadian military camps in England in reserve battalions. When enlisting in No. 2 he gave his occupation as a gardener and his address as Franklin Street, Halifax, Nova Scotia. This *Atlantic Advocate* newspaper carried advertisements for recruits to join No. 2. A full-page advert was in the Volume 1, number 7 edition of January 1917. The advertisement was submitted by Major C. B. Bullen, chief recruiting officer at Halifax. It was headed, '*COLORED MEN!*

Your King and Country Need YOU. A photograph of the commanding officer of No. 2, Lieutenant-Colonel D. H. Sutherland was in the centre.

After extensive recruiting efforts and undergoing some basic training in Canada, this battalion consisting of 19 officers and 605 'other ranks' embarked from Halifax, Nova Scotia on 25 March 1917, aboard the S.S Southland, disembarking at Liverpool, England, on 7 April 1917. However, No. 2 had already lost one of its men, for **John Richard Lambert**, one of the very first to enlist, regimental number 931002, was hospitalised for weeks at Truro, then at Halifax, Nova Scotia, until on on 31 May 1917, he died in the Halifax Military Hospital of pleuro-pneumonia. Some later claimed he died as the result of him and fellow No. 2 soldiers being forced to live in boxcars rather than any kind of proper accommodation whilst training in Nova Scotia. John Richard Lambert had been born on 8 February 1898, at Halifax, so when he died, he was only nineteen years of age. His older brother, **Harold Lambert** also served with No. 2, regimental number 931184. He made it through their time in France and at Kinmel Park Camp, to be discharged from the military at Halifax, Nova Scotia, on 17 February 1919.

Following some further military training at Seaford Camp, East Sussex, England, No. 2 Construction Battalion landed in France on 17 May 1917, and made their way to the Jura Department in eastern France, well known for its mountains and proliferation of trees. Here they became part of No. 5 Canadian Forestry Corps – Jura Group – felling trees and preparing some of the vast amounts of wood needed by the Allies for such vital purposes as trench reinforcing, fencing to put up barbed wire, duckboards and railway sleepers.

In France, because No. 2 Construction Battalion was

under strength, this battalion which has become known as the 'Black Battalion', was reduced to a company – officially now it was No. 2 Construction Company. As a result, its commander Daniel Hugh Sutherland was now only a major and no longer a lieutenant-colonel. These two 'demotions' would have been music to the ears of No.2's many 'white detractors'. But they soldiered on, and like any other battalion or company in the Canadian or British armies they had their share of good soldiers, and not so good soldiers. A number of these black soldiers died of illness and other causes whilst serving in France. There was not always harmony between the white officers, white of course with the exception of Captain William Andrew White, and the black soldiers of No.2. Nor always between the black soldiers themselves. One of the black soldiers, Ernest Garfield Bushfan in Jura, France, on 10 November 1918, threatened a fellow No. 2 black soldier with a knife. For which after being in confinement until 3 December 1918, he was tried by field general court martial for 'conduct to the prejudice of good order and military discipline, and, of

Some Officers of 'The Black Battalion'

threatening a comrade'. He got off lightly with a sentence of three months of field punishment No.1. He did go to Kinmel Park Camp, but a few months after his comrades had been there, left there, and arrived home in Canada.

The majority of No. 2 Construction Company arrived back in England on 14 December 1918, and spent a couple of weeks at Bramshott Camp, Hampshire, and then on to Kinmel Park Camp, the final camp for them before being transported back to Canada.

Their time at Kinmel Park Camp

No. 2 Construction Company had worked alongside white, fellow non-combatants in France, where there had been tension and trouble. Apart from when they had to work together in the saw mills, black and white soldiers were segregated. On at least one occasion at Jura, Captain William Andrew White had to step in with his considerable frame, to stop a serious fight between the men from his No. 2 Company and a group of white soldiers.

However, when No. 2 Construction Company were at Kinmel Park Camp, they were 'cheek by jowl' with fellow soldiers, many, many white ones. The facilities at the camp had to be shared and their time in the camp did not pass without incident.

It may have been as a result of the following 'incident' or not, that No. 2 Construction Company were pretty swiftly away from the camp and embarking for Canada.

After No. 2 Construction Company had been at Kinmel Park Camp for less than two weeks, and they had all undergone the required medical and dental checks, a 'racially charged' melee took place at the camp on 7 January 1919. The circumstances as I have found them, were that a number of black soldiers from No. 2 were in a line waiting to go into the communal bathing facilities at the camp. One white soldier in a group of white soldiers made a verbal 'racial insult' to the No. 2 men, with the inference that they should be going ahead in the queue because 'they were white soldiers'. Insults were exchanged and a nasty fight ensued. During the fight five white soldiers were slashed with knives and a number of black soldiers of No. 2 hurt by stones. A number required medical treatment afterwards.

There is no doubt that on this day a serious incident took place, but I have learnt of another account of what had occurred. This account is that a group of white soldiers with their white sergeant attempted to force the black soldiers of No. 2 to let them go ahead of them in the queue for the baths, accompanied by racial remarks. That Sergeant Edward Sealy of No. 2 had the 'offending' white sergeant arrested and put in the guardhouse and guarded by one of his fellow black No. 2 soldiers. The group of white soldiers taking exception to this, especially the black soldier guarding their white sergeant, tried to release him from custody, and fighting broke out.

Whatever the exact version was, it was a racially charged incident, and one that could easily have had far more serious repercussions.

In 1992, the formation of No.2 Construction Battalion of the C.E.F was designated by the Government of Canada as an 'event of national historical significance' and a commemorative plaque was placed at Pictou, Nova Scotia.

Whilst in February 2016, Canada Post released a fine limited-edition stamp to commemorate the 100th anniversary of the formation of the 'Black Battalion', another formal recognition of its significance, most particularly of course to the black community.

The black officer and some of the black NCO's and other ranks of No.2 Construction Battalion (later Company)

Reverend Captain William Andrew White

William Andrew White, a rather extraordinary man, was born on 16 June 1874, at King and Queen Court House, King and Queen County, Virginia, United States. Post-American Civil War, Virginia was at this time and for many years that followed, a deeply segregated southern state where those who were black, may no longer have been slaves, but they had no civil rights, indeed virtually no rights whatsoever. White's own parents, James Andrew White and Isabella White, nee Walker, were former slaves. Yes, his parents were slaves, victims of the abhorrent abomination that was human slavery – the de-humanising of others for personal gain and gratification (my own term for it). Much of William White's hometown had been destroyed during the bitter civil war between the North and the South. Post-Civil War things did improve to a degree for black people, though I suggest how the hell they could have got any worse for them in the South with full scale slavery I do not know!

Captain William A. White

William White joined the Baptist church and with encouragement and support he moved to Canada and attended Acadia University, Nova Scotia, Canada, only the second black man to do so. William White did well scholastically and on the sports field. He was six feet, four inches tall, though some military records show him as only six feet tall. He stayed in Canada and in 1902, he was the Baptist minister at the Cornwallis Street Baptist Church, Halifax, Nova Scotia, in the African Baptist Association. William White received his B.A. in 1903, and as a Baptist minister he toured the various black settlements of Nova Scotia, establishing a second Baptist church in New Glasgow, Pictou County. He met Izie Dora White (no relation), who was descended from slaves of white New England planters. She was born at Mill Village, Nova Scotia, in 1890, and they married in 1906, at Truro, Nova Scotia, where William was then the Baptist minister. Together William and Izie had thirteen children, one of whom, the third born in 1911, Portia May White, became a fine operatic contralto and was the very first Afro-Canadian to become an international singing success.

Black and White people worshipped at separate churches, and after some ten years as Baptist minister at Zion Baptist Church, Truro, for Reverend William Andrew White, the First World War began. He was now forty years of age and championed the determination of black men in Canada to enlist in the C.E.F and 'fight for King and Country'. Following so many black men being rebuffed when trying to enlist in the C.E.F, he was partly instrumental in the formation of No. 2 Construction Battalion, in which virtually all the NCO's and other ranks were black, but, with the exception of himself, Honorary Captain and Chaplain William Andrew White, all of the officers were white.

Captain William Andrew White served with No. 2 Construction Company, formerly Battalion, in France for the remainder of the war. White soldiers refused to accept him as their minister even when they did not have their own 'white one'.

Post-Armistice, Captain William Andrew White was with hundreds of his men of No. 2 Construction Company at Kinmel Park Camp, all awaiting their repatriation to Canada.

In the early 1930's, Reverend William Andrew White went on radio, making broadcasts of his services of worship from the Cornwallis Street Baptist Church in Halifax, which were heard throughout Canada and in parts of northern United States. He preached a message of hope and unity, not despair and division. That people of every colour had a destiny and no matter what it was, as long as they had a vision to pursue that destiny, they were a success. One of his core beliefs all of his life which he often preached of, was that, 'God created all men as equals, and that Blacks were not put on the earth to be slaves to the Whites'. He tirelessly worked to break down the racial barriers which held back, black men and women in employment, and to remove segregation in schools, theatres and on buses. Sadly, it would take another generation to see this happen due to the likes of Martin Luther King, his wife, Coretta Scott King and Rosa Parks. But having studied him, I believe that Reverend Captain William Andrew White was a torch bearer for racial equality in its embryo stage.

Reverend Captain William Andrew White died on 9 September 1936, at Halifax, Nova Scotia, aged sixty-two. Two documentary films have since been made about him: '*Honour Before Glory*' and '*Captain of Souls*'.

Sergeant Edward Sealy

Sergeant Edward Sealy was born in Barbados, British West

Indies, on 7 March 1876, and had twelve years previous military experience with one of the West India Regiments (WIR), British army infantry regiments recruited from the British West Indies, who served in the Caribbean and in parts of Africa from 1795 to 1927.

Edward Sealy enlisted on 21 July 1916, in the C.E.F at Halifax, Nova Scotia, regimental number 931011, and was later made a sergeant in No. 2 Construction Battalion (later Company). He was described as being five feet, eleven and a half inches tall, of dark complexion, brown eyes and black hair. He had been a labourer residing in Maynard Street, Halifax., Nova Scotia, on his enlistment. By all accounts Sergeant Edward Sealy was 'firm but fair' with the other ranks who served under him.

Edward Sealy died on 15 February 1949, aged seventy-two.

Arthur Seymour Tyler

Arthur Seymour Tyler, known as Seymour, was born at Saint John, New Brunswick, Canada, on 21 February 1898. He was living at Saint John when he enlisted there in No. 2 Construction Battalion. He gave his occupation as horse trainer and teamster, and was described as being five feet, four inches tall, of dark complexion, with dark eyes and dark

A. Seymour Tyler

hair. He was now Private Seymour Tyler, regimental number 931239, and he served in England, France and Wales with No. 2. During his service in France due to an infection he suffered with deafness. He received two blue chevrons for his service. He too was at Kinmel Park Camp in late 1918, early 1919, and was discharged from military service on 17 February 1919 in Canada.

Post-First World War he married Lenetta, did some farming in Minto, New Brunswick, and when the Second World War arrived, he again volunteered for overseas service. Unfortunately, whilst in Britain, he badly broke his leg and was forced to return to Canada. His affable nature endeared him to many people when from 1941 to 1959 he was a pullman porter (sleeping cars) on the Canadian Pacific Railroad, including the routes between Toronto and Vancouver, and Toronto and Regina.

The Toronto Star newspaper edition of 14 November 1982, had a photograph in it of Seymour Tyler now aged eighty-four, proudly wearing his war medals and holding a photograph of No. 2 Construction Battalions/Company's soldiers, including some of the officers, which was taken during the war in 1917. The headline for the story was, '*Battalion of blacks honoured at last*'. There was an account of No. 2 and the work they carried out in France. A reunion had been held for the surviving members of No. 2 and in addition to Seymour Tyler's attendance, **John Wesley Hamilton**, 931072, from Montreal, and **Charles Gordon Wilson**, 931229, of Halifax, were also there. Other surviving members due to illness or infirmity sent relatives to represent them at the gathering organised by The Black Cultural Society of Nova Scotia. Seymour Tyler stated here that the most dangerous assignment No. 2 faced in France was the locating, digging up and defusing of land mines. From what I have learnt of him, he always exuded great pride in having been a 'black soldier in the Black Battalion' during the First World War.

Arthur Seymour Tyler, known as Seymour, died on 17 February 1985, aged just a few days short of his eighty-seventh birthday.

Jamaica born

Two brothers from Jamaica, the British West Indies as they were then called, both enlisted in No. 2 Construction Battalion. They were the Alberga brothers, whose widowed mother Ellen Alberga at the time of their enlistment lived in Montego Bay, Jamaica. **Albert Miller Alberga** was born on 1 January 1894, at Black River, Jamaica. He enlisted in No. 2 at Montreal on 8 September 1916, a civil engineer, described as being five feet, eight inches tall, and for his descriptive features was written, 'colored man'. He was a single man and now Private Albert Miller Alberga, regimental number 931255. Albert Miller Alberga prior to enlisting had been a civil engineering student at McGill University, Montreal, and in 1917, received his degree. He served with No. 2 in England, France and Wales, and was a sergeant. He was at Kinmel Park Camp in late 1918 into 1919, and probably because he was being discharged to a different location to many of his comrades, he returned to Canada embarking on the S.S. Celtic from Liverpool on 10 March 1919.

I have found that Albert Miller Alberga returned to live and work permanently back in Jamaica. For the 4 November 1954 edition of the *Kingston Gleaner*, a Jamaican newspaper, names him as being of Half-Way Tree, in the Parish of Saint Andrew and the assistant director of public works.

His elder brother, **George Frederick Alberga**, born on 29 April 1892, also born at Black River, was also a civil engineering student at McGill University, Montreal. He was described on enlistment as five feet, seven and a half inches tall, giving his address at the time as Strathcona Hall, Sherbrooke Street, Montreal, which was virtually opposite his university. Private George Frederick Alberga was given the regimental number 931308, and also served in England, France and Wales. He was at Kinmel Park Camp prior to his return to Canada. He, like his brother also attained the rank of sergeant.

Searching for him post-war I found that he petitioned for naturalisation in the United States in 1922, and was in New York in the early 1940's, where he wrote songs including one named, 'Searching for You'. I believe that he died aged sixty-eight in the New York area.

I cannot help but feel that whilst many of their fellow black soldiers were labourers, quarrymen, teamsters and the like, not that many 'skilled jobs' were actually open to them at that time, the Alberga brothers were two highly educated men who because of the colour of their skin were utilised 'digging and fixing', rather than leading as commissioned officers, or at worst their civil engineering knowledge being put to good use at the Front.

Black soldiers in No. 2 Construction Battalion, who were born in Barbados, then in the British West Indies, who were at Kinmel Park Camp included:
Leonard Walter Butcher, regimental number 931065; **Lloyd Byer**, 931015; **Grandville Collymore**, 931270; **Adolphus Darlington**, 931068; **Henry Griffiths**, 931063; and **Joseph Harris**, 931057.

Black soldiers in No. 2 born in British Guiana (now Guyana), who were at Kinmel Park Camp included:
Frank Bowers, 931058; **Alexander Bramah**, 931037; and, **Sydney Flood**, 931066.

A black soldier in No. 2 born in Basseterre, Saint Kitts, then British West Indies, at Kinmel Park Camp was **John Bailey**, 931130.

A black soldier in No.2 at Kinmel Park Camp born at Webb Village, Montserrat, West Indies was **Matthew Nathaniel Edwards**, 931028.

Two of those born in the United States

Joseph Roger Butler

Joseph Roger Butler was born at New York City, the United States, on 22 November 1879. He was a baker by profession, residing in Edmonton, Alberta, Canada, when he enlisted in No. 2 Construction Battalion. On his enlistment at Edmonton, Alberta, he stated that he had been in the United States military for a number of years including three years with 9th Cavalry. The 9th Cavalry was one of the few segregated African-American regiments, and served in combat during the Indian Wars and the Spanish-American Wars. They came famously to be known as 'Buffalo Soldiers'. Their regiment motto was and still is, 'We Can, We Will'.

Joseph Roger Butler was six feet tall and described as having a 'colored' complexion, brown eyes and black hair, and was Private Butler, regimental number 931570. He was residing at the time of his enlistment at Calgary, Alberta. His next of kin was his wife, Mary Butler, and on his enlistment, they had two daughters and a son. He reached the rank of corporal serving with No. 2 in France. He was also at Kinmel Park Camp with them.

William Thomas

William Thomas was born at Birmingham, Alabama, the

United States, on 24 March 1892. He was on enlistment in No. 2 Construction Battalion described as five feet, four and a half inches tall, of 'colored' complexion. He gave his next of kin as his mother Melia Thomas, who still lived in Birmingham, Alabama. William Thomas, regimental number 931709, served with No. 2 as a sergeant in France and was at Kinmel Park Camp. On 5 February 1919, he left Britain aboard the RMS Baltic and gave his future address as being in Detroit, Michigan, the United States.

James William Holmes, born in Derbyshire, England

James William Holmes was born in Clowne, Derbyshire, England, on 14 November 1893. He was a coal miner and in Canada he lived with his wife, Phoebe Emma Holmes in Michel, British Columbia, a coal mining town in the Michel Creek Valley which no longer exists as a town. On his enlistment papers for No. 2 Construction Battalion he was described as having a 'medium' complexion, with blue eyes and brown hair. He stated that he had lived with an aunt all of his life and did not know if his mother was alive or not.

He was given the regimental number of 931206, and served in France, and later at Kinmel Park Camp. An interesting fact about him is that on or around 10 August 1918, when serving in France with No. 2, he received what was described as being, 'a gunshot wound (GSW) to the face – lower jaw – severe'. As a result of this he was hospitalised first in France and then back in England for a number of weeks. How exactly he received this wound I am unable to ascertain.

In early April 1979, the Canadian military authorities were informed by I believe his widow Phoebe Holmes, that James William Holmes had died on 23 March 1979, which would have made him eighty-five years of age.

Some of the many black soldiers in No. 2 Construction Battalion (Company), who were born in Canada, and at Kinmel Park Camp, late 1918, up to Summer 1919. A number of those with the same surname are brothers or otherwise closely related to one another, but this does not apply to all of them, despite having the same surnames:

Clarence Allison, 931335; **Kenneth Allison**, 931053; **Walter Roland Allison**, 931358; **William Allison**, 931198; **John Spencer Blizzard**, 931147; **Edward Bowers**, 931035; **George William Brown**, 931163; **Ernest Garfield Bushfan**, 931149; **Harold Frederick Bushfan**, 931103; **Philip Andrew Bushfan**, 931327; **Robert James Bushfan**, 931156; **Henry Francis Courtney**, 931501; **Garrett Wesley Cox**, 931345; **Charles Joseph Cromwell**, 931318; **James Aubrey Cromwell**, 931317; **James Elmer Cromwell**, 931312; **Joseph Herbert Cromwell**, 931315; **Joseph Orvie Cromwell**, 931314; **Neaily Cromwell**, 931302; **Ethelbert Lionel Cross**, 931405; **Clifford William Downey**, 931285; **George Downey**, 931227; **James John Downey**, 931226; **Alexander Elms**, 931189; **Benjamin Elms**, 931109; **Frederick Gordon Elms**, 931089; **John William Elms**, 931274; **Michael Redmond Elms**, 931202; **Walter Howard Elms**, 931092; **Harman Ellison Farmer**, 931397; **Zachariah Farmer**, 931173; **William Kellum**, 931166; **Russell Miller**, 931530; **Clement Parris**, 931056; **Garfield Parris**, 931386; **James Parris**, 931004; **Joseph Alexander Parris**, 931017; **William Winslow Parris**, 931307; **Wallace James Pleasant**, 931085; **Percy James Richards**, 931114; **James Alexander Talbot**, 931046; **James Ivan Talbot**, 931047; **Percy William Thomas**, 931117; **George Washington Tolliver**, 931389; **William Tolliver**, 931003; **Arthur Nelson Ware**, 931657; **Benjamin Washington**, 931555; and **Robert Clarke Whims**, 931613.

The youngest member of No.2 Construction Battalion that I have found who served overseas was **Thomas Goffigan**, regimental number 931248, who was born at Hammonds Plains, Nova Scotia, on 11 August 1901. He was working as a shoe shiner at Halifax, Nova Scotia, when he enlisted there on 11 September 1916, aged but fifteen. He served in France with No.2 for the same period as the other members, namely some nineteen months (from May 1917 to December 1918), and was at Kinmel Park Camp before being returned to Canada and discharged from military service at Halifax on 15 February 1919, when still aged only seventeen years and six months!

A few of those black soldiers of No. 2 Construction Battalion (Company) who for different reasons did not get to go to Kinmel Park Camp

John Lewis Sullivan I am certain would have much preferred to have been at Kinmel Park Camp, despite its many shortcomings than where he was – in prison, serving a sentence with hard labour. John Lewis Sullivan was born on 11 January 1876, at Sheridan, New York, the United States. He had prior to enlistment in the C.E.F served for eighteen years in the United States military with 10th Cavalry, another of the segregated African-American units known also as 'Buffalo Soldiers'. He was a single man and described as being five feet, nine and a half inches tall, of 'colored' complexion, brown eyes and black hair. He must have been an absolute nightmare to have had in your unit. For in France with No. 2, his time there was a litany of being drunk, including on parade; of being violent when put under arrest, using violence against an NCO; and for going AWOL (absent without leave). But he really went 'the whole nine yards' with what he did at Jura, France, in April 1918, as his military record reveals:

In confinement awaiting trial, 24-4-18 to 29-5-18, 36 days. Tried and convicted by Field Court Martial on 30-5-18 for: Offering violence to his superior officer, in that he at Le Jour, Jura, on 23-4-18 threatened to cut Major Sutherland with a knife, and disobeying a lawful command given by his superior officer; in that he at Le Jour, Jura, on 24-4-18 refused to fall-in under escort when ordered to do so by Sergeant-Major Norman. Found guilty and sentenced to 10 years Penal Servitude.

Remission granted of 5 years Penal Servitude conferred by Brigadier-General Phillips on 4-6-18.

John Lewis Sullivan, regimental number 931736, was taken away by the military police to serve his sentence at No.1 Military Prison, France, and he would have been very unwise to have continued his violent conduct when in their charge. In August 1918, John Lewis Sullivan had a lucky break, as on 3 August 1918, the governor of No. 1 Military Prison now further reduced his sentence to one of 2-years penal servitude, with hard labour. In January 1919, obviously not with No.2 at Kinmel Park Camp, he had a gastric ulcer and required hospital treatment. He was transferred to England, and with further leniency shown towards him, on 23 July 1919, at Halifax, Nova Scotia, he disembarked and was discharged from the military.

Belfield Hall, 931342, born in 1897, at Barbados, British West Indies, sadly did not make it back from France. Belfield Hall was seriously ill for a number of months in the Canadian Forestry Corps hospital at Lajoux, Jura, France, and he died at 8.40 am on 22 October 1918, of tubercular peritonitis. On the official C.E.F 'Form of Will' he completed before leaving Canada, he named his mother, Mrs Melvina Hall, Bowling Alley, Saint Joseph, Barbados, as his beneficiary. His mother also received his war medals and his Canadian memorial cross.

Charles Some, known as Charlie, regimental number 931410, was born in 1886, at Natal, South Africa. On 23 September 1918, in the Jura Mountains, France, when with No. 2, his body was found 'dumped' at the side of the road – he had been brutally murdered. He had stab wounds to his body and his throat had been cut across. A French-African soldier who had also been working in the area was a strong suspect for the killing, but no formal charges were ever brought against him, or indeed against anyone for this crime. Charlie Some had gained a reputation for getting involved in serious fights with lumber men and others, and his death could actually have been the result of a vicious fight rather than a 'cold blooded murder'. Charlie Some was a married man and back in Canada had been living in Africville, a primarily Black community located on the outskirts of Halifax, Nova Scotia.

Charlie Some was buried at the Supt Churchyard, Andelot-en-Montagne, Jura, France, in grave number 8.

A total of eight graves of 'Canadian Forestry Corps' soldiers can be found in the south-eastern corner of this Supt Churchyard, including a further three black soldiers of No.2. Each grave has a cross upon it. The three others who all died from illness are:
John Mansfield, regimental number 931378 (not 931328 as shown in some records) buried in grave 1; **Charles Henry Bryant**, 931673, aged but twenty, in grave 3; and, **William Boone**, 931625, born at Tuscaloosa, Alabama, the United States, married with children, in grave 7.

A number of the black soldiers of No. 2 Construction Company who made it back to Canada from France, and latterly from the Spanish Flu ridden Kinmel Park Camp, following the very strenuous work they carried out, sadly died months or just a few short years later. Their toil at Jura being the root cause which sent them to an early grave. One of these was **Joseph Dottin**, regimental number 931067, born on 1 January 1895, at Barbados, British West Indies. Joseph was sent home from France before the Armistice suffering from amongst other things, a spinal abscess. He died on 19 May 1919, at Hartford, Ontario, aged only twenty-four.

Some of the 'white' officers of No.2 Construction Battalion, later Company

The commanding officer himself, Daniel Hugh Sutherland, and the majority of the white officers of No. 2 had experience in building, contracting, engineering, accountancy, storekeeping or forestry. All well suited to a military construction company. An exception was No.2's own doctor, physician, Captain Dan Murray.

Major Daniel Hugh Sutherland

The commander of No. 2 was Major (downgraded from Lieutenant-Colonel when they went to France as a company and not as a battalion) Daniel Hugh Sutherland, born on 10 September 1880, at River John, Pictou County, Nova Scotia. He was five feet, eleven and a half inches tall, a railroad contractor, married to Emily Sutherland and had some previous experience in a Canadian militia when he enlisted in the C.E.F.

He initially enlisted in 193rd Battalion (Nova Scotia Highlanders), then at Aldershot Camp, Nova Scotia, as

Private Sutherland, regimental number 902380. However, whilst working for the Canadian military on a contract in Guysborough County, Nova Scotia, he was offered a new military role, the command in the rank of lieutenant-colonel of a brand-new military entity, an extremely controversial one – No. 2 Construction Battalion, in which virtually every N.C.O and other ranks were black men. Apparently, others had been already offered this command but had turned it down, no doubt in their eyes seeing it as something of a 'poisoned chalice'. It was most probably all done hush-hush for the commander of 193rd Battalion had put Private Sutherland down officially as a 'deserter' from his unit. He was later to write to senior military officers at The Citadel, Halifax, complaining that the now Lieutenant-Colonel Sutherland had been, 'apparently endeavouring to persuade some of the men of this camp by communicating with them directly to transfer or enlist in the unit under his command, a construction corps now being recruited' – It sounds like a case of poaching going on here.

The then Lieutenant-Colonel Sutherland gathered together a number of white officers to serve with this new entity and as their 'Honorary Captain and Chaplain' was the black Reverend William Andrew White. Medical examinations took place on all of those who enlisted and on 17 May 1917, No. 2 Construction Company, with in command, the now only Major Sutherland, arrived in France. He stayed with No. 2 for the duration of the war and was at Kinmel Park Camp with them when they were awaiting their repatriation to Canada. Major Sutherland like many other officers were required to do, returned home to Canada later than his men, and was demobilised on 9 July 1919.

In 2016, a granddaughter of the late Major Daniel Hugh Sutherland, Mary Beth Sutherland, was featured in Nova

Scotian newspapers. In the Autumn of 2015, she had been approached by the 'Black Cultural Centre for Nova Scotia', Cherrybrook, Nova Scotia, and as a result she took a serious look at the contents of a trunk her grandfather had kept. She found many photographs and documents relating to her grandfather's time as the commander of No.2. She said, 'Obviously he treasured his men greatly because he kept these things, he felt they were important'. She has kindly allowed access to these photographs and documents and copies have been made of them.

Captain Doctor Dan Murray

Captain Dan Murray was the doctor for No.2. He was a physician, born on 22 June 1876, at Meadowville, Pictou County, Nova Scotia. He was residing with wife, Morna Murray at Tatamagouche, Colchester County, Nova Scotia, when he enlisted with No. 2 Construction Battalion. He had pre-war served with the Canadian Army Medical Corps. He was in France and England with No. 2, but did not go with them to Kinmel Park Camp, but was sent as a military doctor to another camp, and struck off strength in August 1919.

Captain Dan Murray and wife Morna had a son, James Carson Murray, who also became a doctor. James and his wife, Margaret Marion Murray, nee Burke, had a daughter they named Morna Anne Murray, named after her grandmother. Morna Anne Murray is better known by her stage name of Anne Murray, the very famous Canadian pop and country music singer, who has found international fame and sold over fifty-five million albums worldwide. Her signature song is perhaps 'Snowbird'. In her 2009 book, *Anne Murray, All of Me,* by Anne Murray and Michael Posner, she writes of her grandfather and the 'Black Battalion'. This begins with her speaking of her own father's tolerance back in the early 1960's of rock n' roll, and of men like her two brothers having long hair:

My father probably learned his tolerance from his father Dr Dan Murray. As a medic in the First World War, he'd been the only doctor willing to treat members of Canada's Black Battalion, a group of black non-combatants sent overseas in 1917 to do construction, they would ultimately build 125 hospitals along the Western Front. His best friend in the war was Captain William White, a black Baptist minister and chaplain to the Construction Corps who kept a journal of their experiences. Coincidentally I sang with Reverend White's son, Lorne, on Singalong Jubilee for several years in the late 1960's and celebrated my twenty-first birthday at Lorne's house in Halifax. Lorne's sister, Portia White became an internationally acclaimed contralto concert singer. I knew nothing of this history at the time, and Lorne, though he had read his father's journal and had heard all the stories about Dr Dan, didn't know then that I was Dr Dan's granddaughter.

Other white officers with No. 2 Construction Battalion/Company included the below named. Those who were at Kinmel Park Camp are marked with an asterisk: **Captain Kenneth Allan Morrison**, born on 27 September 1875, at Cleveland, Richmond County, Nova Scotia, a contractor & merchant; **Captain David Anderson**, born on 27 June 1877, at Springhill, Cumberland County, Nova Scotia, a storekeeper; ***Lieutenant Ernest Noel Halton Fyles**, born on 23 December 1885, at Point Levis, Quebec, a contractor & engineer; **Lieutenant Samuel Clifford Hood**, born on 24 April 1885, at Yarmouth, Nova Scotia, a book keeper/accountant; ***Lieutenant Roderick Livingston**, born on 26 September 1873, at Black Brook, Boularderie, Nova Scotia, a civil engineer; ***Lieutenant**

Russell Roderick Rutherford McLean, born on 28 July 1895, at Moncton, New Brunswick, a forester; ***Lieutenant James Stuart Grant**, born on 9 October 1887, at Ottawa, Ontario, a contractor & accountant; ***Lieutenant Gillan Christie Maclean**, born on 10 September 1886, at Beachburg, Ontario, a salesman; ***Lieutenant George Henry Parker**, born on 26 December 1874, at Stewiacke, Nova Scotia, a civil engineer; and, ***Captain Arthur John Gayfer**, born on 26 January 1877, at Uxbridge, Middlesex, England, a civil engineer.

The Edmonton Bulletin, Alberta, Canada, edition of 13 February 1919, reported upon a 'coming together of the races' to honour those who had recently returned from the war:

> COLORED CITIZENS HOSTS AT BANQUET
> Give Enjoyable Reception to Colored Returned Soldiers and White Comrades
> The colored citizens of Edmonton were the hosts of an enjoyable reception held in the Great War Veterans' Club rooms Monday night, in honor of the colored returned soldiers and also of their white comrades. About 250 colored citizens, including a number of colored soldiers who enlisted in the No. 2 Construction Battalion were present, and 100 members of the Great War Veterans' Club. A short musical programme was rendered by the colored musicians and Hart's Orchestra, and was much appreciated. W. G. Cromwell was master of ceremonies and gave a short address. Dr Collins, president of the Great War Veterans' Association gave a short address in which he stated that the association was for the returned soldiers and the colored boys were welcome, and he wished them to become members of

the association. He also paid a tribute to the soldiers of the colored race, and stated that both as individuals and units they had performed acts second to none for bravery, and through the association of soldiers of both races in the great struggle, the race feeling had been considerably softened. After the programme the ladies served the refreshments in banquet style. The large tables were filled several times and that the ladies saw that no one was neglected. After the banquet dancing was enjoyed for some time, music being furnished by Hart's Orchestra. The committee in charge wishes to thank all citizens and business firms who contributed towards making the affair a success, and, also to the ladies and gentlemen who did such good service in carrying out the work of the committee.

Chapter Ten

Some other Canadian soldiers at Kinmel Park Camp

1. John Henry Foster Babcock – Canada's last known surviving WW1 veteran

John Henry Foster Babcock, known to family and friends as Jack, was born on 23 July 1900, on a farm at Holleford, Ontario, Canada, he being one of thirteen children.

Amazingly, he was still alive one hundred and nine years later and what is more, he was widely feted for being so, he being the Last Known Surviving Veteran of the Canadian Military to have served in the First World War. This is his story in which Kinmel Camp played a part.

When he was just six years of age, John Babcock's father, John Thomas Babcock, when aged forty-four, was killed in a tree-felling accident. As a result, the Babcock family was broken up, his mother, Ann Isabel Foster Babcock going to Saskatchewan to find paid employment to try to support the family who were now as it was called, 'dirt poor'. John Henry Foster Babcock found himself being shuttled around various

John H. F. Babcock

relatives for his upbringing and he received little education. He ended up working as a farm labourer on the same farm that his family had lost due to his father's untimely death.

Partly to get away from the humdrum life on the farm and partly because of a yen to see the world, when two recruiting officers, a lieutenant and a sergeant came around his area, he decided to enlist in the Canadian Army and fight in the First World War. He recalled many years later that this recruiting sergeant had quoted to him from the stirring Tennyson poem, 'The Charge of the Light Brigade' and this had helped persuade him by firing his imagination. Another factor could also have been that the army pay he was offered was over double what he was receiving at the time as a farm labourer! So, on 1 February 1916, aged but fifteen years and six months, he attested and enlisted at Sydenham, Ontario, Canada, being assigned to 146th Overseas Battalion of the C.E.F, as Private John Henry Foster Babcock, regimental number 835571. So desperate for 'men' to volunteer were the Canadian military that a blind eye was very much turned all over Canada to the enlisting and sending overseas to fight of mere boys, some as young as fourteen or in the case of John Babcock, just fifteen. Five feet and four inches tall, John Babcock put on his enlistment papers that he was eighteen years of age, yet also put his true date of birth of 23 July 1900, but this was obviously just ignored. He also signed these papers for some reason 'Foster Babcock'. But in fairness, he was picked out as underage whilst still in Canada, but then enlisted in another Canadian regiment and eventually achieved his aim of getting to Europe with the hope of joining in the fighting.

John Babcock in the end received a sea voyage across from Canada to Britain in a troop transport ship and he got to see parts of England, Scotland on a furlough trip, and later Wales, but he never did get to the Front, and he never got to fire a shot in anger. Instead, partly due to public pressure at the deaths of underage soldiers at the Front, John Babcock was 'officially spotted' as being under age. He then spent some time in various military training camps in England, until in the Autumn of 1918, he was in a Canadian young soldier's battalion at Kinmel Park Camp, undergoing eight hours of training every day, to be sent to the Front when he reached the required age to do so of nineteen, as who knew then, when, or even if, their interminable war would end. When many years later asked about his time at Kinmel Park Camp in northern Wales, he described his fellow Canadian soldiers as being, 'a wild bunch'.

After a rather poor time of it in Kinmel Camp, having to wait like so many thousands of his fellow Canadian soldiers for his repatriation to Canada, he finally got back there. However, things were very difficult in Canada in the post-First World War years, economically and jobwise. So, John Babcock in 1920, left Canada for the United States, seeking better opportunities, for a time serving in the United States Army. John Babcock found his way to Spokane, Washington, United States in 1932, and stayed there for the rest of his life – seventy-eight more years!

After the Japanese attack on Pearl Harbour, Hawaii, on the morning of 7 December 1941, John Babcock tried to re-enlist in the United States Army for active service, but due to his age he served out the remainder of the Second World War on home service only.

He had his own plumbing and heating company at one time, and at the age of sixty-five this remarkable man qualified to become a pilot. He worked for and finally gained his high school diploma – at the ripe old age of ninety-five! At the age of one hundred he wrote an autobiography entitled, 'Ten Decades of John Foster Babcock', copies of which were only handed out to his family and friends. He had married twice. His first wife of forty-five years being Elsie who died in 1976, and then he married Dorothy, thirty years his junior and who survived him. In all he had one son, one daughter, two stepchildren and numerous grandchildren and great grandchildren. A younger sister Lucy died in 2002, and she had reached the grand age of one hundred and two.

John Babcock lived a very full life, and in his latter-years had become something of a celebrity, especially in his native Canada. On his one hundred and seventh birthday, he received greetings from Queen Elizabeth II, the Governor General of Canada and the Canadian Prime Minister, amongst others. The Canadian Prime Minister, Stephen Harper also sent him a tie with a poppy pattern upon it.

He was you see, by still being alive on his 107th Birthday, the very last link to all of the 619,636 Canadian men and women who had served militarily for Canada in the First World War. Canada had sustained many military fatalities, with many more injured, both physically and mentally. One of those 'mentally injured' was one of John Babcock's own brothers, Manley Babcock, who served as a sapper with a Canadian Engineers Battalion. Manley Babcock suffered a serious mental breakdown after the War as a result of his wartime experiences.

Canada suffered great losses, but sort of 'came of age' as a result of its involvement in the First World War. In its aftermath, Canada had its own representatives at the Treaty of Versailles, and though Canada remained a part of the British Empire, the Canadian Delegation proudly signed the Treaty as a separate nation.

About three years before his death, an official approach was made by the Canadian Government to John Babcock for him to receive a 'Canadian State Funeral' when he died. Over 100,000 Canadians signed an on-line petition in just three weeks, for him to receive such an accolade. But he declined the offer, mainly on the grounds that he felt that as he had not actually fought in the First World War, that he did not warrant such an honour. Modestly he said, 'I'm sure that all the attention I am getting isn't because of anything spectacular I've done. It's because I'm the last one'.

John Babcock when asked, credited his great longevity to the intense physical training he had received in both the Canadian and later, the United States armies, some of which he had received at Kinmel Park Camp, North Wales, back in 1918 and early 1919. Right up to his death, John Babcock, though afflicted with very poor hearing, most certainly had his wits about him and he would read books and continue to walk. John Babcock died at his home, a ranch type house in Spokane on Thursday, 18 February 2010, aged one hundred and nine. His widow and children were again approached about him receiving a Canadian State Funeral, but they declined the offer knowing that it had not been his wish to receive such a thing. He was instead cremated at a private ceremony and his ashes were scattered across the Pacific North West. Though John Babcock had lived most of his life in the United States and had been very happy to do so, he never lost his love for his native Canada.

The Canadian Prime Minister, Stephen Harper said this on the day of John Babcock's passing: '*I was deeply saddened to learn today of the death of John Babcock, Canada's Last Known First World War Veteran. As a Nation We Honour His Service and Mourn his Passing*'.

2. Sergeant Alexander Picton Brereton, VC

During the First World War, a total of seventy-one Victoria Crosses (VC's) were awarded to soldiers of the Canadian Expeditionary Force (the CEF), including a number awarded posthumously. Two other VC's were awarded to

Alexander Picton Brereton, VC

soldiers from Newfoundland, which was then a separate dominion.

Alexander Picton Brereton was born on 13 November 1892, at Oak River, Westman Region, Manitoba, Canada, to Cloudesley Picton Brereton, a farmer, and, wife, Annie Frazer Brereton, nee Black. Alexander Picton Brereton was a barber, five feet, seven and a half inches tall, when he enlisted at Winnipeg, for the C.E.F. As Private Brereton, regimental number 830651, he arrived in England with a contingent of the C.E.F aboard the R.M.S Olympic on 25 September 1916. After undergoing further military training in England he was at the Front in France & Flanders with 8th Battalion (90th Winnipeg Rifles), an infantry battalion. He received promotion to the rank of corporal and on 9 August 1918, during The Battle of Amiens (8-11 August 1918), east of Amiens, Picardy, France, he performed an act of great bravery on his own initiative, for which he was subsequently awarded the highest military honour, the Victoria Cross (VC). This is the citation for the award:

For most conspicuous bravery during an attack, when a line of hostile machine guns opened fire suddenly on his platoon, which was in an exposed position, and no cover available.

This gallant N.C.O. at once appreciated the critical situation and realised that unless something was done at once, the platoon would be annihilated. On his own initiative, without a moments delay, and alone, he sprang forward and reached one of the hostile machine-gun posts, where he shot the man operating the machine gun and bayoneted the next one who attempted to operate it, whereupon nine others surrendered to him. Corporal Brereton's action was a splendid example of resource and bravery, and not only undoubtedly saved many of his comrades' lives, but also inspired his platoon to charge and capture the five remaining posts.

His actions greatly aided the effort on this second day of what was to become known as 'The Hundred Days Offensive' of the Allies, which resulted in the final victory and defeat of Germany and the Central Powers.

Alexander Picton Brereton was deservedly promoted to the rank of sergeant and he survived the war. Post-Armistice he spent some weeks at Kinmel Park Camp on M.D. 10 Wing, awaiting his return to Canada. He sailed on the HMT Empress of Britain on 17 February 1919, disembarking on Canadian soil on 25 February 1919.

On 17 June 1925, he married Mary Isabel McPhee, and they had three children together. He and his family farmed some 640 acres of farmland at Elnora for many years.

During the Second World War, Alexander Picton Brereton, VC was a company quartermaster-sergeant (CQMS), regimental number M34083. He died on 10 January 1976, aged eighty-three, at the 'supportive living' Golden Hills Lodge, Three Hills, Alberta, Canada, and was buried at the Elnora Cemetery, Elnora, Alberta, Canada. His Victoria Cross and his other medals from both world wars are on public display at the Lord Ashcroft Gallery, the Imperial War Museum, London. The local branch of the

Alexander Picton Brereton, VC, in later life

'legion' is named in his honour – The Alex Brereton, VC, Royal Canadian Legion Branch, Elnora, Alberta.

On 18 June 2016, at a special re-dedication ceremony, a new headstone was placed on the grave of Alexander Picton Brereton, VC, one which now included further details of his military career. Indeed, the CWGC (the Commonwealth War Graves Commission) are in the process of providing new headstones for all of the Victoria Cross recipients from the First World War.

3. Colonel Malcolm Alexander Colquhoun, CMG, DSO

The commandant of Kinmel Park Camp during the riots/disturbances was the highly respected and experienced Canadian soldier, Colonel Malcolm Alexander Colquhoun, CMG, DSO, from Brantford, Ontario, Canada, who had been at the camp since September 1918. He was only too aware that from Armistice Day, Kinmel Park Camp was now but a staging camp, a temporary holding camp, for the eventual repatriation of thousands of Canadian soldiers.

Colonel Malcolm Alexander Colquhoun was born in 1869, at Mulmur, Dufferin County, southern Ontario. He was pre-1914, for a number of years an officer with the locally based 38th Dufferin Rifles (founded on 28/9/1866 as 38th Brant Battalion of Infantry), a Canadian militia regiment. Though his day job was as a foreman at the huge Massey-Harris Company Limited, agricultural equipment makers works at Brantford, Ontario. In 1891, Massey Manufacturing had merged with the company of A. Harris & Son, to then become Massey-Harris. Massey-Harris later merged with the Ferguson Company, farm machine manufacturers to become the iconic 'Massey Ferguson' Company, for the company to develop into the largest makers of agricultural type equipment in the entire British Empire. Being particularly synonymous with farm tractors and combine harvesters.

Col. M. A. Colquhoun

At the outbreak of the First World War he was Captain Colquhoun of 38th Dufferin Rifles, and just a few days into the war he joined with fellow local men the C.E.F to be a part of the newly formed, 4th (Central Ontario) Battalion, Canadian Infantry. Captain M. A. Colquhoun embarked with 4th Battalion from Gaspe Harbour, Quebec, on the S.S. Tyrolia, disembarking at Devonport Royal Dockyard (formerly known as Plymouth Dock), Devon, England, on 23 October 1914. They landed in England with 44 officers, 1,121 other ranks and some horses. The 4th Battalion underwent military training in England which included some time on Salisbury Plain. On 11 February 1915, 4th Battalion, including Captain M. A. Colquhoun disembarked from the S.S. Atlantian at St. Nazaire, France – they were soon, after a train journey and some marching, to be near the Front.

These extracts are taken from letters written with a mixture of sadness, but also great pride by Colonel M. A. Colquhoun, to his wife back in Brantford, Ontario, in the days following the 'Mad Fourth's Charge' on 23 April 1915. This was during the Second Battle of Ypres (22 April – 25 May 1915). In these letters, he writes of the hell that the battle was, of the bravery of the soldiers who served under him, and of the sad loss of the many who fell that day on the battlefield:

> ... Don't know the date. Have been at it for two days and two nights. The Germans broke through the line we were going to take over. We were ordered at 1 a.m. to stop the German advance. At 5 a.m. I was ordered to lead the advance with my company. The Germans had entrenched themselves one thousand yards in front. We had to advance over open ground with no cover at all. I led the firing line, Captain Collins, (36th Y.R.) the supports. We advanced to within 400 yards of the Germans, when I received orders to go no further until I received reinforcements. I only had about half of my company left then. We dug ourselves in the best we could, under heavy fire, and held the line until nine o'clock that night, when we were relieved by the East Kent's. Had nothing to eat all night and all day. My boys

were pretty well played out. In this action our battalion was cut to pieces. As for myself, I had a man shot down on my right and left at the same time. All I can say, it must be the prayers of you people at home that saved me, as where we went through, it was almost impossible for a man to live. Two-thirds of my company were killed or wounded. Not time yet to find out as we are still at it.

... Lieut. Jones got buried by a Jack Johnson (*nickname for the German artillery shell that on impact produced a great deal of black smoke*). It took three men to dig him out. He is all right. I can't speak too highly of the Brantford boys. I feel sure, that anywhere I lead they will follow to a man. They had to face the hardest attack of the war and not a man flinched. Just feel terrible over my losses. I had no chance to save them. We just had to face that fire. It was as thick as hail and the artillery fire was fearful. To put it plainly, it was perfect hell.

... People here have quite a different opinion of the Canadians now. They want to have the Canadians in the fighting all the time. We are now classed amongst the very best troops.

... While writing on Sunday I was stopped short by an order to fall in. The Germans made another attempt to break through our line and we were sent up at once. They are still using gas. We met hundreds of men coming back, completely knocked out. We were there all night but they did not succeed in breaking through. I did hope they would. We were waiting for them and I'm anxious for an opportunity to get a square chance since I lost so many of my good men. I cannot speak too highly of the splendid discipline of all ranks of my company. I wish you would

> extend my sympathy to all the bereaved ones at home as I will not get a chance to write to them all.
>
> ... Tell them I feel most highly honoured in commanding such a brave lot of men. It nearly broke my heart to see so many of them go down.

The *Brantford Expositor* newspaper edition of 15 December 1915, included extensive coverage to date then of the involvement in the war of so many of its local fighting men. Of Lieutenant-Colonel Malcolm Alexander Colquhoun. the *Brantford Expositor* first published back in 1852, and still going strong today, had this to say:

> First on the list of Commanders from Brantford is Lt-Col M. A. Colquhoun, Commander of Fourth Battalion, which through its splendid fighting record against the Huns, won the name of The Mad Fourth! He left Brantford with the first contingent, becoming Company Commander in 4th under Col. Labatt. So severe were the losses at Langemarck that the Regiment was greatly reduced in strength. He took command of the remnants of the 4th and later received promotion to Lieut-Colonel. 'Mac' Colquhoun was one of the most popular officers with the Dufferin Rifles, being a favourite with officers and men – and his record for efficiency when in command of A Company was of the very high order – a Crack Company.

Colonel M. A. Colquhoun and his wife, Mary, lived for many years at 237, Dalhousie Street, Brantford. They had one son, Wyndham John Colquhoun, born in 1895 at Barrie, Ontario. Upon completion of his education, Wyndham John Colquhoun known by family and friends as Wyn, entered employment with the Bank of British North

America. Wyn aged twenty enlisted in August 1916 in 120th Battalion, the Canadian Infantry and was granted a commission as a second lieutenant. On his arrival in France he was transferred to 15th Battalion (48th Highlanders of Canada). Second Lieutenant Wyn Colquhoun managed to survive many months at the Front physically unscathed until 27 September 1918. On this day at Marquion, France, he led his platoon into action during an attack upon the German enemy in a concerted advance towards Cambrai and he was severely wounded.

It was at 8.45 a.m. on 27 September 1918, that Lieutenant Wyn Colquhoun and 15th Battalion had advanced towards the canal at Sains Les Marquion. German gunfire from a location known as Keith Wood had prevented the Canadian Engineers from building more than one bridge across the canal for the attack. Under constant fire, 15th Battalion dashed across the canal by a makeshift plank bridge and entered the village of Marquion, where they were involved in house to house fighting with the German defenders. The 15th captured the village, taking some 300 German prisoners, but suffered 153 casualties, a number which included Lieutenant Wyn Colquhoun. He was evacuated from the Front to a hospital at Matlock Bath, Derbyshire, England, where sadly on 8 November 1918, he died from double pneumonia that had developed from influenza he had contracted soon after being wounded. Very unusually, the body of twenty-three-year old Lieutenant Wyndham John Colquhoun was returned to his family in Brantford, Ontario, though of course he had died in England and not on the Western Front. He was buried on 8 December 1918, '*with Military Honours*' as the local newspapers put it, at Greenwood Cemetery, Brantford, Lot 0 – 16. At this time his father, now Colonel M. A. Colquhoun was in command at Kinmel Park Camp and probably arranged his son's body being returned to Canada, but I am sure he would not have been able himself to return for the funeral.

Colonel M.A. Colquhoun was for a time the commander of the Canadians at Shorncliffe Military Camp, Kent, until in September 1918, he took up command at Kinmel Park Camp. The camp was receiving thousands of Canadian soldiers, initially a segregation and military training camp, but following the Armistice, for the Canadians it was a staging camp.

As the commander of Kinmel Park Camp post-Armistice, there was nothing he could do about the deaths from the Spanish Flu pandemic which occurred at the camp. It was not in his power to get these Canadian soldiers returned home, instead he had to try to deal with the desultory repatriation of them and the resentment and bitterness that grew day by day, as they waited to board troopships back to Canada.

He did at the time and in the years since, receive a portion of the blame for the deaths during the riots/disturbances, but he had made personal attempts by going amongst the men to try to dissuade them from causing further mayhem in the camp. He had also categorically stated that he wanted no blood shed during the riots/disturbances, but the 'ringleaders of the mob' and a number of 'the defenders' had different ideas.

In the 1920's, Colonel M. A. Colquhoun was the commanding officer of 38th Dufferin Rifles at Brantford. He was a greatly respected member of his community, with many being only too aware of his exploits with the so called 'Mad Fourth Battalion' back in 1915 and 1916 on the Western Front.

He was a member of the executive committee which oversaw the creation of the fine Brant War Memorial in

Brantford, which was officially unveiled on 25 May 1933, and dedicated to the areas 'Fallen in The First World War', which of course included his own son. The official unveiling was carried out by His Excellency, The Governor General of Canada, the Right Honourable, The Earl of Bessborough in a very well attended, highly symbolic and impressive ceremony. Colonel M. A. Colquhoun had the great honour of being the Mayor of the City of Brantford for 1935.

Colonel Malcolm Alexander Colquhoun, C.M.G., D.S.O., known affectionately by many as 'Mac', died in 1950, aged eighty-one and was buried, like his son so many years before him at Greenwood Cemetery, Brantford, Ontario. His funeral service held at the Park Baptist Church was attended by hundreds of people, many of them veterans of the First World War, especially ones from 4th Battalion (Central Ontario), proudly wearing their war medals. Over his grave, three rifle volleys were fired by fourteen soldiers – a fitting finale to a soldier who had been a genuine war hero and a very decent man indeed.

4. Sergeant Alfred James Dasher – born in England

Alfred James Dasher was born at Birkenhead, England, on 12 April 1894. Pre-First World War he worked on ships in the merchant service, including in the Far East, as a result of which he ended up in Canada. He was a single man, employed as a fireman on merchant ships, when he enlisted in the C.E.F at Victoria, British Columbia, giving his address at this time as The Manitoba Hotel, Victoria, British Columbia. He was described as being five feet, five and a half inches tall, of sallow complexion, with brown eyes and hair. He gave his religion as Church of England and his next of kin as his mother, Mrs Rebecca Dasher, of 54, Cathcart Street, Birkenhead, England, who was born in Liscard, Cheshire, England. His father, Henry Augustus Dasher, who was born in Yarmouth, Nova Scotia, Canada, had been a stationary engine driver before his death in 1911. Alfred James Dasher allotted to have his Canadian Army separation allowance paid to his widowed mother.

He embarked for England from Halifax, Nova Scotia, on 23 July 1916, aboard the gigantic R.M.S. Olympic, sister ship of the ill-fated Titanic, disembarking at Liverpool on 31 July 1916. After undergoing some further military training in the south of England, he landed in France on 23 December 1916, and served with 2nd Battalion Canadian Mounted Rifles in France & Flanders, regimental number 707253. His military medical record includes the following: *Date of admission to hospital – April 2nd 1917. With GSW (gunshot wound). Left lower extremity, severe flesh wound. Cause – Raiding Party. Place – Vimy Ridge. Admission – Flesh wound, 3 inches by one and a half inches side of left thigh, wound clean. V.A.D. hospital recommended.*

He had initially been treated at No. 26 General Hospital, Etaples, France, and then in England at 1st Southern Military Hospital, Stourbridge, West Midlands, a converted former workhouse. On his medical records it also showed that on two occasions in the past he had suffered bouts of malaria, no doubt from his time pre-war in the Far East with the merchant service.

Post-Armistice he was at Kinmel Park Camp awaiting his discharge, not in his case was he awaiting shipping transport back to Canada, for he was staying in Britain.

The War Diary entry of 27 May 1919, for M.D. 3 at Kinmel Park Camp shows that the writer of it had a sense of humour:

Kinmel Park Camp. 27-5-19. Sgt. Dasher looking very dashing in his 'civvies' paid a visit to the camp today. Probably to give us ocular proof that it is actually possible to receive a discharge from this army. He then dashed back to Liverpool, where we understand he has a wife.

Sergeant Alfred James Dasher had officially been discharged from military service the previous day. A few weeks earlier he had married at Birkenhead, Teresa Humphreys, and in 1920, they had a daughter together, Gertrude Marion Dasher. In 1939, Alfred James Dasher was a married man, residing in Chester Street, Birkenhead, England, and employed as a fitter's labourer in a local shipyard. Alfred James Dasher died in Birkenhead, in 1944, aged fifty.

5. Captain Robert James Davidson, MC

Robert James Davidson was born on 6 December 1883, though some records show it as 1881, at Ottawa, Ontario, Canada. Prior to the First World War, he had served as a member of the Canadian militia regiment, the 43rd Regiment, D.C.O.R. (Duke of Cornwall's Own), and with the Royal Canadian Regiment. He volunteered for war service with the C.E.F on 9 November 1914, when employed as a machinery salesman. He gave his next of kin as an aunt, Mrs Robert Davidson of 95, Henderson Avenue, Ottawa. He was single, by religion Church of England, and was Private Davidson, regimental number 59240 (temporary number 827). After further military training and kitting out in Canada, on 6 May 1915, from Montreal aboard the S.S. Metagama, he embarked with a draft of the C.E.F for England. Arriving in England on 15 May 1915, and was initially at the West Sandling Camp, near Hythe, Kent. Whilst here, he showed leadership qualities and was promoted on 1 July 1915, to company sergeant-major. On 14 September 1915, he embarked at Folkestone for the Western Front with 21st Battalion (Eastern Ontario),

Robert J. Davidson, MC

C.E.F. On 12 January 1916, in France, he was granted a commission and was made a temporary lieutenant. At the Front in France & Flanders he was to distinguish himself in the face of the enemy. On 15 September 1916, he was admitted to a casualty clearing station suffering from shrapnel wounds to his back and right arm. He had been blown up by an enemy shell and his hearing became defective, for he had sustained a perforated eardrum. He was invalided back to England and was treated at several hospitals including the Fort Pitt Military Hospital, Chatham, Kent. The London Gazette, number 29890 of 2 January 1917, records him having been 'Mentioned in Despatches'. After a period of recuperation and leave he was back at the Front, and for a time he acted as 'brigade bombing officer'. On 2 April 1917, he received promotion to temporary captain. The London Gazette, number 30188 of 8 July 1917 records that he had been awarded the high military honour of the Military Cross. This is the citation for it:

Lt. Robert James Davidson, Canadian Infantry
For conspicuous gallantry and devotion to duty. His company was on two occasions held up and disorganised by hostile

machine-gun fire. He rallied his men and led them to their objective, capturing a machine-gun and crew, and saving a very dangerous situation.

He was again to be wounded in action when on 15 August 1917, he was treated for having shell fragments in his left hand, which necessitated him being taken by field ambulance to No. 1 British Red Cross Hospital, Le Touquet, Northern France, also known as The Duchess of Westminster Hospital. He was later returned to England and received further treatment at the Royal Free Military Hospital for officers, Grays Inn Road, Holborn, London. After a period of recuperation leave which was extended, he was examined and found to be unfit to return to active duty. Following this he attended the Eastern Command Musketry School and he qualified as a 1st class instructor.

Post-Armistice, on 6 January 1919, he was attached to Kinmel Park Camp, and two days later he was made acting-major and second in command of 'C Wing' of M. D. 2 Wing at the camp. Following the riots in the camp, at the subsequent court of enquiry he was named: *Not all officers were forewarned of potential unrest. Captain R. J. Davidson of the 21st Battalion and second in command of M. D. 2 said, 'I was surprised at the outbreak. I knew there was unrest about the sailings, but I did not expect any outbreak. I do not think the outbreak was organised to any great extent'.*

On 13 August 1919, Captain Davidson was on his way back to Canada, after to say the very least, a difficult wartime experience.

He died on 17 May 1936, aged fifty-two, and was buried at Prospect Cemetery, Toronto, also known as 'the Cemetery on St Clair'. Also buried in this fine cemetery are two Victoria Cross recipients from the First World War, namely, Colin Fraser Barron and Walter Leigh Rayfield. The gravestone of Robert James Davidson has the following inscribed upon it:

> 21ST BATTN. C.E.F.
> IN LOVING MEMORY OF
> ROBERT J. DAVIDSON M.C.
> DIED MAY 17, 1936
> AGED 52 YEARS

6. Chester Arthur Greenwood

Chester Arthur Greenwood was born on 15 July 1895, at Brantford, Ontario, Canada, to Peter and Bertha (Bertie) Amanda Greenwood. This family resided for many years in Park Road, Brantford. Chester Greenwood was a market gardener and five feet, six inches tall when he enlisted on 8 May 1918, at Brantford in the C.E.F. He arrived in England on 25 September 1918, on board HMT Themistocles. Though he never saw action, it can be fairly said that he personally witnessed several deaths, some of them being of his friends. For, after arriving at Kinmel Park Camp he was on 16 October 1918, admitted to the camp's military hospital suffering from influenza – the deadly Spanish Flu. Whilst in hospital he would have witnessed a number of deaths of fellow young Canadian soldiers, particularly in the latter part of October 1918. But he survived and was discharged after twenty-three days of hospitalization on 7 November 1918 – he was one of the lucky ones.

Chester Greenwood returned to Canada and married in 1920, and the couple had a total of four children. In his retirement he resided in Park Road North, Brantford, Ontario. In 1978, when aged eighty-three he travelled over the Atlantic to make a visit to the Kinmel Park area, especially to the St Margaret's Churchyard, Bodelwyddan, to pay his respects to those friends and former comrades who died of illness whilst with him at the nearby Kinmel Park Camp. He told a local reporter that he remembered watching the riots at the camp unfold from the camp's hospital.

Chester Arthur Greenwood died in 1981, aged eighty-five having completed a 'veteran's pilgrimage' to North Wales three years earlier.

7. Thomas William Holmes, VC

Thomas William Holmes was from a humble background, being born on 27 October 1898, at Montreal, Canada, to John and Mary Edith Holmes. Just prior to the outbreak of the First World War he was a single man, employed as a 'chicken picker'. He had never before undergone any kind of military service or training when on 20 December 1915, he enlisted at Owen Sound, Ontario, Canada, in the C.E.F. He stood just over five feet, seven inches tall. Gave his religion as being 'Salvation Army', his home address at this time was 380, 9th Street East, Owen Sound, Grey County, Ontario. Private Thomas William Holmes, known as

Thomas William Holmes, VC

The Victoria Cross

'Tommy' regimental number 838301 was sent to the Front in France & Flanders. He was here initially with 147th (Grey) Battalion, but was moved as a replacement to the 4th Canadian Mounted Rifles on 7 April 1917, though it was now acting purely as an infantry battalion. Two days later, on Easter Monday, 9 April 1917, during the now iconic Battle of Vimy Ridge, he sustained a gunshot wound to his left forearm, as a result of enemy machine-gun fire. He received treatment in a military hospital in Bristol, England, and this is how it was 'officially' recorded: '*It was a through and through bullet wound, causing a fracture of the ulna. The wound having healed and the bone united. The patient is feeling fit*'. Then followed a period of convalescence at the then Canadian Convalescent Hospital in Epsom, England. He re-joined the battalion on 13 October 1917, in time for the sheer hell of the latter stages of The Battle of Passchendaele (31 July – 10 November 1917), also known as The Third Battle of Ypres.

It was for his remarkable actions here on 26 October 1917, that he was subsequently awarded the Victoria Cross (VC). This is the 'official' announcement of this award, which appeared in the London Gazette, No. 30471, of 8 January 1918.

4TH CANADIAN MOUNTED RIFLES
VICTORIA CROSS
No. 838301 Private, Thomas William Holmes.
For most conspicuous bravery and resource when the right flank of our attack was held up by heavy machine-gun fire and rifle fire from a pill-box strong point. Heavy casualties were producing a critical situation when Pte Holmes, on his own initiative and single-handed, ran forward and threw two bombs, killing and wounding the crews of two machine-guns. He then returned to his comrades, secured another bomb, and again rushed forward alone under heavy fire and threw the bomb into the entrance of the pill-box, causing the nineteen occupants to surrender.
By this act of valour at a very critical moment, Pte Holmes undoubtedly cleared the way for the advance of our troops and saved the lives of many of his comrades.

That is the 'official' record for what had occurred. In a letter home to his mother, 'Tommy' Holmes had intimated that he had been nominated for a medal, but his family back home in Owen Sound only learnt that it was the Victoria Cross, the highest honour, when in mid-January, 1918, a local reporter from the *Owen Sound Sun* newspaper visited them and told them. By this time Tommy Holmes was already in possession of this coveted medal.

Tommy Holmes ended the war as a sergeant, and after a period at Kinmel Park Camp, it was on 30 March 1919, that he left the camp, the scene only a few weeks earlier of the riots/disturbances, to return to Canada. Aboard the S.S. Saturnia from Glasgow, he returned to Owen Sound on 14 April 1919, arriving aboard a private train car provided in his honour by the Canadian Pacific Railway. Thousands of people turned out to welcome home a hero, but sadly this fine day for him was to be followed by darker days.

An elder brother, Roy Holmes who had enlisted in 58th Battalion, the C.E.F was also wounded in the war and as a result he suffered the loss of an eye. The two brothers actually met up in hospital in England, when they were both being treated for their respective wounds.

Tommy Holmes was to suffer from TB, tuberculosis, a debilitating illness and then he was stricken by cancer. In 1935, a despicable low-life committed burglary, ransacking Tommy Holmes' home in Owen Sound and stole his Victoria Cross. Whilst it is of course possible to have exact replicas made, it would never be the actual one he was so deservedly awarded. I understand that his stolen Victoria Cross has never been recovered. In 1936, whilst working for the Toronto Harbour Commission he had helped to save three lives from an overturned boat. He had with his wife, one son and one daughter.

Tommy Holmes, VC, following a ten-year battle with cancer, died on 4 January 1950, at the Sunnybrook Hospital, Toronto. Three days later, he was buried with 'full military honours' at The Greenwood Cemetery, Owen Sound, Grey County, Ontario, memorial I.D. 7032960. His funeral was attended by three other Victoria Cross winners from the First World War. He is most certainly not a forgotten man and locally at Owen Sound in 1986, the Owen Sound Armoury, the home of The Grey and Simcoe Foresters was renamed, 'The Tommy Holmes, VC, Memorial Armoury'. Whilst a replica of his bravely won Victoria Cross is proudly on display at The Owen Sound branch, of The Royal Canadian Legion. At the superb Canadian War Museum in Ottawa, Ontario, is the portrait painting of Thomas William Holmes VC, by the noted Canadian war artist, Ernest George Fosbery (born 29/12/1874 – died 7/2/1960), who himself had served in the First World War with the Canadian Grenadier Guards, was wounded in action and

Mentioned in Dispatches. He left the military with the rank of Major. At one time he was the President of the Royal Canadian Academy. Fosbery painted this fine work in late 1918/early 1919, and depicts a young looking, fresh-faced Tommy Holmes wearing his sergeant's stripes and with his soldier's cap at an angle.

8. Major William Ennis Kidd, MC

William Ennis Kidd, M.C. (Military Cross), a Clerk in Holy Orders, was born on 23 February 1879, at Burritts Rapids, Eastern Ontario, Canada. He enlisted early in the war on 1 November 1914, at Kingston, Ontario. He arrived in England with the C.E.F from Montreal on 15 May 1915, aboard the S.S. Metagama, and landed in France on 15 September 1915. Here he suffered for a time with bronchitis, requiring his admittance to No. 5 Canadian Field Ambulance. Records show that during his time on the Western Front he was awarded the Military Cross and on another occasion was Mentioned in Dispatches when he served with 21st Battalion (Eastern Ontario), C.E.F. The citation for his having been awarded the Military Cross stated

William Ennis Kidd, MC

that he had, '*Tended and dressed the wounded continuously for three days under very heavy fire, displaying great courage and determination*'.

He arrived for service as chaplain at Kinmel Park Camp on 6 October 1918, when it was pre-Armistice. Then post-Armistice when it became a staging camp for returning Canadian soldiers he was officially attached to this new entity on 29 November 1918. It was not until the very end of the Canadian presence at Kinmel Park Camp, that he left it to return home, embarking for Canada on 3 August 1919. Being officially discharged from military service on 14 August 1919, at Quebec.

He returned home to his wife, Margaret Louise Dealtry Kidd at Trinity Rectory, Brockville, Ontario, and to being an Anglican minister. Between 1939 and 1945 he served as the President of the 21st Battalion Association. In the early hours of 5 April 1970, aged 91, he died. His wife of over sixty years having died only a few months earlier in the Winter of 1969. A service attended by many military and ex-military personnel for the much loved and respected William Ennis Kidd was held on 8 April 1970, at Kingston, Ontario, prior to his being buried at the Anglican Cemetery, Brockville, Ontario.

9. Charles Clarence Laking – The very last of the Canadian 'Old Sweats'

Charles Clarence Laking was born on 21 February 1899, in Campbellville, Ontario, Canada. His father, Charles Laking (senior) was totally opposed to the war and as a pacifist openly made this view known, much to the chagrin of his son. Charles Clarence Laking (junior) was known to family and friends as 'Clare', a name his grandmother used for him to avoid confusion with his father, and the name stuck for the rest of his very long life.

'Clare' Laking

Rather embarrassed by his father's anti-war stance, and being a teenager, he rebelled and obtained a lift to Guelph, a city in Ontario, where on 14 April 1917, he enlisted for the C.E.F. Learning of this, his father said that he disowned his son and wanted nothing whatsoever in future to do with him. 'Clare' Laking was just over eighteen and stood a tad over five feet, three inches. After some initial military training in Canada, on 2 June 1917 he sailed on the Canadian troop transport the RMS Olympic, arriving in England on 10 June 1917. He was now Gunner Laking, regimental number 33514, with the Canadian Field Artillery (the C.F.A.). He served in France & Flanders as a signaller with 27th Battery, C.F.A. His duties at the Front included stringing telephone wires along the trenches – often referred to as communication trenches, and going into the frontline trenches when a Canadian barrage took place, in order to telephone back to the Canadian gunners manning 'the big guns', as to the accuracy of their opening shelling upon enemy positions.

He had a few close calls when at or near the Front. On one occasion on 4 November 1918, exactly one week before the Armistice, a German shell hit a house where he and some comrades were seeking shelter. A flying brick smashed into his steel helmet leaving a large dent in it. He was unconscious for a short time and when he regained consciousness he assisted wounded comrades. He later recalled: '*We were carrying Baldy Craig down to a dressing station when I asked another soldier if there was a hole in my tunic. I was told that my right shoulder at the back had shrapnel embedded in it*'. It was officially recorded as a GSW (gunshot wound) to his right arm, which necessitated hospital treatment at a nearby clearing station and then at the Etaples Military Hospital. Sadly, he later recalled, after spending a few days in a military hospital his steel helmet with the large shrapnel dent in it had disappeared. He suspected it had been stolen, and he had wanted it for a souvenir – after all it had almost certainly saved his life or at least avoided him having a very serious head injury.

Clare Laking arrived at Kinmel Park Camp on 5 May 1919, and was placed on M.D. 2 Wing. He was just passing through, for by now, post-Kinmel Park Camp riots/disturbances, most of the Canadian soldiers had gone, quickly moved on from this staging camp back to Canada.

Post-First World War there was a reconciliation between Clare Laking and his father. Clare Laking went to work for timber companies in Toronto. In 1929 he married Helen Patterson, a legal secretary. A marriage which was to last for some sixty-four years until wife Helen died in 1993, aged ninety-four. The couple had two children, a boy and a girl, and had 'at least' eight grandchildren and twenty-three great grandchildren.

Clare Laking by all accounts was quite an amazing man. He took over and then ran for many years a company called 'Danforth Wallboard and Insulation Limited', which he sold when he was sixty-five. He stopped smoking at eighty; stopped playing his favourite indoor sport of curling at the age of ninety-six; gave up his season ticket to his favourite professional ice hockey team the Toronto Maple Leafs aged one hundred; and perhaps most amazingly of all, he finally gave up his driving licence aged one hundred and two. Although, he insisted he could still drive capably, his doctor advised him that at that age if he was ever to be involved in a road traffic accident, his age would 'be a suspect as to the cause'!

Clare Laking admitted over the years that he was troubled by his vivid memories of exploding shells and of seeing his comrades wounded. But he took great heart when he remembered that when he and his unit passed through liberated French villages, the villagers would come out, and wave, cheer and throw flowers at them. Later in life Clare Laking was fittingly awarded the French Legion of Honour and the Golden Jubilee Medal. I am sure that this fine 'old sweat' would have proudly received these awards not for himself, but for all those who served with the C.E.F during the First World War.

Charles Clarence 'Clare' Laking died peacefully, of well, old age, on 26 November 2005, aged one hundred and six – The very last of the 'Old Sweats' – Canadian soldiers who had seen combat in the First World War.

10. Captain Cyril Geoffrey Lloyd

The *North Wales Chronicle* of 20 June 1919, had this rather different 'post-war' story:

> A KINMEL OFFICER AND HIS BABY
> Capt. C. G. Lloyd, 1st Canadian Mounted Rifles, Kinmel Camp, writing to the Daily Mail says:
> 'At Cardiff Station on June 10th, when my wife and baby, accompanied by the nursemaid, were returning from Rhyl to Haverfordwest, they were refused entrance to a

> first-class carriage because of the baby, although both had first-class tickets. Is this one of the rules of the country or is it a crime to have children? I may say, that such a thing has never occurred in Canada'.

The Canadian soldier concerned was Captain Cyril Geoffrey Lloyd who was born on 27 May 1887, at Morden, Manitoba, Canada. He was a farmer by occupation, and served pre-First World War with 18th Mounted Rifles, Manitoba, a Canadian army reserve militia.

On 10 January 1915, he enlisted at Yorkton, Saskatchewan, Canada, to fight overseas with the C.E.F, sailing to England on 12 June 1915.

Whilst on active service in France & Flanders with 1st Battalion Canadian Mounted Rifles he was seriously wounded, both physically and mentally on 2 June 1916, suffering a GSW (gunshot wound) to his back and shellshock (neurasthenia), and was admitted to No.7 Stationary Hospital, Boulogne, France. His mental condition at this time was worse than his physical one, and he was returned to Canada on 1 August 1916. A medical report upon him at this time stated: *'A little dizzy and somewhat deaf from an exploding shell'*. It is no surprise that Cyril Geoffrey Lloyd suffered shellshock, for 2 June 1916 was the opening day of a major offensive by the German army in a battle known as The Battle of Mount Sorrel (2 June to 14 June 1916) in the Ypres Salient. Here the Canadian Third Division which included the 1st Battalion Canadian Mounted Rifles had to undergo a 'tornado of shellfire', so devastating that it destroyed whole lines of trenches and decimated a whole area and every living thing there. Thousands of Canadian soldiers were killed, with Lieutenant Lloyd's own battalion particularly taking a heavy loss in lives. After this German bombardment, the German's first attacking wave met little opposition, and many Canadian soldiers died fighting or were taken prisoner.

After an extended leave in Canada in order for him to recuperate, he returned to overseas duty, returning to England in late 1916, and he married Gladys Lillian Rowe, at Hastings, Sussex. Gladys of course was what we call a 'Canadian War Bride'.

In 1917 and 1918, he again served at the Front in France & Flanders. On 24 May 1919, Captain Cyril Geoffrey Lloyd was at Kinmel Park Camp, M.D. 10, having arrived from the Ripon Camp. Then on 24 June 1919, he embarked for his return to Canada on the S.S Cassandra. He was Mentioned in Despatches in Sir Douglas Haig's post-war 'M.I.D' recognition list of 11 July 1919.

Post-war, Cyril Geoffrey Lloyd joined the Royal Canadian Mounted Police and was constable 11741. He died on 22 March 1938, aged fifty, and was buried at the Elmwood Cemetery, Winnipeg, Manitoba. His widow Gladys died in 1966 and was buried in the same cemetery. One of their children, Lance-Sergeant Charles Henry Oswald Lloyd, regimental number L/53700, 14th Canadian Hussars, died of his wounds on 6 April 1945, aged twenty-two, and was buried in the Holten Canadian War Cemetery, Holten, in the Netherlands.

11. Captain William Christopher Sprague – military dentist

William Christopher Sprague was born on 25 December 1874, at Shediac, Westmorland County, New Brunswick Canada. When he enlisted in the C.E.F on 11 August 1916, at Vancouver, British Columbia, Canada, he was a dentist by profession, married to Jane Sprague, and residing with her at 1530, Barclay Street, Vancouver. He enlisted as a private, and was Private Sprague, regimental number 646205. He served in the Canadian Army Dentistry Corps in Canada, England and Wales. He was promoted to the rank of acting sergeant on 16 February 1917. He most probably did not serve in France & Flanders due to his age, for he was aged forty-two when he arrived in Britain.

On 7 January 1919, he was transferred from Bramshott Camp to Kinmel Park Camp and placed on M.D. 4 Wing to await his own eventual return to Canada, but not before he had dentally examined hundreds, perhaps even thousands of the many Canadian soldiers and nurses at this 'staging camp', post-Armistice. At the camp he had influenza which required his hospitalisation at the camp's military hospital from 11 May 1919 to 15 May 1919. This Spanish Flu was a virulent strain of flu, taking a particularly heavy toll in lives on the younger, fitter persons who contracted it, and Captain Sprague may at forty-four have survived for this reason. Though also the fact that he had not served at the Front, and of course not in the trenches meant his constitution may have been stronger to resist it.

Once back in Canada, on his discharge papers it is marked that he now reverted back to the rank of lieutenant from that of captain.

William Christopher Sprague died on 6 April 1947, aged seventy-two.

Post-Armistice, Kinmel Park Camp had many Canadian officers there either in command or second-in-command of the various M. D. Wings who were highly decorated and greatly respected men. They included: **Acting Major C. Stevenson**, MC, the officer in command of M. D. Wing 4 – Alberta Regiment, and his second-in-command, **Captain Samuel Parkinson Lough**, MC; **Acting Lieutenant-Colonel H. W. Harbord**, DSO, OiC of M. D. Wing 13; **Acting Lieutenant-Colonel E. V. Collier**, DSO, OiC of M. D. Wing 5, the Canadian Engineers.

Chapter Eleven

Canadian Nursing Sisters

Canadian nurses had nursed in relatively small numbers during the Boer War, but now in August 1914, a far more global war had broken out and Canadian soldiers all over the vast expanse of Canada were forming themselves into battalions to go to war overseas against Germany and the Central Powers. Margaret Clothilde MacDonald (born 26 February 1873 – died 7 September 1948), a nursing sister, born at Bailey Brook, Pictou County, Nova Scotia, Canada, was in Ottawa two weeks after war was declared. She was busy gathering together qualified nurses to join the Canadian Army Medical Corps. Some ninety-eight nurses were at Valcartier, Quebec, on 23 September 1914, ready for overseas service. Here they were medically examined to ensure that they were fit and healthy ready for what they knew would be the rigours of overseas war service. After being vaccinated they were given their distinctive, striking uniforms which were: A sky blue coloured uniform dress made of cotton, over which they had white aprons, crossed at the back. Whilst on duty, they wore a sheer, white veil. The dress uniform was of navy-blue serge, navy blue jacket which had a high round collar edged with scarlet and white. They were also supplied with some 'bad weather' clothing of a long navy coloured coat, or for some, a navy-blue coloured cape which had scarlet coloured lining. They were also issued with black coloured army type boots, which must have been most uncomfortable when on their feet for hours on end when on duty. But no doubt essential wear for those nursing at locations such as near to the Front, or in the muddy quagmire that was often Kinmel Park Camp. Over one hundred nursing sisters actually left Quebec Port, Canada, bound for England on 23 September 1914, aboard the S.S. Franconia, including Matron MacDonald herself. Unlike their British nursing counterparts these Canadian nurses were called 'nursing sisters' and all of them held the minimum rank equivalent to 'lieutenant', shown by their wearing of two 'first lieutenant rank stars' on the shoulders of their uniforms. Those nurses of 'matron' rank were equivalent to 'majors'.

The Canadian nursing sisters were sent to serve in a variety of hospitals: Casualty clearing stations' which were to be found nearer the Front, such as the first two in France which were at Etaples and Le Treport; what were called stationary hospitals, despite their name they were actually mobile hospitals which could be moved around as the fighting and the Front lines altered; plus a number of hospitals around Britain – general hospitals, including ones to be found at military camps. Some of the Canadian nursing sisters went further afield than France & Flanders and Britain.

A total of some 2,504 Canadian nursing sisters served overseas during the First World War in Britain, France & Flanders, Gallipoli (in Eastern Turkey, often referred to as The Dardanelles), Alexandria, Egypt, and the Salonika Front (Macedonia Region). Of these 2,504, fifty-three are known to have been killed by enemy fire, by disease, or through accidents. On at least two occasions in 1918, Canadian field hospitals in France were hit by enemy bombing raids, with several nurses losing their lives. When on 27 June 1918, the German U-Boat, the U-86 despicably torpedoed the clearly marked and lit Canadian hospital ship the Llandovery Castle, all fourteen Canadian nursing sisters on board lost their lives.

Canadian nursing sisters during the First World War

were affectionately nicknamed 'Bluebirds' by Canadian soldiers because of their blue coloured uniforms with white coloured veils. Though they were more correctly known as 'Sisters of Mercy', or as 'Angels of Mercy'. These Canadian nursing sisters, greatly admired and appreciated by those they nursed, cared for not only wounded and gassed patients, but also of course ones with ailments and illnesses such as dysentery, malaria, meningitis, frostbite, trench foot, and influenza, the latter especially during the Spanish Flu pandemic. When trawling through the military records of many of the nursing sisters the most common ailments I came across for them to suffer from during their wartime nursing were influenza, which is not surprising with the Spanish Flu pandemic; debility – defined as physical weakness after illness; and, nervous exhaustion. Many nursing sisters were physically 'run-down' from their toil nursing soldiers, with the added strain of nursing those wounded in war, some horrifically – poison gas victims, gunshot wounds, shrapnel injuries etc., and of course particularly those nursing at the Front with many soldiers dying as they tended to them.

Some Canadian Nursing Sisters who served at Kinmel Park Camp

Margaret Katherine Beard (later on her marriage – Gillam)

Margaret Katherine Beard was born on 9 April 1881, at Gould, (now named Lingwick, a township which incorporates the former villages of Gould and Sainte-Marguerite), Quebec, Canada. Her parents George W. Beard and, wife, Mary Beard, when she enlisted as a nursing sister with the Canadian Army Medical Corps, resided in Scotstown, Quebec.

Nursing Sister Beard was nursing at Bramshott Camp until on 16 October 1918, she was sent to serve at Kinmel Park Camp's military hospital, which was then called a segregation camp. She is the 'Miss Beard' referred to in the diary entry for 16 October 1918, of Clare Gass. Three days later she was in her own hospital at the camp suffering from influenza, almost certainly the Spanish Flu strain. She managed to recover from this, which so many at the camp, sadly were unable to do. However, it left her with debility and she received further treatment at the Canadian Red Cross Special Hospital, Buxton, Derbyshire. Nursing Sister Beard then returned to nurse at No. 9 Canadian General Hospital, Kinmel Park Camp, until on 8 July 1919 she 'retired in the British Isles'.

There was a reason for her retiring, for she had married locally to the camp, one Major George Joshua Gillam, a physician with the Canadian Army Medical Corps, whom she had met whilst they both served at Kinmel Park Camp. George Joshua Gillam, born 21 November 1887, at Norwich, Oxford County, Ontario, had been well travelled during the war. He began at Mudros, on the Island of Lemnos, tending to the soldiers who were involved in the military catastrophe that was the 'Dardanelles Campaign'. He contracted paratyphoid there but made a good recovery from it. He was then sent to work as a physician at a hospital in Boulogne, France, where he had diphtheria, but again made a good recovery, until post-Armistice, on 27 December 1918, he was at Kinmel Park Camp on M.D. 2 Wing. Major (may have been a temporary rank) Gillam was discharged from the military at Kinmel Park Camp.

After a time in the British Isles, the couple, Mr and Mrs Gillam, returned to Canada to permanently reside there. Margaret Katherine Gillam, nee Beard, died in 1974, aged ninety-three, and was buried at Malvern Cemetery, Lennoxville, Estrie Region, Quebec.

Margaret Currie Drew

Margaret Currie Drew was born at Liverpool, Nova Scotia, Canada, on 19 June 1885. As a professional nurse she enlisted at Halifax, Nova Scotia in the Canadian Army Medical Corps for service with the C.E.F, on 4 February 1915.

She went on to serve as a nursing sister in France, England and Wales. On 8 September 1917, she arrived in France for frontline duties in a Canadian casualty clearing station (C.C.C.S.). On her return to England she served at No. 9 Canadian General Hospital, Shorncliffe, and she moved with it, when it was moved to Kinmel Park Camp, where she was placed on M.D. 6 Wing.

On 14 April 1919, Nursing Sister Margaret Currie Drew had a serious bout of bronchitis which kept her hospitalized until her discharge on 15 May 1919. She was honoured as was Mary Georgina Fox in the same awards: *DREW, SISTER, MISS M.C., 9th General Hospital, Kinmel Park.*

Nursing Sister Drew returned to her homeland on board the S.S. Aquitania, disembarking at Halifax, Nova Scotia, on 22 June 1919.

Margaret Currie Drew died on 11 August 1959, aged seventy-four.

Margaret Vitaline Foster (later on her marriage – Harston)

Margaret Vitaline Foster was born on 28 July 1894, at Bancroft, Hastings County, Ontario, Canada, to Ira Foster and, wife, Agnes Foster, nee Brown. The Foster family lived in a farmhouse which had no electricity and no indoor plumbing. Margaret went to school at a one-room schoolhouse, to get to which each day she had to walk three miles (and back). She decided to become a professional nurse and qualified at the Belleville Nursing School,

Belleville, Ontario, in early 1917. After some three months of nursing there, she enlisted at Kingston, Ontario, on 5 May 1917, to go overseas with the Canadian Army Medical Corps. She was a Canadian nursing sister, nursing in England at the Duchess of Connaught Canadian Red Cross Hospital, for sick and wounded soldiers, on the magnificent Cliveden Estate, Taplow, near Maidenhead, Buckinghamshire. The wealthy Astor family had kindly given part of their estate grounds for the hospital to be built.

This entry is a sort of 'joint entry', for Nursing Sister Margaret Vitaline Foster met Ernest Harston whilst in England, and on 11 January 1919, at Maidenhead they were married. Ernest Harston was born at Manchester, England, on 5 May 1889. He was a Methodist minister of religion who was in Canada when he enlisted for the C.E.F at Toronto, on 7 February 1917. He was initially Private Harston, regimental number 1102311. He arrived in France on 29 March 1917, and after a few days was made up to acting sergeant. Though he was soon made an honorary captain in the Canadian chaplain services. After a period of leave and duty in England, most probably during which Margaret and he met, he returned to duties in France & Flanders. He was at Kinmel Park Camp as a chaplain in early November 1918, when it was still called a segregation camp. When it became a staging camp for the repatriation of Canadian soldiers he remained at the camp. He spent a few days in the Canadian military hospital here suffering from a 'carbuncle on his back'.

Margaret and Ernest now married, served in their capacities at Kinmel Park Camp until Margaret resigned her commission, and went to live nearby at a property known as Llais Afon, High Street, Abergele, North Wales. The couple were awaiting their own repatriation to Canada, and both were at Kinmel Park Camp during the riots/disturbances of

4/5 March 1919. On 24 May 1919, the couple were discharged from military service in Wales (records show as per usual 'England'), prior to sailing for Canada aboard the S.S. Metagama, disembarking on 1 June 1919, at the Port of Quebec.

Margaret Vitaline Harston, nee Foster, was a housewife for some twenty-three years of married life, until following the death of husband Ernest, she returned to nursing, firstly at Toronto East General Hospital, now renamed The Michael Garron Hospital, and then at The Lockwood Clinic, Toronto. Margaret died on 1 May 1990, at the age of ninety-five.

Mary Georgina Fox (later on her marriage – Elliott)
Mary Georgina Fox was born on 11 December 1884, at Victoria, British Columbia, Canada. She became a professional nurse and on 16 September 1915, in London, England, she enlisted in the Canadian Army Medical Corps (CAMC).

In 1916, she served as a nursing sister at a military hospital in Salonika. Here the survivors of the disastrous 'Gallipoli Campaign' came, many wounded, with many others suffering from dysentery. Here, Nursing Sister Fox after months of 'nursing at the sharp end' one might say, suffered debility, brought on it was later agreed in a report compiled by three doctors, 'by the strain of her nursing duties', and from her having dysentery, a form of gastroenteritis. She was sent to Malta and then back to England for a period of recuperation, before continuing her nursing duties in England and Wales. Dysentery claimed the lives of many in Gallipoli, Salonika and in Malta during the First World War.

Nursing Sister Fox arrived at the now recently renamed No. 9 Canadian General Hospital, Kinmel Park Camp, on

27 December 1918. A few months earlier whilst nursing at a military hospital in England she had suffered with neuritis to the left side of her neck and left shoulder. At Kinmel Park Camp she was on M.D. 11 and remained here until 13 June 1919.

The Journal of Nursing, Issue 1,640, dated 19 August 1919, had this in its pages: *HONOURS FOR NURSES OVERSEAS; NURSING SERVICE; MENTIONED FOR VALUABLE SERVICE; DOMINION OF CANADA – FOX, SISTER, MISS M. G., 9th Canadian General Hospital, Kinmel Park.* This was the nursing equivalent of being 'Mentioned in Despatches'. On 4 January 1919, she had been awarded the 1914–15 Star & Riband. Nursing Sister Fox sailed back to Canada from Liverpool on sailing No. 93, aboard the S.S. Carmania, on 5 July 1919.

Mary Georgina Elliott, nee Fox, died on 26 August 1959, aged seventy-four.

Clare Gass

Clare Gass was born at Shubenacadie, Hants County, Nova Scotia, on 18 March 1887. She was a graduate nurse when on 13 May 1915, she enlisted at Montreal, Canada for overseas service with the Canadian Army Medical Corps as a nursing sister. She was five feet, five inches tall and had a fair complexion, blue eyes and red hair. She was sent to France & Flanders, nursing firstly at No. 1 Canadian General Hospital, Etaples, France, and later at No. 3 Canadian General Hospital, Boulogne, France. She also nursed in England and Wales, and this extract is taken from her own war diary entitled, *The War Diary of Clare Gass 1915–1918*, edited and introduced by Susan Mann:

1918 – October 16

Four of our sisters at Bishopsdale were told they were to go to the

segregation camp in North Wales to help out with this awful plague of Spanish Influenza which has broken out there. I offered my services in place of another who does not wish to go.
1918 – October 17
Kinmel Park Military Hosp. We arrived 10.00 pm last night in Rhyl. Met by Can headquarters car & went to bed in a ward hut. A very busy day today, Miss Beard and I on a 30-bed ward. Such sick sick sick men. Many of them will die.

After being at Kinmel Park Camp for a number of weeks, Nursing Sister Clare Gass moved to another Canadian military establishment, and then on 9 January 1919, on board the RMS Olympic she sailed for Canada and there continued her nursing career.

Nursing Sister Clare Gass was not the only one of her immediate family to enlist in the C.E.F. Four of her brothers were at the Front in Europe, one of whom, Lance-Corporal Blanchard Gass, regimental number 69064, was killed in action attacking Hill 145, on 9 April 1917, during The Battle of Vimy Ridge. The three other brothers survived the war, namely, Corporal Gerald Gass, 2479; Lance-Corporal Cyril Gass, 67097; and Private Athelstan Gass, 901864.

Nursing Sister Clare Gass

Clare Gass though, has what may fairly be called a 'genuine claim to fame', for in her diary entry for 30 October 1915, she has an early version of the classic 'Great War poem', 'In Flanders Fields', by Major John McCrae. Clare Gass nursed alongside Doctor, Major McCrae when they were both at No. 3 Canadian General Hospital in France. They became friends and he showed her his poem. She wrote down an early version, and is said to be the one who suggested he submit it for publication, as she thought it was a worthy poem. He sent it to the *Spectator* magazine who returned it to him unpublished. However, *Punch* magazine in their 8 December 1915 edition did publish it. Major John McCrae, physician and surgeon, born on 30 November 1872, at Guelph, Ontario, sadly died of pneumonia at the Front in France & Flanders on 28 January 1918, following his long periods of 'medical toil' of operating on and treating the wounded.

Clare Gass died on 5 August 1968, at the Camp Hill Veterans' Hospital, Halifax, Nova Scotia, aged eighty-one, and was buried at the place of her birth, Shubenacadie.

Annie Elizabeth Green

Annie Elizabeth Green was born at Soperton, Ontario, Canada, on 11 October 1882.

Annie Elizabeth Green became a professional nurse having undergone her nurse training at Kingston General Hospital, Kingston, Ontario. On 10 January 1917, at Kingston, Ontario, she enlisted to serve as a nurse overseas with the C.E.F, and came over to Britain to carry out her military nursing duties. Things health wise proved difficult for her and on 19 July 1917, a medical board held in London accepted that she had contracted diphtheria due to her then current military service. Diphtheria being a potentially life-threatening illness usually spread by human contact or airborne, particularly via coughs and sneezes by an infected person. Their report included that, *'she has improved slowly, but she still tires very easily'*.

Nursing Sister Green was able to return to her nursing duties and was posted to No. 9 Canadian General Hospital, Kinmel Park Camp. Whilst there she had a bout of influenza, most probably the so called 'Spanish Flu', and was admitted to her own No. 9 hospital on 18 February 1919. She was one of the lucky ones, for after eleven days of hospitalization she was discharged and returned to her nursing duties at the camp on 28 February 1919. She was nursing at Kinmel Park Camp when the riots/disturbances' of 4 and 5 March 1919 took place.

On 24 April 1919, at Kinmel Park Camp, Nursing Sister Green underwent medical and dental examinations in preparation for her being returned to Canada.

On 8 July 1919, she left No. 9 hospital to temporarily go to No.16 hospital, and from there on 8 August 1919, she sailed back to her native Canada on the S.S. Megantic.

Annie Elizabeth Green died in 1929 aged forty-seven, and a collection of her letters, souvenir albums and assorted ephemera are held at Queen's University, Kingston, Ontario.

Rebecca McIntosh – who died at Kinmel Park Camp

Rebecca McIntosh (sometimes recorded as being spelt Macintosh) was born on 29 June 1892, at Pleasant Bay, Inverness County, Nova Scotia, Canada. Her parents both born in Nova Scotia were Peter Macintosh, a farmer, born in 1845, and his wife, Christie, born in 1853. Rebecca's paternal side grandmother, Annie Macintosh was born in Scotland in 1817, emigrating to Canada in 1843. Her paternal grandfather, James Macintosh was an early settler from Scotland in Nova Scotia, in the early 1800's – an early

Nursing Sister Rebecca McIntosh

pioneer. Pleasant Bay was all about farming and fishing.

Rebecca McIntosh graduated from high school and then graduated from nurse training college. In 1914 she was stricken with a serious bout of scarlet fever, from which she recovered well. In 1917 she heeded the call for nurses to sign up for overseas service with the Canadian Army Medical Corps. She signed up for 'the duration of the war, plus six months afterwards'. When she enlisted in April 1917, she was twenty-five years of age and gave her next of kin for record purposes as being an elder brother, John Peter McIntosh. Rebecca was a tall young woman at nearly five feet nine inches. Her father at this time had died, but her mother was still alive and resided in the town of Bridgewater, Lunenburg County, Nova Scotia.

On 25 April 1917, she set sail for Britain on the hospital ship the HMHS Letitia. A week later the ship arrived at Liverpool, England, and Rebecca was assigned to No. 10 Canadian General Military Hospital, Brighton, (formerly the British Indian Army 'Kitchener Indian General Hospital') now run by the Canadians. This military hospital received wounded soldiers from the front only, who arrived via ambulance trains which were 'unloaded' of their human cargo at the nearby Brighton Railway Station. In November 1917, Rebecca McIntosh became a patient herself at this hospital, suffering from severe abdominal pains – acute appendicitis was diagnosed, but though debilitating for her, it did not require her to undergo an operation. Rebecca returned to her nursing duties weeks later and in December 1918 she was posted (now post-Armistice) to No. 9 Canadian General Hospital, Kinmel Park Camp. A very different posting than the bright lights of vibrant Brighton – London-on-sea as it was often referred to. Kinmel Park Camp was now almost exclusively a staging camp. December 1918, and indeed the following four or so months were cold and difficult ones at Kinmel Park Camp. The Spanish Flu pandemic was rife in the camp and a coal strike resulted in fuel shortages. It was freezing cold in the camp which of course consisted of wooden huts, so cold that the pipes had burst in the hospital and water could not pass through them. The war diary of 5 February 1919 for No. 9 General Hospital at the camp reads: *Influenza is increasing rapidly in camp. Central part of hospital almost full – we have over 600 patients now. Admitted 49 yesterday and 55 today, practically all influenza.* On the following day the war diary included this in it: *Seventeen of the personnel of this unit are in hospital.*

On 10 February 1919, Nursing Sister Rebecca McIntosh had the early stages of this often-deadly form of influenza, and her ability to breathe properly became a problem, and she was admitted to her own hospital at the camp. Whilst the riots/disturbances of 4 March and 5 March 1919 took place at Kinmel Park Camp, Rebecca was oblivious to what was occurring, for she was fighting for her life in a bed in the camp's hospital. Sadly, in I believe the early hours of 8 March 1919, she lost this fight and died, aged but twenty-six.

The War Diary of the hospital for 8 March 1919

recorded this: *Nursing Sister McIntosh of this unit died in hospital today – Influenza. This Sister was very popular with the unit; a true nursing sister devoted to her duty. She will be greatly missed by all*

On 12 March 1919, Rebecca McIntosh was buried at the nearby St Margaret Churchyard (The Marble Church), Bodelwyddan in grave reference 508. The inscription on the base of the stone on her grave reads: *Erected by the Nursing Sisters of 10th Canadian Hospital, Brighton and 9th Canadian Hospital, Kinmel Camp*. She is also commemorated on the memorial to 'foreign nurses who died in the First World War at the Elizabeth Garrett Hospital Nurses' House (Home) in London. Her memorial nursing cross was sent to her mother, Mrs Christie McIntosh. Whilst her elder brother, Reverend J. P. McIntosh of Brookfield, Nova Scotia, recorded as her next of kin on her enlistment papers, was sent her war service medals and memorial scroll. But he would never receive them. For as fate would have it, he had also died of influenza back in Brookfield, Nova Scotia, only a couple of months earlier – in I believe late December of 1918.

Anna Clarke Crera De Wolfe

The interestingly named Anna Clarke Crera De Wolfe, known as Annie, was born on 25 June 1893 at Halifax, Nova Scotia, Canada, to Captain Fred Turner De Wolfe and his wife, who sadly I believe due to 'birth complications' died the same day that she gave birth to her.

Annie De Wolfe became a professional nurse and during the early years of the First World War was a graduate nurse at the Halifax Military Hospital, Nova Scotia. Until on 15 February 1918, she enlisted at Montreal, Canada, for overseas service with the Canadian Army Medical Corps. It was on 17 December 1918, that Nursing Sister Annie De

Wolfe began her service at the now re-named and under Canadian control, No. 9 Canadian General Hospital, Kinmel Park Camp. She was to nurse here through the Spanish Flu epidemic which took a heavy toll on those at the camp, and also during the riots/disturbances of 4 and 5 March 1919, and their aftermath of injured soldiers, some seriously.

On 26 February 1919, Nursing Sister De Wolfe was herself hospitalised at her own Kinmel Park Camp, but not due to influenza. She was suffering from Vincent's angina, described as being a pharyngeal infection, accompanied by an ulcerative gingivitis. She recovered and on 5 March 1919, was discharged and returned to her nursing duties at the camp's hospital.

She left Kinmel Park Camp on 4 July 1919, and after a brief spell at No. 6, Canadian General Hospital, Orpington, returned home, arriving back at Halifax, Nova Scotia, on 5 August 1919, aboard R.M.S. Adriatic.

Records show that it was not until 1928 that her well-deserved war medals were sent to her Vancouver, Canada home for her fine service in Welsh and English military hospitals during the First World War.

Chapter Twelve

Crimes, misdemeanours and accidents

The *Denbighshire Free Press* edition of 8 March 1919:

> Took the Wrong Coat
> Private Charles Edward Oldale, 2 Coy, M.D. No. 10, Kinmel Camp, was charged with stealing a coat at Rhyl on Saturday. Prisoner said he made a mistake in taking the wrong coat, Prisoner was fined 17 shillings.

Private Charles Edward Oldale was born in Derby, England, on 20 September 1889, and had emigrated to Canada some years earlier. He attested at Fort William, Ontario, Canada on 25 April 1916, and joined 94th Canadian Overseas Battalion, C.E.F, regimental number 199338. On his attestation papers he is shown as a grain inspector by occupation, five feet, five inches tall and gave his next of kin as being his wife, Gertrude Oldale of 645, North Harold Street, Fort William, Ontario.

The *Aberdeen Press and Journal* of Monday, 21 April 1919 had this:

> Rowdy Canadians
> Rowdy Canadians, Rhyl – Rhyl Magistrates on Saturday fined Private James Shannon, a Canadian soldier from Kinmel Camp £4 16 s for breaking hotel windows at Rhyl. Four Canadians were refused drink at closing time.

The *North Wales Chronicle* of 9 May 1919:

> SOLDIER KNOCKED OVER BY A TRAMCAR
> A Canadian soldier named G. A. Deestelmeyer of the Headquarters Staff Camp, Kinmel Park, who was visiting Llandudno, was knocked down by an electric tramcar in Mostyn Street on Wednesday night. He walked right in front of the tramcar, the driver of which applied the emergency brake, but could not stop it until it had run over the soldier. The tramcar reversed and Deestelmeyer was seen lying between the rails. He was conveyed to the Cottage Hospital and was attended by Dr Goldsmith without delay. Shock and severe facial wounds were inflicted, but no other injuries.

This soldier was in fact George Albert Diestelmeyer (not Deestelmeyer), born on 29 July 1893, at Kitchener, Ontario, Canada. He is shown in 1911 to be a deliverer of groceries. He enlisted in the C.E.F in 1915, and gave his next of kin as his widowed mother, Wilhelmine Diestelmeyer, known as 'Minnie', who lived in Kitchener, Ontario. His father, Albert Carl Diestelmeyer had died on 9 September 1913. George Albert Diestelmeyer was described as being five feet six inches tall, of fair complexion, with blue eyes and brown hair. His religion all of his life was Lutheran.

Initially he enlisted on 19 January 1915, regimental number 7051, gave his occupation as a teamster and served overseas. He returned to Canada, but re-enlisted in the C.E.F, returning to Britain on I believe 12 October 1918. He did not leave Britain and on 3 December 1918, he was at Kinmel Park Camp awaiting his return by ship to Canada, and placed on M. D. Wing 1. He now had the regimental number 4005055.

But it was not just this tramcar accident that delayed his return to Canada, for prior to this whilst at Kinmel Park

Camp he was in an 'official' boxing bout and fractured his ribs, seriously enough to require hospitalisation at the camp's military hospital.

Happily, George Albert Diestelmeyer fully recovered from his 'bout with the tramcar' and being in the military hospital from 1 May to 12 May 1919, for what were described as being face and head injuries. He was eventually able to return home to Kitchener, Ontario.

The city of Kitchener was known as 'Berlin' until the onset of the First World War, and in 1916 the city's name was changed to the patriotic and non-Germanic, Kitchener. George Diestelmeyer was for many years a fireman with the Kitchener Fire Department. On 29 November 1921, George married Fanny (Frances) Linder at the St Peter's Lutheran Church in Kitchener. They lived for many years at 140, Weber Street East, Kitchener.

George Albert Diestelmeyer died on Monday, 24 July 1972, at the Kitchener-Waterloo Hospital, a few days short of his seventy-ninth birthday. He was buried at the Woodland Cemetery in Kitchener. His widow Fanny (Frances) died in 1974, aged eighty-six.

The *North Wales Chronicle* of 16 May 1919, reported in the same article upon two separate, serious and violent criminal incidents which had occurred. One at Kinmel Park Camp and the other close to the camp:

EXTRAORDINARY INCIDENTS AT KINMEL CAMP
Stores Assistant Robbed Of £40
And, Masked Soldiers Attack Motor Driver
Two extraordinary cases are being investigated by the police in connection with a robbery of £40 and an attempt to steal a motor car near the Kinmel Camp by soldiers.

The first case is that in which Mr Arthur Bazinatti,

assistant in one of the stores in 'Tin Town' adjoining Kinmel Camp was held up. He was in his stores late at night when two soldiers entered and asked for coffee. He was about to serve them when one produced a revolver and covering him, demanded money. The other man then went through his pockets and relieved him of £40, the whole of his savings, which he was in the habit of carrying on his person. Fortunately, they did not find the key of the safe which was in Mr Bazinatti's pocket, and having secured such a good haul they cleared out, and no trace has been found of them.

The second case occurred near the camp on the high road. Mr Vaughan of John Street, Rhyl, who drives a Ford car to and from Kinmel Camp, left Rhyl at 11.15 p.m. with passengers for the camp. On his return, and when near No. 9 Camp, three soldiers barred his way, and after asking for a match they asked him to drive them to Rhyl. He at once asked them what they wanted in Rhyl at midnight, adding, there would be no places open at such an hour. The men replied that they had to get to Rhyl, and without further arguing jumped into the car and told him to drive on. The road leads from Kinmel Camp through the village of Bodelwyddan, and then it passes under an avenue of trees. Here one of the three men tapped the driver on the shoulder from the back of the car, with the remark, 'stop boss, I have lost my cap'. The driver pulled up at once, and the three men then jumped out of the car. Two immediately went to the side and one switched off the engine, with the remark, 'we want this car'. Mr Vaughan then noticed that the three men wore masks made of handkerchiefs which covered all but their eyes. He realised that he was in a difficult position, but hoped to be able to reach a cottage a short distance away, where military police stop. He then said, 'alright, take the car', and proceeded to get out and in doing so had the presence of mind to take off the key of the switch, without which the engine could not be started. As he got out, the three men boarded the car. He started to run for the cottage, and put the key in his pocket. Finding that they had been checkmated, the three men followed him and attempted to surround him. He dodged them until one struck him a violent blow on the side of his head, with what seemed to be a piece of iron. Mr Vaughan shouted for help, and at the same time dealt his assailant a sturdy blow in the pit of his stomach, knocking him to the ground. At that moment someone from the direction of the cottage shouted that he was coming to the driver's assistance. Mr Vaughan, who is a well-built man, then turned on the other two, but they ran away, and the man he had knocked down also cleared off. Mr Vaughan says he was afraid to close with the man he knocked down through fear of the other two. Assistance came from the cottage and it was found that Mr Vaughan's head had been badly cut. He returned to his car and proceeded to Rhyl, reporting the occurrence to the police on duty. He says he fears he will not be able to identify the assailants owing to the darkness of the night and the handkerchiefs the men were wearing.

A number of newspapers around the country including the local ones reported upon a 'bank robbery' having taken place at 'Tin Town', Kinmel Park Camp during the first weekend in June 1919. The general heading for these accounts was 'Daring Bank Robbery'. Shortly after the arrival of the bank manager Mr Edwards from nearby Abergele and another member of the bank's staff to the Kinmel Park Camp branch office of the National Provincial Bank, two soldiers in uniform wearing face masks and carrying rifles entered the bank. They threatened the two bank officials and forced them to hand over a sum of £90 in cash. The bank officials subsequently told the police who attended this bank robbery that they believed that the two perpetrators by their accents were Canadian soldiers from the very nearby 'Canadian dispersal camp'.

The *North Wales Chronicle* of 13 June 1919:

> Army Blankets at 1s 6d each
> Canadian soldiers in trouble at Rhyl
> At the Rhyl Police Court yesterday, Privates Patrick Martin, Milton Rentoul and Guy Patrick, Canadian soldiers from Kinmel, pleaded guilty to stealing 59 Army blankets from Kinmel Camp.
>
> Deputy Chief Constable Lindsay stated that the blankets were worth £40. It appeared the three men were in Rhyl on Monday and asked a taxi driver if he wanted to buy 400 blankets. The man refused to have anything to do with the defendants. The men then saw a Mrs Gizzi, who was in the habit of visiting the camp and collecting things. They offered to sell her 400 blankets and said they had sold a quantity to a man at 1s 6d each, and that he made a profit of £50. They explained that the blankets in the camp had been counted that day, but 400 were put on one side in the disinfecting section. Mrs Gizzi at once reported the matter to the military police, and acting on their instructions she arranged to buy the blankets. At midnight the defendants brought 59 blankets from Kinmel in a taxi cab, and were arrested. They then disclosed where 75 other blankets were placed ready for removal.
>
> The defendants pleaded for leniency as they were ready to return home. Deputy Chief Constable Lindsay stated that Rentoul had already been in prison for one month for stealing a dangerous drug and supplying it to other soldiers.

> The Bench sent each defendant to prison for two months with hard labour.

The *Sunderland Daily Echo* of Thursday, 19 June 1919, had a brief account of what appeared to be a most disturbing matter:

> At Rhyl yesterday, Private Herbert Rogers, a Canadian soldier was remanded without bail, charged with administering a drug to women at Kinmel Camp.

I have been unable to follow this story up, which certainly was something which appeared out of the ordinary – even for Kinmel Park Camp back then!

A small piece in one of the North Wales newspapers told a most sad story. It concerned the death of a Canadian soldier at Rhos-on-Sea, North Wales, when attempting to rescue a couple from the sea. Though this Canadian soldier, Lieutenant Samuel Yardley Cook was never I believe actually stationed at Kinmel Park Camp, his parents resided in Colwyn Bay, North Wales.

Samuel Yardley Cook was born on 17 June 1886, at Darlaston, Staffordshire, England. He emigrated to Canada and he and his wife Mary resided in September of 1915, in Vancouver, British Columbia, Canada. He was an analytical chemist, when on 23 September 1915 he enlisted in British Columbia with 72nd Battalion (The Seaforth Highlanders of Canada) to go overseas with the C.E.F. Samuel Yardley Cook was five feet, nine and a half inches tall, of fair complexion, blue eyes and fair hair. Having had some previous military experience with a Canadian territorial regiment, he rose up the ranks and was soon in the highly respected army rank of C.Q.M.S. (Company Quarter

Master Sergeant), regimental number 129488.

Whilst at the front in France & Belgium in October 1917, he received a shrapnel wound to his lower right forearm. Then in early November 1918, he received a GSW (gunshot wound) to his left forearm.

His war service consisted of seven months in Canada, mainly training; one year and eleven months in England, a portion of it in military hospitals; and, one year and three months in France & Belgium at the Front. On 23 November 1918, he received his commission to become an officer, a lieutenant.

On 20 May 1919, he was medically examined at the Seaford Camp prior to him returning to Canada to continue his life there. His wife Mary was staying with his parents at their home of 2, Kingsway, Prince's Drive, Colwyn Bay, (then in Denbighshire), North Wales. They went to stay with them whilst awaiting his sailing back to Canada, which proved to be a very fateful decision indeed. For on 3 July 1919, only days before he and Mary were to sail for Canada, he drowned carrying out a brave and selfless act. The West Denbighshire's coroner's report of 5 July 1919 provides us with the salient details:

> *I hereby give notice that the body of a male, aged about 33 years is lying Dead at No. 2, Kingsway, Prince's Drive, Colwyn Bay. Name: Lieut Samuel Yardley Cook. Time of death: 3.PM., 3rd July 1919.*
>
> *Deceased was a Lieut in the 72nd Seaforth Highlanders of Canada; an analytical chemist, staying along with his Wife at the above address, with his parents prior to returning to Canada.*
>
> *It appears about 3. PM this day deceased was on the promenade, Rhos-on-Sea, opposite the Rhos Abbey Hotel, when he saw a young lady and a gentleman bathing about*

20 yards from the sea wall and calling for help. The sea was rough and at high tide. Quite unfit for any bathing. He immediately went to their assistance, but failed to reach them, and disappeared. His body was subsequently found at 7.PM by Walter Chubb, Bathing Tent Proprietor, about 150 yards from where he went down.

The lady and gentleman who were in difficulties, were rescued by two other Gentlemen, Rev P. L. Adams, and his brother F. A. Adams, The Rectory, South Reddish, Stockport.

It was a very informal inquest which was held at the Colwyn Bay home of the deceased's parents, and where the body was lying. There was no form of coroner's jury and the report upon the death had been completed by Police Sergeant William A. Thomas, the station sergeant at Colwyn Bay Police Station. The official verdict was: 'Death by drowning. Mis-adventure'.

Lieutenant Samuel Yardley Cook was buried at the Colwyn Bay (Bronynant) Cemetery, grave reference B.358.

One cannot help but be saddened by this story, for he had survived being wounded twice in the hell of the Front and was about to return to his civilian life in Canada with wife Mary when his selfless act cost him his life. I just wonder if perhaps the wounds he had sustained, and the rigours of the war had taken a physical toll upon him causing him to be unable to swim as well as otherwise he may have done.

Records show that in 1920, a war gratuity was paid to the widow Mary Cook, then of 1220, Georgia Street, West, Vancouver, Canada.

Sadly, for this Cook family, a younger brother of Samuel's, Lieutenant Herbert Cook, born on 7 November 1890, had previously died in the war. Lieutenant Herbert

Cook had initially enlisted at Weyburn, Saskatchewan, Canada, in 152nd Battalion, (Weyburn-Estevan), but was killed in action, on 17 October 1917, when serving with 70th Squadron, a fighter squadron of the Royal Flying Corps.

The *Denbighshire Free Press* of 5 July 1919:

> £10 FINE FOR STEALING A BICYCLE
> CANADIAN'S LAME STORY
> At Rhyl on Tuesday, the magistrates fined a Canadian soldier £10 and 18s costs for stealing a bicycle valued at £5. The prisoner was Nicholas Landy, of Kinmel Camp. Mr R. Lake of Waen, St Asaph, rode to Rhyl on his bicycle on Friday night, and left it for a few minutes outside a shop, and it disappeared. On Saturday, P.C. Lewis, of Trefnant, found the man trying to dispose of the machine at Trefnant, and, being suspicious, detained him. The man said he had bought the bicycle from a civilian and wanted to get back to camp at once, as his time was up. P.C. Lewis said it was strange the prisoner was in a hurry to get back to camp and yet was ready to sell his bicycle, the distance to the camp being about eight miles. While detaining the man news came of the loss of the machine. Prisoner declared his innocence and said he travelled back by train from Rhyl on Friday, but two witnesses he called failed to confirm his story. He said he used the machine to go to Denbigh to see his lawyer, but did not sell the bicycle as his conscience told him that it did not belong to the man he bought it from and he meant to inform the police after seeing his lawyer. He was of good family and well brought up.

Chapter Thirteen

Sport, leisure and entertainment

The Canadian Military Athletics Association (the CMAA)

The fighting men in the First World War from North America – the Canadians, and later in the war, the Americans, had their own sports to take part in and to watch whilst they served in England, Wales and on the Western Front. Football (soccer) and rugby football were really not their sports, though they did take part in them on occasions. During the second half of the First World War the Canadian Military Athletics Association (the CMAA) arranged many of their 'favoured sports' for their Canadian soldiers, often from 1918, with American opponents.

The CMAA held its inaugural meeting at Argyll House, London, in January 1918 and invited all the Canadian military units in England to send representatives. From this meeting the CMAA declared that they would 'inaugurate Athletics and Athletic related competitions between the various Canadian units in Great Britain'. Also, to 'standardise Athletics content of all kinds.' The president of the CMAA was the Canadian, Lieutenant-General Richard Turner. Baseball, soccer (association football), boxing, athletics and wrestling being sports to the fore. The various competitions were financed by the paying of a quarterly subscription of £1 per Canadian unit to the CMAA. Payable initially by the six Canadian command areas in Britain – namely, Shorncliffe, Bramshott, Seaford, 5th Canadian Division, Bexhill and London.

The war showed no sign of ending and the Canadian

military authorities believed it was going to be a long haul, and that their soldiers needed sports, not so much for entertainment but to be played to occupy time and to help keep the men physically fit.

To provide just a few examples of what the CMAA organised in Britain in 1918 and post-war in 1919: The CMAA organised in England a proper baseball season which began on Easter Monday, 1918. When at Reading 7,000 spectators attended a match between the 'All Star Canadian and American Baseball Teams'. A few weeks later the same teams met at Swansea, South Wales, in front of 13,000 spectators. On 25 May 1918, the Canadian Pay Corps played the American Pay Corps in a baseball match. But the most famous of all Canadian military sporting events of the First World War took place on 1 July 1918, not in England or Wales, but in France. Despite the war raging not that far from them, a sports stadium was especially constructed in Paris, to which the Canadian Prime Minister Sir Robert Borden, Canadian Corps Commander Sir Arthur Currie, other dignitaries and a crowd of some 70,000 flocked to watch a variety of highly competitive sports. Here before them was an afternoon of running races, wrestling, boxing, all capped off with a baseball match between 'All Star' teams representing the 1st and 3rd Canadian Divisions.

Baseball

The baseball season in Britain and on the Western Front during 1918 for the Canadian, and for the more recently arrived American soldiers had three great impediments to contend with. The least of which was an acute shortage of baseballs. Much greater impediments were the Spanish Flu pandemic and the German Spring Offensive of 1918, which nearly proved to be a critical success for the Germans.

When the war ended and the Canadians were being pulled out from the Western Front, the number of baseball matches declined as Canadian soldiers were slowly being returned to their homeland.

At Kinmel Park Camp in early March 1919, a baseball sub-committee was formed under the auspices of the Canadian Military Athletics Association (the CMAA) and a proper baseball league structure was set-up within this vast camp which now at any one time held around a figure of 17,400 Canadian soldiers. At Kinmel Park Camp baseball diamonds were constructed and medals for awarding to participants were commissioned ready for Easter Monday 1919. The vast numbers of Canadian soldiers 'passing through' the camp would now be able to take part in properly organised and equipped baseball matches. As was the case at other camps such as at Seaford in East Sussex, England, also 'home' to thousands of Canadian soldiers. This camp was being wound up and the last baseball league game took place there on 5 June 1919, as part of a special 'Peace Day Sporting Gala'.

But generally post-Armistice, baseball and other athletic sports were increasingly being seen by the Canadian military authorities as a means of keeping the men fit, healthy, and even more importantly occupied! Most of these Canadian soldiers were hardened battle veterans, fighting men no longer keen to submit to the daily routine of drills and route marches. So, it was no wonder that in March 1919, a really concerted effort was made to get all the Canadian units still in Britain to join the CMAA and get actively involved.

The Kinmel Park Canadian Athletics Association organised a series of baseball games for the thousands of C.E.F men passing through the camp before being shipped back home. It is said that: *Canada's First World War baseball story began on the Salisbury Plain, England, in 1914, and ended at Kinmel Park Camp, North Wales, in the Summer of 1919*. It was also said: *For many Canadian soldiers their last act as a soldier was when they stepped up to the plate in a military baseball game at Kinmel Park Camp.*

The War Diary for M.D. 3 Wing at Kinmel Park Camp for 2 March 1919 includes this: *The Officer's Indoor Baseball Team of this wing today defeated Officers representing M.D. 13 in a game in which the heavy hitting of Major McCormack featured.*

The War Diary entry for M. D. 10 Wing for 6 March 1919, had this:

Interesting indoor-baseball match M. D. 10 vs M. D. 6 resulted in a win for M. D. 10 by a score of 11-5.

The War Diary for M.D. 3 Wing at Kinmel Park Camp for 7 March 1919 recorded: *The Indoor Baseball Game scheduled to take place today between the officers of this wing and those of M.D. 13 is postponed on account of rain.* I rather suspect the real reason for cancelling this 'indoor event' because of rain was that only a couple of days earlier mayhem had taken place at the camp with the riots/disturbances of 4/5 March. Some M. D. Wings at the camp were affected more seriously than others.

There was a concerted effort in late 1918, and into 1919, by the American and Canadian soldiers stationed in Britain to try to establish baseball as a leading sport in Britain, most particularly in England and Wales.

Whilst many of the baseball games held in Europe by the Canadian and American soldiers were primarily to entertain and to aid fitness, a number of so called 'exhibition baseball games' also took place, including one at Aberystwyth, Wales, in May of 1919, which was advertised in the *Cambrian News* and *Merionethshire Standard* edition of 9 May 1919:

> BASEBALL
> The American National Game
> Two teams of American Students at the Aberystwyth University will give an Exhibition Baseball Match on The Vicarage Field,
> On Saturday, 10th May
> Game called 2.30. ADMISSION FREE

Also, so called 'baseball display games' were held to which the general public as well as serving military personnel were invited to attend. The *North Wales Chronicle* of 13 June 1919 had this:

> BASEBALL DISPLAY
> Teams of Canadian soldiers from Kinmel Camp engaged in a baseball match on Bank Holiday, on the football ground of Rydal Mount School, lent for the occasion. Several-hundred people watched the play, but the finer points of the American national game where unappreciated as far as the majority were concerned. It would have been well if leaflets of instructions on the rules could have been distributed. As it was, people left the ground confident that baseball was only 'glorified rounders'!

Football

The War Diary of M. D. 10 Wing has this entry for 4 March 1919:

Football match M. D. 10 vs M. D. 7. Results in win by M. D. 10 – 8 goals to NIL.

The *North Wales Chronicle* edition of 25 April 1919:

> Caernarfon News
> Football – The local team played the Canadians from Kinmel Park at The Oval on Saturday and defeated them by nine goals to one.

Denbighshire Free Press of 26 April 1919:

> FOOTBALL MATCH
> CANADIANS v Denbigh
> A grand victory football match was witnessed on a field near Captain Bridge, which was kindly lent for the occasion by Messrs Jones and Wynne, between Denbigh Town and a team of Canadians from Kinmel Camp, on Good Friday. The teams were lined up and the kick off was taken promptly at 3 o'clock. There were several of the old town players in the Denbigh team. The Canadians at once worked down the field towards the Denbigh goal, and the custodian Sam Griffiths had a busy time of it but managed with his old style to keep out the ball every time. After a pressing five minutes for the Denbigh custodian, the play returned to midfield, and a ding-dong game was witnessed for some time, when the Canadian forwards broke away and swept down the field and managed to net the ball after twenty minutes play. In about ten minutes, Denbigh equalised through Glyn Thomas (Henllan), who shot with a beauty leaving the Canadian custodian with no chance whatever. Half-time was reached with the score even; Denbigh 1; Canadians 1.

> Commencing the second half, Denbigh attacked the Canadian's goal with renewed vigour, but the Canadian's sound defence kept them out every time. Denbigh gained a penalty, but failed to score. The play was now of a very even nature, and remained so until ten minutes from time, when there was a melee in the Denbigh goalmouth and the Canadians managed to score the winning goal. Evans, the left back did some admirable work and cleared again and again. Final score; Canadians 2; Denbigh1.

A further article in the same edition:

> FOOTBALL
> Canadians V Denbigh.
> Another football match will be held at Denbigh tomorrow (Saturday) in field as on Good Friday, when Denbigh will meet a team of Canadians from Kinmel Park. Kick off at 3 o'clock.

Entertainment

The *North Wales Chronicle* had this in their 24 January 1919 edition:

> The Bangor Ladies Choir visited Kinmel Park Camp yesterday week to entertain the Canadian Troops stationed there. They had a cordial reception and every item on the programme was encored. The soloists were Mrs Lowe, Miss Gladys Owen, Miss Eva Jones and Miss Jennie Edwards. Duets were sung by Mrs Dobbs and Mrs Lowe, and by Misses Jones and Amy Owen. Among some of the selections sung were 'Sleep, gentle lady': and 'Happy Miller'. The choir were met by a party of soldiers at Abergele Station and were entertained to tea at the

> Cambrian Hotel, afterwards proceeding by motor to Kinmel Park.

The *Denbighshire Free Press* newspaper, North Wales, reported in their 19 March 1919 edition of 'A Brilliant Programme' of entertainment to be had two days hence, on Easter Saturday, at the Rhyl Pavilion. This day was the start of the 'Summer Season' in Rhyl and Miss Margaret Cooper, a prominent it was said entertainer at the piano, would appear with her 'Party of entertainers'. Then the following day, Easter Sunday it stated: *The services have been secured of the 3rd Canadian Reserve Military Band. This band was exceedingly popular in Folkestone last season, and they have arranged a capital programme, both for the concert in the Gardens in the afternoon and for the great concert in the Pavilion in the evening, when Mr Ben Davies the world-famous tenor, will be the vocalist.*

The article alluded to the fact that bookings had been very strong for the Easter weekend at the Rhyl Pavilion. There is no doubt that many of the audience for these Easter Weekend concerts would have been Canadian soldiers and perhaps also some Canadian nursing sisters from Kinmel Park Camp, travelling there and back on the KCR, the Kinmel Camp Railway.

Chapter Fourteen

Canadian War Brides

Close to 80% of the C.E.F for overseas service, were single men on their enlistment. When going on furlough (leave) from the Front or military training; receiving hospital treatment or convalescing in England and Wales, many Canadian soldiers met and subsequently married British women. Nothing surprising in that perhaps, but what I suggest was surprising is that they did so in such great numbers.

It is estimated that between July 1917 and November 1918, around 17,000 Canadian soldiers' dependants returned to Canada. These soldiers' dependants, their wives and children did not receive free transportation, but did pay a reduced fare. Many of these had already been residing in Canada, but had come over to Britain, being British born themselves, to either be nearer to their Canadian soldier husbands or to be with their war wounded husbands who were in British hospitals or convalescent homes.

Post-Armistice and up to the end of 1919, an estimated 37,748 Canadian soldiers' dependants travelled from Britain to various parts of Canada. Many of these were 'Canadian War Brides', women who had never before set foot on Canadian soil. These 'War Brides' in late 1919, dependants of Canadian soldiers, could claim reimbursement from the Canadian Authorities for the cost of their passage to Canada. The reimbursement was based on the 3rd class fare – often called steerage.

There are no official figures that I have found for the total number of British women who married Canadian soldiers in Britain, then went out to Canada permanently to forge new lives for themselves in the growing 'Dominion of Canada'.

Many of the 'Canadian War Brides' of Canadian soldiers, some with children, who had already lived in Canada, then returned to Canada on the same troop ships as their soldier husbands. These ships were known as 'dependant's ships.' But despite being husbands and wives they were not permitted to be berthed in the same part of the ship. But it was rather nice that 'couples', in many cases along with their children could meet up on the ship's deck in the mornings, spend the day together, even taking their meals together. In the evenings it was said, 'weather permitting', they would stroll along the deck together, 'many a wartime romance was rekindled' with the couples dancing together on 'Deck C', before their disembarkation in Canada.

These British women, 'Canadian War Brides' crossed the Atlantic to Canada on a number of ships including: The Corsican; Grampian; Megantic; Melita; Metagama; Scandinavian; and Tunisian. These ships regarded as smaller transport ships could carry around 2,000 passengers, whilst the larger of the transport ships such as the Olympic, the sister-ship of the ill-fated Titanic, could carry over 5,000 passengers, or almost 6,000 soldiers. Shipping transport on the Atlantic route post-Armistice was at a premium and a 'War Bride' could be given a berth on any ship that had a space for her.

The voyage from Britain across the Atlantic Ocean to Canada generally took from seven to ten days, varying, depending on which British ports and which Canadian ports were used. Many of the Canadian troop ships left from Liverpool Port – the Prince's Landing Stage. It was the use of Liverpool Port and its location in relation to Canada which attracted the Canadian authorities to using Kinmel Park Camp as a staging/transit camp for thousands of Canadian soldiers awaiting their repatriation to their homeland. However, due to dock strikes and other factors in 1919, other British ports such as Glasgow and Southampton were also utilised. Especially during the Winter months these transport ships would dock at two eastern ports of Canada – namely, Halifax, Nova Scotia and Saint John, New Brunswick. When the mighty St Lawrence River thawed in around late April, these ships could again use the Port of Quebec, an inland port located in the city of Quebec, the oldest port in Canada.

The wives and children on these Atlantic voyages to Canada post-Armistice had two main immediate concerns. One was more of an unwelcome irritant – sea sickness – never to be underestimated. The Atlantic Ocean was rarely calm and most passengers would suffer sea sickness, but some suffered sea sickness for the entire voyage. Those who travelled 3rd class (steerage) had less opportunity to move around, were crowded and had less facilities, making sea sickness more of a problem.

The second concern was a far more serious one, for during the Winter of 1918 and Spring 1919, the deadly influenza epidemic known as 'Spanish Flu' was at its zenith, taking a terrible toll worldwide. Medical officials did check passengers at ports of embarkation such as Liverpool for 'obvious signs' of 'Spanish Flu', but it was no more than a cursory examination due to the sheer volume of passengers involved, both military and non-military.

The *Abergavenny Chronicle* of 13 December 1918 had this:

> 1,000 MARRIAGES A MONTH
> There were animated scenes at Liverpool on the occasion of the departure of the liner 'Minnedosa' for St John, New Brunswick. Every berth was occupied by returning Canadian soldiers, and women and children.

The latter the advance guard of some 50,000 women and children who are going to Canada during the next few months. Many of the women have never seen Canada, having married their husbands in this country. In fact, it is said that Canadian soldiers are steadily marrying British girls at the rate of 1,000 a month.

Canadian soldiers who were at Kinmel Park Camp, who married British Women

John Robert Lunny

The *Denbighshire Free Press* edition of 16 November 1918, reported upon a military wedding at Bodelwyddan:

> MARRIAGE
> On Saturday, at Bodelwyddan Marble Church, a very pretty but quiet wedding took place, the contracting parties being Sergeant J. R. Lumley, of the Canadian Training School, Bexhill-on-Sea, and Miss Helen Elizabeth May West, Battersea, London. The best man was Staff Sergeant T. Swain, Canadian Postal Corps and the bridesmaid was Miss Ruby Hamlin, Blodwen Cottage, St Asaph. This is the first Canadian soldier's wedding within the precincts of this beautiful church. The officiating clergyman was the Reverend J. H. Hope, M.A., vicar. The happy couple were the recipients of many congratulations and the best wishes for a long life of happiness. As the wedding party were leaving the church the Guards marched passed and many cheers and hurrahs were given to the bridal pair. They were also the recipients of numerous presents.

By this date, the 'Marble Church' at Bodelwyddan had already held burial services and burials in the churchyard for

Canadian soldiers from the nearby Kinmel Park Camp. This was a much happier event of course.

The Canadian soldier who had married was in fact John Robert Lunny (not Lumley), born on 18 June 1885, at Belturbet, County Fermanagh, Ireland. He had emigrated to Canada, and he attested for military service at Winnipeg, Manitoba, Canada, on 6 April 1916. On his attestation papers he gave his address as being c/o The Commercial Hotel, Winnipeg, and his occupation as being a fireman. He stated that he had previous 'military experience' having been at a naval training school for four years. He gave his next of kin as being his mother, Lizzie Lunny of Killymachen, County Fermanagh. John Robert Lunny was of dark complexion, dark eyes, dark hair and six feet tall. During his standard medical at Kinmel Park Camp it was noted that he had two tattoos on his body – one an unfurled Union Jack and the other his initials J.R.L. At Kinmel Park Camp he was Sergeant Lunny regimental number 871697.

Lionel John Middleton

It was announced in the *Denbighshire Free Press* of 8 March 1919, in their 'St Asaph News' column that a marriage had taken place the previous Saturday, St David's Day, at St Asaph Parish Church, between Private Lionel Myddleton, one of the Canadians who was stationed at Kinmel Park Camp, and Miss Muriel Tomlinson, the seventh daughter of Mr and Mrs William Tomlinson of 2, May Terrace, St Asaph. The best man was Sergeant Smith of the Canadians, and the bridesmaid was Miss Gertrude Tomlinson, a sister of the bride. The bride 'charmingly dressed' was given away by her father and the ceremony was performed by the Reverend D. J. Williams. A reception afterwards was held at the bride's home, and included the bride's mother, father, family and friends. Also, in attendance were Sergeants Dow and Chapel, Corporal Heggie, and several other Canadian soldiers from the nearby Kinmel Park Camp. The wedding presents were said to have been 'both numerous and costly', and the happy couple were the recipients of numerous congratulatory messages for their future happiness.

The bridegroom was in fact Private Lionel John Middleton, who was born on 16 October 1897, at Ancaster, Ontario, and was a mason by occupation, a son of contractor John Middleton, who had been born at Kirkcudbright, Scotland. Private Lionel John Middleton enlisted in the C.E.F at Hamilton, Ontario, on 28 July 1915, described as five feet, seven inches tall, of dark complexion, with brown eyes and brown hair. He served at the Front in France & Flanders with 4th Battalion (Central Ontario), regimental number 141508. In action on 5 August 1916, he suffered a slight gunshot wound to his right hand. Then on 13 December 1917, he was admitted via field ambulance to a casualty clearing station suffering from 'shell gas poison and gas sores', as it was put on his military record.

He arrived at Kinmel Park Camp in early January 1919, and was placed on M.D. 2 Wing. However, when he and Muriel Tomlinson married on 1 March 1919, he gave his address as 'Kinmel Park Camp Hospital'.

The couple post-war went to live in Canada, a far cry for wife Muriel from the small city of St Asaph in North Wales, to the rugged area of Ancaster, located on the Niagara Escarpment. They had at least three children together, two boys and one girl. By the early 1940's or possibly before, they were living at West Seneca, Erie County, New York, the United States. Muriel Middleton, nee Tomlinson, died on 11 April 1944, at Lincoln, Ontario, aged forty-seven. In 1954, Lionel John Middleton became a naturalised citizen of the United States. He died in February 1975, at Buffalo, New York State, the United States, aged seventy-seven.

Douglas Herman McPherson

The *Denbighshire Free Press* of 10 May 1919:

> MILITARY WEDDING
>
> A very pretty, but quiet wedding was solemnised at St Mary's Church, Denbigh, on Wednesday. The contracting parties being Miss Florence Mary Evans, third daughter of Mr and Mrs T. Parry Evans, Bryn Tegid, Townsend, Denbigh, and Private D. H. McPhearson, 4th C.M.R., Kinmel Camp, Abergele, whose home is at Aylmer, Ontario, Canada. The bride was given away by her father, and attended as bridesmaid by her sister, Miss Maria Evans. Private Alec McDicken, 13th Canadians, Kinmel Park, is a native of Coleman, Alberta, Canada, acted as best man. Canon Redfern officiated. After the ceremony, the party motored to the bride's home, where the wedding breakfast was served. Mr and Mrs McPhearson will sail for Canada next month and will do so with hearty good wishes of numerous friends.

Florence McPherson, nee Evans

The Canadian soldier who married here was in fact Douglas Herman McPherson (not McPhearson), who was born in Elgin

County, Ontario, Canada, on 16 June 1897. Prior to his military service in the First World War he was a shoemaker, residing with his mother, Lottie McPherson at Aylmer, Ontario. Douglas Herman McPherson enlisted with 91st Battalion, C.E.F, regimental number 190168. In France & Flanders at the Front, he served with 4th Canadian Mounted Rifles, getting trench foot in 1916, and in January 1917 he was according to his military records, 'dangerously ill with pneumonia'. Happily, he recovered and survived the trenches.

The married couple went to live, at least for a time, at 34, Hiawatha Street, St Thomas, Ontario, Canada.

The bride was born in 1894, and her father was Thomas Parry Evans, a tailor, who on the 1911 Census was shown as residing at 6, Albert Terrace, Vron, Denbigh.

A lady I have known for many years, Margaret Etoile Parry from Denbigh, is a granddaughter of Douglas and Florence McPherson. She informs me that sadly this 'Canadian War Bride' story did not ultimately have a happy ending. Margaret's mother, Doris Lottie McPherson, was born in St Thomas, Aylmer, Ontario, on 18 February 1920, to Douglas and Florence, the only child born to them. However, two years later, sometime in 1922, Florence returned to Wales with the now two-year-old Doris to visit her family, without husband Douglas. Florence was very homesick and she and Doris did not return to Canada, neither ever seeing Douglas again. The couple were divorced a few years later, with Douglas McPherson re-marrying and having four children with his second wife. Florence McPherson, nee Evans never re-married herself, and was a professional nurse for all of her working life. She died in Denbigh, North Wales, on 27 January 1989, aged ninety-four.

Douglas McPherson kept in touch with his daughter

Doris via letters until she was six. Douglas McPherson became known as a carver of wood, especially diamond willow, which he turned into 'works of art'. He also made fine walking canes (sticks). He died at Great Falls, Montana, the United States, on 24 July 1985, aged eighty-seven. A few years ago, the Welsh and Canadian sides of Douglas and Florence's families had a get-together in Canada, and keep in touch from time-to-time.

British newspapers the length and breadth of the country reported upon British women marrying Canadian soldiers and other Canadians, such as Canadian farmers, then going back with them to live permanently in Canada. A few examples of these:

The Wigston Advertiser, Cumberland, edition of 11 January 1919, reported this:

> A large number of Scottish girls have left Glasgow for Canada to marry Canadian farmers.

The *Western Times*, Devon, edition of 3 February 1919:

> War Brides accompanying their husbands to Canada – 250, with 200 children sailed from Liverpool on the S.S. Tunisian.

The Hastings & St Leonards-on-Sea Observer, edition of 29 March 1919:

> The War Brides were given a warm reception after landing here. The Dominion of Canada has opened wide her gates to the young wives of her heroes, who fought for freedom and right.

Dundee Evening Telegraph, edition of 21 April 1919:

> Twenty-thousand Canadians married British wives during the war, and they are still marrying in their hundreds. Buxton is the clearing station for the married soldiers.

Annette Fulford from Maple Ridge, British Columbia, a Canadian genealogist, and an authority on 'Canadian War Brides' of the First World War says that over 35,000 European women travelled over to Canada as 'War Brides' following the Armistice. The majority of these were British women, but a number of them were French or Belgian.

I am indebted to her for her research work, in particular for the 'War Bride' marriages relating to the Port Haney/Maple Ridge area, British Columbia, which I have followed up with my own research. But most of all for this account of her own grandmother:

Grace Clark, nee Gibson and Hugh Clark

A personal account by Annette Fulford:

Grace Clark was one of the many British city girls who married a Canadian soldier from a rural farming community, and embarked upon a completely different way of life.

My grandmother, Grace Gibson (born 1898 – died 1968,) met Canadian soldier Hugh Clark, who was stationed at the Ripon Military Camp in North Yorkshire, early in 1919. Grace was a city girl from Sheffield, England. Hugh met Grace's younger sister first, but fell in love with Grace when he visited their family home for a meal.

Hugh Clark, a farmer from Saskatchewan, was drafted into the C.E.F in May 1918, and travelled to England in August of that year. He got caught in the Spanish Flu pandemic at Bramshott camp in October 1918, and by the time he recovered,

Hugh and Grace Clark in Canada

the war was over. He never saw action at the Front, but at Canadian military camps in England he would entertain his fellow troops by taking part in exhibition boxing bouts.

Grace Gibson was born in Clydebank, Scotland, in 1898, and was the eldest child of Francis Oliver Gibson and Jane McCalman. The family moved to Belfast, shortly after her birth where Grace's three siblings were born, two brothers and one sister. Later the family moved to Sheffield, England, where her father worked in the iron industry as an iron founder.

Hugh and Grace were married with the required permission from the Canadian military on 15 April 1919, at Sheffield, England, and came to Canada in September of that year on board the R.M.S. Melita, a Canadian Pacific Railway ship. While on her journey to Canada she wrote a letter to her parents back in England that chronicles her maiden voyage on a troopship carrying returning Canadian soldiers, military dependents and civilians in 1919.

Grace found herself living in a rural community where the mode of transportation was horse and buggy, and cooking on a wood stove was common. For the first four years of her marriage she lived with her husband and his parents in a small house on

Hugh and Grace Clark (Wedding Photo)

a farm in Southern Saskatchewan. Grace, a city girl from a quite affluent middle-class family in England, had a lot to learn about living on a farm. She told her daughter later in life, 'I had hardly seen a cow before, let alone milk one.' She lived without the aid of basic amenities such as electricity, running water or an indoor bathroom for the first half of her marriage. It wasn't until the family moved to Langley, British Columbia in 1942, that life became easier when they purchased a house with these necessities.

Despite the lack of amenities, she learned how to run a farm household successfully and was able to produce enough food for the family for each year. She kept three gardens and became proficient at preserving what she grew.

Grace raised four children who all went on to lead productive lives in Canada. Grace and Hugh also had 18 grandchildren, 23 great-grandchildren and 13 great-great-grandchildren. She supported her local community through her many volunteer activities and made many life-long friends during her lifetime here. Grace died in 1968, having lived in Canada for a total of 49 years.

One of Hugh's cousins, later reflected on meeting Grace that: 'She was a very strong, courageous woman. Beautiful and lovely'.

Annette Fulford also provides this:

The First World War brides met their Canadian soldiers at local churches, social events such as dances, and while a soldier was in hospital recovering from his wounds, or on leave in Britain. Peggy Lewis met and married her school friend's older brother Alfred Holmes when he returned to England from Canada with the C.E.F. Whilst Dorothy Allard worked as a VAD, voluntary aid detachment nurse, when she met her future husband, the British born now Canadian soldier, Edward Weir Abraham. Annie Farthing was one day 'dressing' a millinery shop window in London, when a soldier in uniform standing outside smiled and waved at her. Annie smiled and waved back, so he boldly entered the shop and duly introduced himself as Melvin Aldis Steer, a Canadian soldier. This was the beginning of a two year 'courtship' that culminated in their marriage in 1920, at Moose Jaw, Saskatchewan.

Whilst Canadian Sapper Walter Brindle wrote home about his life while overseas, and said the following about England: 'It was not all work, however. We had our evenings and weekends, when we were invited to homes, churches, entertainments and concerts, and some of our men found their way to the beauty spots of nature, which are very plentiful around here, with members of the fair sex, and there told them the story that never grows old, and some of these soldiers now that the war is over, are showing the same ladies the beauties of our fair Canada'.

After the war ended, Canadian soldiers at demobilization camps in England had more free time to meet young women in Britain. If the soldiers wanted to take advantage of the free transportation for their wives, they had to submit the paperwork and wait for an available ship to Canada. Consequently, the average courtship was shortened because they had no idea when they would be shipped back home. My own grandparents married within three months of meeting.

Canadian soldiers, married in England, France or Belgium, were sent to Buxton Camp in Derbyshire, England, to await their repatriation after the war. Some war brides were sent to a hostel in Buxton to meet up with their husband's shortly before being shipped home. However, this proved to be costly, so they changed it so that the British war brides arrived at Liverpool on the day of the sailing and they met their husbands on-board. This created a few anxious moments until they were reunited.

The **Melvin Aldis Steer** referred to in the above piece by Annette Fulford was born at Markdale, Ontario, Canada, on 29 March 1897, but on enlistment was residing at Gouverneur, Saskatchewan. He enlisted in the C.E.F at Moose Jaw, Saskatchewan, being described as five feet, eight inches tall, of dark complexion, with brown eyes and black hair. He arrived in England on 18 April 1917, aboard the S.S. Northland, and served in France & Flanders as Private Steer, regimental number 1009862, with 46th Battalion (South Saskatchewan). In France he received a shrapnel wound to the right shoulder which required his hospitalisation in England, followed by some weeks of convalescence. It was perhaps during the latter that he had his 'chance meeting' with Annie Farthing, followed by their two year 'courtship' and subsequent marriage in 1920, at Moose Jaw, Saskatchewan. But getting home for Melvin after being at Kinmel Park Camp for a few weeks did not 'prove to be plain sailing'. For during the voyage back to Canada on the impressive RMS Empress of Britain, he had a nasty fall on some steps of a stairway of the ship, as a result of which he had contusions to his back and head. He was then hospitalised in Halifax, Nova Scotia, for thirty-three days. An example of 'the course of true love never did run smooth', as the great bard once wrote.

Edwin Marklin Kendrick, who was also at Kinmel Park Camp. Another soldier from Port Haney (also known as Haney), who married a British 'War Bride' was Edwin Marklin Kendrick. He enlisted in 29th Battalion of the C.E.F on 12 November 1914, at Vancouver. Edwin served on the Western Front and met and married Annie Littleworth in England in 1917. The couple travelled to Canada on the S.S. Melita in May of 1919.

On his attestation papers Edwin Marklin Kendrick is shown as having been born at Haney, Maple Ridge, British Columbia, on 10 October 1894. He gave his next of kin as being his mother Agnes Kendrick of Haney, Maple Ridge. His Kendrick family were of Irish descent. He was a teamster by occupation and received the regimental number of 75503. He was just short of six feet tall, with a fair complexion, grey eyes and dark brown hair, and Presbyterian by religion. Following some military training in Canada, Private Kendrick sailed to England from Canada with his unit on 20 May 1915. Following further military training and kitting out in England, on 7 December 1915 he was at the Front in France & Flanders with 29th Battalion (Vancouver), of the C.E.F, an infantry battalion known during the First World War as 'Tobin's Tigers', as their first commander was Lieutenant-Colonel H. S. Tobin.

On 8 July 1916, at St Eloi, Private Kendrick sustained a GSW (gunshot wound) to his left leg – '*wound by bullet, severe*', his medical records state. During his convalescence in the London area, he met an English woman, Annie Littleworth who was born at Yiewsley, Hillingdon, London. On the 1911 Census, Annie Littleworth was a scullery maid at 23-25 Great Cumberland Place, Marleybone, London, in the large household of Vice-Admiral Sir George Warrender.

Edwin and Annie had a son together they named Jack Edwin Kendrick, who was born in the London area on 29

June 1917. On 2 March 1918, Private Kendrick was granted permission to marry Annie Littleworth, which he did a few days later. It was then back to the trenches at the Front in France & Flanders for him with 29th Battalion. On 3 April 1919, he was for a short period of time at Kinmel Park Camp on M. D. 2 Wing. On 3 May 1919, he embarked at Liverpool on the S.S. Melita, disembarking at Quebec Port on 12 May 1919.

Annie Kendrick, nee Littleworth died on 8 October 1937, at Nanaimo, Vancouver Island, British Columbia, aged forty-nine. Edwin Marklin Kendrick died at the Shaughnessy Hospital, Vancouver, British Columbia, on 28 January 1967, aged seventy-two.

The **Edward Weir Abraham** mentioned in Annette Fulford's last piece was born on 25 September 1887, at Risby, Suffolk, England, the son of a reverend. He was living in Canada, when on 10 September 1914, early in the war, he enlisted in the C.E.F at Valcartier, Quebec. He was five feet, nine and a half inches tall, of fair complexion, blue eyes and brown hair. He gave his next of kin as residing on Vargas Island, Tofino, British Columbia. He served for a time in France with 7th Battalion (British Columbia), regimental number 16739, was wounded in France & Flanders, and was shipped back to hospital in England, which is where no doubt he met his future wife, as Dorothy Allard was a VAD, voluntary aid detachment nurse. Edward Weir Abraham was granted a commission and made a second lieutenant in the Cheshire Regiment. He and Dorothy married in the Summer of 1917, in the Oswestry area of Shropshire, England.

On 4 May 1954, aboard 'The Empress of Scotland', Edward Weir Abraham and Dorothy Evelyn Abraham, nee Allard, returned to Britain as tourists, arriving at Liverpool from Montreal. Edward Weir Abraham died on 7 February

1981, at Victoria, British Columbia, aged ninety-three. Whilst wife, Dorothy, who was born in 1894, died in 1990, aged ninety-five.

When Edward died, the couple had been married for over sixty-three years – not bad for a 'whirlwind wartime romance'! They are buried together in the Ross Bay Cemetery, Victoria, British Columbia.

Vaughan Haliburton Webber, a long-term prisoner of war, was born on 28 September 1887, at Port Haney, Maple Ridge, British Columbia, Canada. He enlisted early in the war at the Valcartier Camp, Quebec, Canada, on 23 September 1914, and received the regimental number of 17180. He was described as being five feet, eleven inches tall, of fair complexion, brown hair and brown eyes. He was by religion Church of England and his occupation was a steam engineer. He gave his next of kin as his father, David C. Webber of Port Haney. Private Vaughan Haliburton Webber, regimental number 17180 sailed with his battalion, 7th Battalion (1st British Columbia) from Quebec, aboard the S.S. Virginian, arriving in England on 14 October 1914. The battalion sailed with 49 officers and 1083 men (other ranks). Private Webber was quite soon at the Front in France & Flanders with his battalion.

On 24 April 1915, on the first day of The Battle of St Julien (24 April to 4 May 1915), Private Vaughan Webber was taken prisoner by their German enemy. This battle was the second of four battles in the Ypres area, which are referred to as being part of The Second Battle of Ypres. These four separate battles heralded the German's first use on a large scale on the Western Front of chemical weapons – here it was chlorine gas, the even viler mustard gas was to follow later. Initially Private Vaughan Webber was reported as 'missing in action'. At that time, it was believed that he was most probably 'a goner', lying dead somewhere on the battlefield. Then a message came from the Germans that Private Vaughan Webber was now a prisoner of war. I understand that he was held for at least a large portion of the time at the Giessen Allied Prisoner of War Camp, Giessen, Hesse, Germany. Giessen is in central Germany and north of Frankfurt. This camp was described by one who was a prisoner of war there as, 'well ordered and sanitary'. Here Canadian, British, French and other Allied soldiers were held. In 1918 the belligerents in the war agreed that those prisoners of war who had been incarcerated for a long time would go to 'neutral Holland', The Hague, where they would be interned and receive a 'kinder form of wartime imprisonment'. Private Webber was one of those to benefit from this. Post-Armistice on 18 November 1918, he was 'safely' in England at a military camp and receiving treatment for what for him personally had been a terrible three and a half years of being a POW, and latterly an internee. Following the Armistice and his being freed, he was sent to England to recuperate from what had been a difficult ordeal. Whilst recuperating he met Agnes Dukes and they married in England, before travelling over to Canada. His bride Agnes Dukes was Agnes Julia Dukes, born in 1881, to Job Charles Dukes, an electrician's labourer, and Mary Ann Dukes, nee Gibson. This Dukes family came from Watford.

Vaughan Webber returned to Canada aboard the S.S. Metagama, disembarking at Quebec Port on 12 August 1919.

A few Maple Ridge, British Columbia born soldiers returned home with new brides. *The British Columbian* newspaper reported that: *Vaughan Webber of Haney, who left with the first contingent of the C.E.F in 1914, spent most of the war as a prisoner of war in a prison camp.*

Ernest Beckham – born in England
Ernest Beckham was actually British born, and as a single man went to Canada to make a new life for himself, having been born at Battersea, London, on 28 December 1881, to James Beckham a master tailor, and, wife, Eliza Beckham, nee Flanders. This Beckham family lived for many years at 101, High Street, Battersea, London.

War ensued, and when residing in New Westminster, British Columbia, he enlisted in the C.E.F in January 1916, at Vancouver, British Columbia, to return to Europe to fight. He did survive the war, but he was to return to Canada as 'an invalid'. On his attestation papers he was described as being just short of five feet, six inches tall, of dark complexion, brown eyes and black hair. He was a labourer and named his next of kin as his sister, Mrs Florence Parkes of Whonnock, Maple Ridge, British Columbia.

He was now Private Ernest Beckham, regimental number 645600, and he arrived in England on 20 November 1916, aboard the gigantic White Star transatlantic cruise liner, RMS Olympic. The RMS Olympic was the sister ship of the ill-fated Titanic, and both were built at the Harland and Wolff Shipyard, Belfast. The Olympic was requisitioned for use as a troopship and she underwent 'alterations' to say the least, from her peacetime fittings and appearance. She was painted grey, had her many portholes blocked, and was fitted with 12 pounder guns and 4.7 inch-ones. She could carry comfortably as a troopship up to an amazing 6,000 troops for the crossing of the Atlantic, and is credited with having carried more Canadian troops back and forth over the Atlantic during the First World War than any other ship, and earned the sobriquet, 'The Old Reliable'. Another 'claim to wartime fame' one might say was when on 12 May 1918, the RMS Olympic was under torpedo attack from the German U-Boat, the U-103, under the command of Kapitanleutnant Claus Rucker. This U-Boat on its five previous patrols had sunk seven British ships, damaged one British ship, and sunk one French ship, causing a total loss of life of approximately one hundred crew on these ships. The RMS Olympic purposely rammed the attacking U-103 and sank it, with the loss of some ten of its crew, with the remaining thirty surviving. Sadly, after continuing as a cruise liner post-First World War, she was in 1935 scrapped, with her fine interior fittings auctioned off.

Private Ernest Beckham fought with 7th Battalion (1st British Columbia) in France & Flanders, and on 9 April 1917, at Vimy Ridge, he received a gunshot wound to the lobe of his left ear. However, much worse was to come for him, for on 10 November 1917, at the now 'infamous' Passchendaele, during The Battle of Passchendaele (31 July – 10 November 1917), he was very seriously wounded. A rifle bullet had entered his head on the right side, travelled through his right eye and had emerged below and behind his left eye. It resulted in him having to have his right eye removed and it was stated by a doctor who was treating him: *Right eye removed. Left, counts fingers at one yard with head turned. This man to all intents and purposes is blind and he wishes to go to St Dunstan's as soon as possible.* Private Beckham did indeed go for a short time to the St Dunstan's Hospital for the Blind. In January 1918, he also was to suffer from trench fever, a major medical problem especially for those fighting in the trenches of the First World War. It was a highly contagious, body louse transmitted, rickettsial, infectious disease.

Whilst in England convalescing, he married in late 1918 Hannah Downing, who travelled to Canada on the S.S. Melita in September of 1919, with their ten-month-old daughter Joan to join him. Hannah was fortunate that she made the journey to Canada in an intermediate class cabin rather than the steerage, third class, most 'War Brides' had to endure. Steerage was the overcrowded, below deck section of a ship which lacked to say the least, the proper amenities for a mother with a baby.

Hannah Downing was born on 17 September 1880, at Dudley, then in Worcestershire, England, to Thomas Downing, a bricklayer and, wife, Eliza Downing, nee Rogers. This Downing family resided for a number of years at 41, Churchill Road, Willesden Green, Cricklewood, London. Prior to her marriage, Hannah was a dressmaker by occupation. I have found that Ernest, Hannah and daughter Joan, over the inter-war years, on at least two occasions travelled over to England to visit her Downing family, including one in 1924, when Ernest described himself as being a pensioner. On the 1939 War Register, Ernest, Hannah and daughter Joan are residing back in England at 18, Ivanhoe Drive, Harrow, Middlesex. Ernest is described as being 'retired on pension', Hannah as a housewife and daughter Joan as a shorthand typist, and also part of an ARP first aid section.

Hannah Downing died on 28 September 1959, at Prince George, British Columbia, aged seventy-eight, most probably when on an extended visit to daughter Joan who was married and living permanently in British Columbia, Canada.

Ernest Beckham died whilst at St Dunstan's, Ovingdean, Brighton, England, on 16 November 1960, aged seventy-nine. His home address was 14, Lenham Road West, Brighton. St Dunstan's, now called 'Blind Veterans UK' opened their wonderful centre at Ovingdean, which overlooks Brighton and the English Channel in October of 1938. It was, and indeed still is a tremendous facility for visually-impaired veterans.

Recently, I found in an obituary piece, that Joan Beckham, Ernest and Hannah's daughter, herself died after a short illness on 6 December 2014, at Victoria, British

Columbia. She was Joan Crockett, having married the late W. Gordon Crockett. The piece included the details of how Joan had travelled over to Canada post-First World War with her parents. Joan and her parents it said, had endured the London Blitz, and Joan during the Second World War had been a Wren in the Women's Royal Naval Service, granted a commission, and worked in Ceylon (now called Sri Lanka), as a teletype operator decoding secret messages.

The *Cambria Leader* of 12 April 1919:

> CANADIAN WOMEN JEALOUS
> Toronto – Thursday: A proposal by Lady Muir-Mackenzie to send Britain's 1,500,000 surplus women to get husbands overseas is received here with open hostility. 'Does she not think overseas girls may need husbands too?', asks *The Telegram*.
>
> Many women, including Lady Hearst, the Ontario Premier's wife, disapprove of the scheme in interviews – *Daily Mail*.

The *North Wales Chronicle* of 15 August 1919:

According to Lieutenant-General Sir Arthur W. Currie, G.O.C., of the Canadian Forces who left England on Saturday for Canada, thirty-five thousand, of these soldiers have taken English wives home with them to the Dominion.

First Nations Canadian War Brides

Fred Gaffen in his fine book, '*Forgotten Soldiers*', has this piece on First Nations Canadians during the First World War:

The experience of serving overseas had a noticeable effect. Some learned to speak, read and write English for the first time. A few took brides from the British Isles.

Further Reading

1. *Forgotten Soldiers,* Fred Gaffen, Theytus Press, 1985.

2. *The Black Battalion 1916–1920: Canada's Best Kept Military Secret,* Calvin W. Ruck, Nimbus Publishing Ltd, Halifax, N.S.

3. *The Blacks in Canada – A History,* Robin W. Winks, McGill – Queen's University Press, Montreal & Kingston, 1997.

4. *The War Diary of Clare Gass 1915–1918,* edited and introduced by Susan Mann, McGill-Queen's University Press, Montreal, 2000.

5. *Sister Soldiers of the Great War: The Nurses of the Canadian Army Medical Corps,* Cynthia Toman, UBC Press, Vancouver, 2016.

6. *War Brides,* Melynda Jarratt, History Press, 2007.

Acknowledgements

1. The Canadian War Museum, 1. Vimy Place, Ottawa, Ontario.
2. The London Gazette.
3. Personnel Records of the First World War – Library and Archives Canada.
4. Annette Fulford, Maple Ridge, British Columbia.
5. ww1warbrides.blogspot.ca.
6. University of Alberta Libraries – Peel's Prairie Provinces newspapers resource.
7. Andrew Horrall's article of 2001, entitled: 'Keep-A-Fighting! Play The Game!' – Baseball and the Canadian Forces during the First World War.
8. Government of Canada Veteran Affairs.
9. Great War Centenary Association of Brantford, Brant County and Six Nations (GWCA), Ontario.
10. Glenbow Museum and Archives, Calgary, Alberta.
11. Nova Scotia Archives, Halifax, Nova Scotia.
12. Margaret Etoile Parry, Denbigh, North Wales.
13. Thank you to Myrddin and all the staff at Gwasg Carreg Gwalch, especially Dwynwen.

Other titles by the author:

The Story of Kinmel Park Military Training Camp 1914-1918

£8.00

www.carreg-gwalch.cymru

This is an account of life – and illness and death – in and around the military training camp at Kinmel Park near Abergele in northern Wales that was set up in 1914. Soldiers were trained and detained there, and Conscientious Objectors found themselves based there. The camp had an effect on the surrounding area, too, with road accidents, burglaries, and musical entertainments being visited on the local population! The author Robert Graves was at Kinmel Camp for a time.

This readable book is as much as anything the author's tribute to three members of his family who were involved in the First World War, including Robert Owen, who died aged eighteen before completing his initial military training at Kinmel Park Camp.

Welsh Soldiers, Civilians and Eisteddfodau in WW1

£9.00

www.carreg-gwalch.cymru

Through extensive research the author has unearthed truly interesting stories of bravery, endeavour, struggle, tragedy and loss during the Great War.

These stories are of Wales and its people in the tumultuous war years of 1914 to 1918, with the emphasis on the northern part of the country.

North Wales had combatants in all of this war's major battlefield conflagrations, and the losses at sea, including the notorious sinking by a German U-Boat of the passenger liner RMS *Lusitania*.

You will read of Welsh munitions factories and their workers, and of Welsh soldiers away from their homeland reinforcing their Welsh identities through the holding of Soldiers' Eisteddfodau.

Welsh National Eisteddfodau, the great Welsh cultural festivals struggled greatly during these war years and here those difficulties are explored, and involved some of Wales' most iconic figures of the early 20th century including David Lloyd George and Ellis Humphrey Evans, 'Hedd Wyn'.

The Enemy Within
'German POW's and Civilians in North Wales during WWI

£8.50

www.carreg-gwalch.cymru

In this, his third First World War related book, with the emphasis on the northern part of Wales, Robert H. Griffiths provides fresh insights into a plethora of themes and topics which make for absorbing reading.

The decision to intern long-term, thousands of 'alien men', mainly Germans, residing in Britain at the outbreak of war, produced serious humanitarian and logistical problems.

The Welsh and English born wives and children of such interned 'alien enemies' found themselves branded as 'The Enemy Within', and treated as such by the British authorities, and by their fellow citizens. Many having to endure great hardships, and for some it was the dreaded workhouse.

Germanophobia and spy fever abounded in Britain. Now anyone and everyone, especially those having a 'foreign' sounding name or accent were suspected of being a German spy.

Britain was also forced to deal with enemy prisoners of war on a large scale, including 'dangerous' commanders and officers from German U-Boats. Such intelligent, focused, highly motivated and resourceful officers were interned at Dyffryn Aled, in north-eastern Wales. From here escapes were made, including probably the most audacious one of the entire war – on either side.